UNDERSTANDING ARMS CONTROL
THE OPTIONS

Published simultaneously in Canada by Penguin Books Canada Ltd., 2801 John Street,
Markham, Ontario L3R 1B4.
Printed in the United States of America.

The text of this book is composed in Trump Book, with display type set in Eras Demni. Composition by Vail-Ballou. Manufacturing by The Maple-Vail Book Manufacturing Group. Book design by Margaret Wagner.

First Edition
Library of Congress Cataloging-in-Publication Data

McCain, Morris.
     Understanding arms control / by Morris McCain.—1st ed.
       p. cm.
     1. Nuclear arms control. 2. United States—Military relations-—
     Soviet Union. 3. Soviet Union—Military relations—United States.
     I. Title.
     JX1974.7,366 1989
     327.1'74—dc19   88-21134

ISBN 0-393-95650-4 PAPERBACK
ISBN 0-393-02687-6 HARDCOVER

W. W. Norton & Company, Inc., 500 Fifth Avenue, New York, N.Y. 10110
W. W. Norton & Company Ltd., 37 Great Russell Street, London WC1B 3NU
1 2 3 4 5 6 7 8 9 0

UNDERSTANDING
ARMS
CONTROL
THE OPTIONS

MORRIS McCAIN

THE COLLEGE OF WILLIAM AND MARY

W · W · NORTON & COMPANY

NEW YORK   LONDON

CONTENTS

—

v

AUTHOR'S PREFACE

—

When the United States Senate gave its consent to ratification of an INF Treaty in May 1988, the ninety-three to five vote meant more than removal of a class of nuclear weapons from Europe. It gave new life to a process which had drawn Washington and Moscow into common effort over a period of thirty years. That process—arms control—had sometimes been the sole, slender thread of cooperative endeavor in a fabric of East-West conflict. At times the hostility to arms control had grown so strong that the process seemed near to abandonment in favor of an unregulated arms race.

I began work on this book at such a time, the early 1980s, when the second SALT Treaty had recently been withdrawn from Senate consideration and a new American President, deeply suspicious of cooperation with the Soviets, had just been inaugurated. The book survived the collapse of arms control negotiations in Geneva at the end of 1983 and lived to see a new, younger Soviet leadership—one more attuned to the opportunities for cooperation—rise to power. As it goes to press, the President of the United States has returned from a meeting with that leadership in Moscow, carying an INF Treaty under his arm.

That we have come through the New Cold War of the 1980s

and caught hold once again of the thread which ties us to our international rivals shows much about the character of the American public. We are a nation of optimists, whose hope for a better future outlasts our discouragements and whose instinct for cooperation eventually triumphs over our fits of anger. We are also a public willing to inform itself and give guidance to its leaders, to master subjects like arms control despite their technical jargon and the forbidding prospects of nuclear holocaust they force us to confront. Were it not for that willingness this book would be wasted, and so, for that matter, would American democracy.

The book is dedicated to all who strive to inform us. It owes much to the students and faculty at the College of William and Mary, where I have taught for more than ten years. In 1982 I set out to offer a senior seminar on arms control at the college, and my inability to find a short, introductory work which could serve as a starting point prompted me to write one myself. As it has turned out, the book can provide a core for such a specialized course, a supplementary reading for introductory courses on international relations, or a guidebook to the inquiring citizen. It assumes no prior acquaintance with the subject, giving the reader a brief introduction to nuclear weapons and the strategies of nuclear war, before discussing arms control itself. Technical terms indispensable to understanding the topic are italicized the first time they occur and explained both there and in a glossary at the end of the book. To the many colleagues and students at William and Mary who helped me toward an intelligible product, my warmest thanks.

I am also indebted to those who informed me about arms control and who often did battle with my views on the subject: to the Center for Science and International Affairs at Harvard; to the Ford Foundation, which allowed me to work there for a year; and to Harvard's Russian Research Center, where I have spent countless summers studying our relations with the Soviets. My associates at Harvard will find much that is theirs in this book. Such errors and misjudgments as remain are, however, my own.

I suspect that the fondest acknowledgments for any book go to the friends who sustain an author through its creation. In this regard I have been particularly fortunate, in Williamsburg, in

Boston, and among my neighbors in Vermont. I will mention by name only Charlie Byron, who devised most of the book's illustrations and read every word of each successive draft. But to everyone who lent encouragement, my profoundest gratitude.

UNDERSTANDING ARMS CONTROL
THE OPTIONS

INTRODUCTION: WHY ARMS CONTROL?

—

The current era in world affairs took shape at the end of the Second World War. With the destruction of Japan and Germany and their unconditional surrender to the Allies, two of the most expansionist powers of the twentieth century were removed from international competition. The simultaneous exhaustion in victory of Great Britain and France—rival empires from an earlier day—left the field clear for domination by the United States and the Soviet Union. The relationship between the "superpowers," whether hostile or cooperative, was to form the central issue for the rest of the century.

For a brief moment at the end of World War II it seemed as if a new, cooperative mode of interaction were possible. The United States and the USSR, though of radically different ideological persuasions, had joined forces to defeat fascism. Because they lay in different hemispheres, conveniently separated by thousands of miles and without a common land border, they could hope to pursue their interests with less conflict than previous world powers. Because each was richly endowed with resources and territory, there was no urgent need to compete for colonies outside their boundaries. The United Nations, established in the optimism of the war's last year, was a prescription for world condominium—cooperative decision making—by the victors, with the Soviets and Americans at the helm.

It took only a year or two, however, for the prospect of cooperation to fade. Russia and the United States transformed themselves with remarkable swiftness from the introverted, isolationist giants they had been in the 1930s into world actors whose interests were essentially global and usually at odds. From Berlin to Greece to Iran to Korea—wherever Stalin's expansionism sought gains—there Washington felt its security to be threatened. From 1946 forward the dominant mode of East-West relations was a "cold war" between Moscow and Washington, a sustained conflict without resort to all-out military hostilities.

For the political realist, the Cold War came as no surprise. Efforts to replace international competition among sovereign states with some form of world order had been going on since the end of the nineteenth century, and they had failed repeatedly. Even if the United States and the Soviet Union could afford to act differently in the international system from earlier emergent powers like Germany and Japan, there was little reason to expect they would. They quickly developed classic power politics conceptions of national interest, racing each other in arms, assembling "alliances" of weaker client states, and generally defining their ambitions in terms of extending their own influence at the expense of their rivals'. In all these ways their behavior was identical to that of other world powers before them.

But in one way the superpower rivalry was different from its predecessors. In the course of forty years it produced no world war. Despite dozens of lesser actions involving the armed forces of the United States or the USSR, each kept its troops where they would not directly engage the other's. And the nuclear weapon, which both sides possessed by 1950, was never used between them. The nuclear age, with its incomparably greater means of destruction, had so altered the nature of war as to reduce the chances of its outbreak between nuclear-armed states.

A REGULATED RIVALRY: TACIT COOPERATION

How was this salutary effect achieved? What regulatory mechanisms govern this fundamentally conflictual relationship, keeping East and West from stumbling into a war that could easily become a global nuclear calamity? The answer lies in two forms of cooperative behavior: the first tacit, involving rules that are understood rather than spelled out; the second explicit (or formal), structured around treaties and other agreements.[1] Of the two, tacit cooperation has probably been the more important at most points in the past forty years. Moscow appears to believe, as it has repeatedly stated, that any conventional conflict between capitalist and socialist camps will soon escalate to all-out war. The USSR uses a great variety of techniques, including armed force, to achieve its international goals, but it withholds its troops from situations where they are likely to confront American forces directly. Thus in the Korean War, with U.S. forces pouring northward, it was Beijing, not Moscow, which sent its army to the rescue of the Communist regime. More recently, in the Middle East, the USSR has several times refused to aid clients like Egypt and Syria with Soviet ground forces, even though this meant humiliating losses in those countries' wars with Israel in the 1960s and 1970s. The dangers of direct U.S.-Soviet military engagement in the Middle East have put a check on Moscow's operations there.

The United States has been a little less cautious in this regard than the Soviet Union. Though most of its military interventions in the postwar period have been confined to Latin America, where the risk of direct conflict with Moscow's troops is very slight, Washington has sometimes operated closer to the brink. In Korea in the 1950s, in Vietnam between 1965 and 1973, and in Lebanon as recently as 1984, it has deployed its troops even where direct Soviet involvement could not be ruled out. When it mined the North Vietnamese harbor at Haiphong, through which Soviet ships were supplying Communist forces, the United States was stretching the limits of tacit cooperation to the breaking point.

American cooperative behavior to avoid war with Moscow takes a slightly different form. Despite rhetoric to the contrary, the West allows the Soviet Union a sphere of influence in Eastern Europe where it can use armed force with impunity. When Warsaw Pact troops invaded Hungary in 1956 to suppress an anti-Communist rebellion, and when they intervened in Czechoslovakia in 1968 to end the liberalizations of the "Prague Spring," the West retaliated in various ways, but military action was not one of them. From its side, the USSR has generally left the United

States a sphere of influence in the Western Hemisphere, where Moscow encourages anti-American movements but keeps its own military profile low. The greatest exception—Nikita Khrushchev's 1962 decision to place missiles in Cuba—brought the postwar world as close to nuclear war as it has ever come.

EXPLICIT COOPERATION: ARMS CONTROL IN THE ERA OF DÉTENTE

In one aspect of the superpower rivalry, however, tacit cooperation made little sense, and the opportunity to regulate East-West competition depended on explicit, negotiated agreements. This was the nuclear arms race. As soon as Joseph Stalin learned that the United States had the atomic bomb, he began his own crash program to build one. Once the United States discovered that Stalin had succeeded, President Harry Truman authorized a new, many times more potent American weapon: the hydrogen bomb. By the mid-1950s Moscow had that, too. The race then shifted to faster and more accurate delivery vehicles: from strategic bombers to ballistic missiles, from intermediate-range missiles to ones with intercontinental range, and from single-warhead missiles to ones with multiple warheads.

The arms race could not be brought to an end by tacit arrangements because in that form of bargaining each side counts on the other's taking a cue from its own actions and responding with the behavior the first side wants. If one of two cars approaching a head-on collision swerves to the left, its driver has reason to hope his counterpart will notice this maneuver and behave in a cooperative way. If not, both are destroyed. The same principle applies to tacit East-West bargaining to avoid a military collision. But in the case of an arms race, if one contestant stops racing unilaterally—or simply decides not to build an especially threatening weapon—the opponent can gain an advantage by racing right ahead. Before either side can rationally restrain its own actions, it needs some reliable assurance that the other will follow suit.

Of the past forty years, the period from about 1963 to about 1980 may be seen as a hiatus in the Cold War, in the sense that governments in both Moscow and Washington acknowledged the opportunity for regulating their rivalry by explicit agreements. One stimulant to détente—or, as the Soviets call it, a "relaxation of tensions"—was the death of Stalin and the revised formulation of foreign policy by his eventual successor Nikita Khrushchev. From 1956 onward the new Communist party leader spoke in terms of "peaceful coexistence," a concept explored in detail in a later chapter. It implied that war between capitalist and socialist camps would be disastrous for both and could be avoided, even though the East-West relationship remained competitive.[2]

In the United States it was not until the early 1960s that official opinion began to focus on an end to the Cold War. Senator J. William Fulbright was one of the first and most forceful advocates of East-West cooperation, but the American President who endorsed the concept was John Kennedy. In his American University speech of June 1963, the President advocated an improvement in U.S.-Soviet relations he called "more practical, more attainable" than the dream of universal peace and disarmament. Appealing for a peace based on "a series of concrete actions and effective agreements which are in the interest of all concerned,"[3] Kennedy announced the series of high-level discussions involving Moscow, London, and Washington which, only a few weeks later, produced the Limited Nuclear Test Ban Treaty, the first major landmark in the arms control process.

Like later agreements, the test ban of 1963 represented both failure and success in the negotiating process. It was not the comprehensive ban on nuclear explosions many had hoped for in advance of the treaty. Britain, the United States, and the USSR—the parties to the agreement—could still test nuclear devices underground, though not in the atmosphere, space, or the oceans; France, the latest nuclear power, did not sign. The Limited Nuclear Test Ban Treaty did halt all but a small number of atmospheric tests, freeing the earth's population from radioactive fallout, but it let the development of new, more accurate warheads go ahead.

So it has been with the whole series of major arms control agreements of the 1960s and 1970s:

• An Outer Space Treaty (1967) kept nuclear weapons from being placed into orbit but did not prohibit antisatellite and other space-based weapons using conventional explosives.

- A Nuclear Nonproliferation Treaty (1968) slowed the spread of nuclear weapons to additional nations but did not stop India or, apparently, Israel from gaining them.[4]

- SALT I, the most far-reaching treaty when it was signed in 1972, froze the numbers of U.S. and Soviet strategic missiles but let each side go on adding warheads to each missile.

- The last agreement of the détente era, SALT II (1979), set ceilings for warhead numbers, but at such high levels that both Moscow and Washington could continue building up for years.

By the end of the 1970s East-West relations had entered what some are now calling a "New Cold War"—a period of conflict and recrimination unmitigated by agreements to cooperate, at least formally. SALT II, like some of the lesser arms control agreements of the 1970s, remained unratified, and its expiration date passed at the end of 1985 with no successor in sight.

In part, the decline of détente was due to the limitations of arms control itself, which had come under attack from both right and left. On the conservative side, commentators like George Will call arms control "a process barren of achievements," preferring an unregulated arms competition in which the United States would return to the position of superiority it held in the early 1960s.[5] To the extent possible under budgetary constraints set by Congress, the Reagan administration has followed this line, breaking out of what would have been the SALT II limits in an effort to outstrip the Soviet militarily. To do so, however, required a doubling of defense spending and a consequent doubling of the national debt, making the economic merits of cooperation with Moscow somewhat clearer by 1987 than they were in 1981, when a balanced federal budget was projected within three years.

From the left, arms control has been viewed with mounting impatience, as each new agreement under détente blocked some avenues of the arms race only to drive it forward in other directions. Until the intermediate-range nuclear forces (INF) agreement of 1988, arms control meant agreeing *not* to do certain things rather than the more active and courageous commitment to cut back the arsenals already accumulated. "A question we would like answered," the British *Guardian* editorialized in 1980, "is whether arms control as opposed to disarmament is not too modest a goal for the nations to set themselves."[6]

WHY ARMS CONTROL?

The fruits of arms control may be meager, and its hesitant progress a trial to the impatient, but we have good reason to prefer it to its most likely alternative: an unbridled, multinational arms race. Nor is there any instant way to replace it with a conflict-free world, to "sweep away," as Michael Howard puts it in *The Causes of War,* "the whole tangled web of international rivalries and suspicions like so many cobwebs left over from the past."[7] Among the options presently facing us, arms control offers advantages of several sorts: From a military standpoint, it may simplify difficult choices among competing weapons, not all of which can be built at once; in economic terms, it can mean stable or declining defense budgets instead of skyrocketing expenses that force societies to give up other priorities; and if pursued consistently and with success, it may improve the longer-term chances for a fundamentally reformed world order less dominated by conflicts among sovereign nation-states.

The Military Logic of Arms Control

Harold Brown, defense secretary under President Jimmy Carter, and Lynn Davis, professor of military strategy at the National War College, state the military case for arms control agreements as follows:

> They can provide greater confidence as to the future characteristics and size of the nuclear force postures of each side than would exist in the absence of any agreements. They can reduce the number of nuclear weapons, to decrease both the cost of maintaining a nuclear balance and the reliance of governments on nuclear weapons in their foreign and defense policies. They can constrain modernization, either overall or of the most destabilizing kinds of threats, e.g., accurate intercontinental ballistic missiles (ICBMs), which can destroy missile silos in a preemptive strike. They can improve crisis stability by reducing the vulnerability of each side's nuclear forces.[8]

As Brown and Davis suggest, some forms of nuclear delivery systems are more threatening than others; these are the ones a nuclear power could use to destroy another's weapons by striking first. Arms control, by restricting these accurate delivery systems sufficiently, can enhance *crisis stability*, making nuclear war less likely, even if other nuclear weapons remain in superpower arsenals.

Furthermore, since each side in an arms race reacts in advance to what it expects the other to build—devising ways to attack, circumvent, or defend against prospective new weapons—a treaty banning a type of weapon may also stop a race to build countermeasures against it. One current example is the looming competition in antisatellite systems. Devices which can home in on an opponent's satellites in orbit have now been tested by both the United States and the Soviet Union. Unless agreement is reached soon to prohibit their deployment, the superpowers will find endangered their one source of information about each other's military activities: satellite reconnaissance. The most likely result will be a race not only to develop more and better antisatellite technologies but also to find ways of defending satellites against attack. Both could be prevented, and the intelligence capabilities of both sides secured, by a treaty banning further testing and all deployments of antisatellite weapons.

Some leaders at the Pentagon, such as Robert McNamara and Harold Brown (secretaries of defense to Presidents Kennedy, Johnson, and Carter), have been impressed with these arguments for arms control, while others have not. The more common attitude within defense establishments in both Washington and Moscow seems to involve skepticism about arms control and an eagerness to pursue weapons development without restrictions, in the hope of coming out on top in the arms race. In view of each side's superiority in some forms of military technology— the Soviet lead in lasers, for example, or American computer superiority—the temptation is strong to embrace weapons competition at the expense of arms control.

The Economic Rationale for Arms Control

Over the past two decades the two nations which have invested the most in the nuclear arms race—the Americans and the Soviets—have suffered declining growth rates in their economies and an embarrassing inability to compete in world markets. The superpowers remain militarily dominant in the international system, with navies and air forces to "project" their power worldwide and nuclear arsenals dozens of times the size of any other nation's. But they have watched with dismay the resurgence of German and Japanese influence in world affairs, based not on the armed might of these reemergent powers but on their economic capabilities. Can there be a relationship between the arms race and the declining relative positions of the nuclear giants?

Beyond a doubt, investment in defense has its economic costs. Developing the increasingly sophisticated nuclear delivery systems of recent decades—intercontinental missiles with multiple warheads, intermediate-range weapons with extraordinary accuracy, radar-evading bombers, and elaborate space-based defenses —drains skills and supplies from the high technology sectors of the civilian economy. As Leonid Brezhnev declared in announcing his support for the SALT process early in the 1970s, "the favorable outcome of these talks would make it possible to avoid another round in the missile arms race and to free substantial resources for constructive purposes."[9]

The findings depicted in Figure A suggest an inverse relationship between military investment and productivity growth in a country's civilian economy. For the Western industrial countries, at least, the larger the share of an economy's output spent on defense, the lower the growth rate in civilian productivity. Governments like America's or Britain's, spending 6 to 8 percent of gross domestic product for military purposes, have also been contending with anemic economies, growing at rates of only 2 to 3 percent per year. West Germany, which devotes a smaller share to defense, has a productivity growth nearly twice as high. And Japan, devoting a scant 1 percent of its output to military purposes, easily outpaces the productivity growths of all other nations shown. The Soviet Union is not included in Figure A, but its economy shows the same kind of result: With defense spending estimated at 12 percent or more of its overall output in the 1970s, the USSR experienced steadily declining economic growth, until by the 1980s annual productivity gains were hovering near zero.

It is often argued that nuclear arms control can do little to reverse the deterioration in Soviet and American economies since the budget for nuclear weapons makes up only a small part of

Figure A—Military Spending and Productivity Growth

MILITARY SPENDING AS A SHARE OF
GROSS DOMESTIC PRODUCT
VS.
GROWTH IN OUTPUT PER HOUR
IN MANUFACTURING (PRODUCTIVITY)

(Average Percent, 1960–1979)

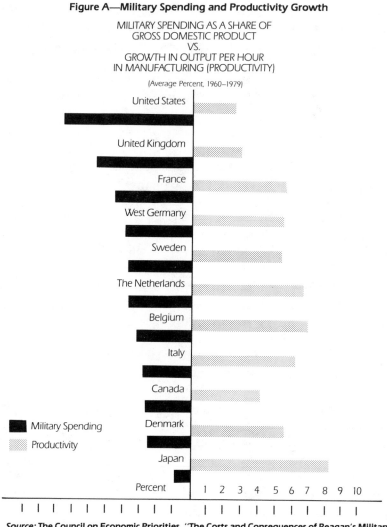

Source: The Council on Economic Priorities, "The Costs and Consequences of Reagan's Military Buildup," 1982

total defense expenditures by Washington or Moscow. In a sense, this argument is valid. If the nuclear arms race were ended, only to be supplanted by a more intense competition in conventional weapons technologies, defense budgets would rise rather than fall. Nonnuclear weapons have also become highly complex, and they generally require more troops to use them than do nuclear forces. Even if spending for conventional arms remained flat, nuclear arms control could affect defense expenditures only marginally. But that may be exactly what is needed to reinvigorate overburdened economies—not the sharp dislocation of a sudden military retrenchment but a gradual, orderly decline in the share of output diverted from productive purposes to the demands of defense.

Arms Control and the International System

In his *Fate of the Earth,* Jonathan Schell engages in a prolonged battle with the logic of nuclear deterrence, concluding that the security policy of the nuclear powers now threatens Earth's human population with complete annihilation. In the ironic logic of nuclear deterrence, according to Schell, the United States and the Soviet Union must maintain the fiction that they could fight and win a nuclear war, acquiring weapons which they intend not to use, but which, if used, could destroy not only the opponent but humanity as a whole. Schell's argument leads him to demand complete nuclear disarmament and, since that might only make conventional war more likely, complete conventional disarmament as well. Schell recognizes, though, that these goals are unattainable in a world of sovereign nations, with no international order to impose disarmament or police it: "The terms of the deal that the world has now struck with itself must be made clear. On the one side stand human life and the terrestrial creation. On the other side stands a particular organization of human life—the system of independent, sovereign nation-states."[10]

This may seem a frustrating conclusion. Only complete disarmament will meet our needs, but it must wait for a new world order. Is Schell correct, though? In one way, he probably is. The present world of conflicting nations does not allow complete disarmament as an option. On the other hand, something short of world disarmament may still be helpful. I have already argued that arms control, a set of agreements among sovereign governments, can stabilize the nuclear balance, making the genocidal war Schell fears less likely. Arms control may have a further, more far-reaching effect. Because it involves the experience of cooperation among rival nations, cooperation that is explicit and visible to all, it may hasten the day when sovereignty can be transcended by an international system attuned to the common interests of its component nations. Arms control pursued successfully over time may have exactly that effect of "establishing, through experience, the conviction that cooperative action will benefit all of the participants" which Kenneth Waltz in *Man, the State, and War* points out is missing from our current anarchic international system.[11]

Such has not been the experience of arms control so far. Because of shifting public attitudes toward détente, the arms control process over the past thirty years has sometimes highlighted cooperation and sometimes focused attention on conflict. It has created no enduring sense that the rivalry between world powers masks opportunities for cooperation of a permanent sort. Yet we have ample history of conflict yielding to coexistence and then to consensus. The American colonies functioned as rival entities for a century or more before discovering the benefits of confederation and then union. The European Community, for all its blemishes, now conjoins in a cooperative order nations that nearly destroyed one another fewer than fifty years ago. If arms control is to lead the nuclear powers in a long-term advance toward a new, cooperative international system, it will have to develop more consistently than in the past, providing a sustained experience of successful cooperation. This may be the answer to the *Guardian*'s question of whether arms control is not too modest a goal. The step-by-step process of arms control, building each small advance on the basis of the last, may be valuable not only in itself but also as the path to a fundamentally different future.

THINKING ABOUT ARMS CONTROL

To introduce the subject of arms control, this book provides three types of information: technical, logical, and historical. My teaching experience suggests that most minds are better at grasping some aspects of the topic than others. Some students become fascinated with the technical characteristics of weapons, expecting to find a solution to the arms race in technology. There is probably none there. Others, with a talent for reason, become deeply involved in strategic logic, trying to locate and clear away some intellectual logjam which accounts for the mistakes of the past. But logic alone offers no solution either. Finally, there are those who leap to the task, presented in the last chapter of this book, of imagining arms control agreements preferable to the ones we have signed so far. Vision can be a fine tool in shaping the future, but only if guided by a knowledge of the past.

All three kinds of study—technical, logical, and historical— are a part of understanding arms control. It is possible in a relatively short time, nonetheless, to master the basic elements. Each chapter in this introductory work offers the essentials a reader needs to grasp one aspect of arms control. Each concludes with a short controversy section, pointing up one or two of the most contested issues in the chapter's materials. And it refers the interested student to some of the best sources for more detail on its part of the subject. But each chapter is predicated on no more knowledge than is contained in preceding chapters, so that the book may be read straight through without stopping to consult additional sources.

Part I describes the weapons involved in nuclear arms control. Beginning with the basic physics of nuclear explosions and their effects in Chapter 1, it moves on to describe the main strategic delivery systems for nuclear weapons: the bombers, ballistic missiles, and cruise missiles which carry them to their targets. This book examines only nuclear delivery systems with ranges long enough to let one nuclear power use them against the territory of another. They are the ones most arms control agreements have been concerned with so far, and they are likely to form the subject of future agreements as well. Chapter 2 makes the crucial distinction between highly accurate delivery systems, able to destroy an enemy's weapons in a first strike, and those which can annihilate only "soft targets" like population centers. Part I concludes with a chapter on intermediate-range weapons in the European theater, ones the Soviet Union considers strategic but the United States does not. These, too, have become a subject for arms control in recent years.

The second part of the text—Chapters 4 and 5—explores the intricate logic of strategic doctrine, the ways Washington and Moscow think of using their nuclear weapons. It describes simple strategies that threaten a single type of response to expected aggression by the other side, and it details more complex strategies that require a greater variety of responses, including the possible first use of nuclear weapons. Drawing the distinction between countervalue retaliation and counterforce targeting, Chapter 4 indicates which weapons are most valuable for each type of strategy. It also considers the logic of strategic defense and the arguments for and against the proposed American Strategic Defense Initiative. Because students in the West are likely to look at these issues only from their own side, Chapter 5 examines strategic doctrine from the Soviet perspective. It emphasizes that in the Kremlin, as in the Pentagon, strategic logic can become a weapon in the political battle over defense budgets.

With this technical and logical background, Part III turns to arms control itself, presenting in Chapter 6 the history of achievements and failures through the end of the détente era in 1979. The main terms of treaties from the Limited Nuclear Test Ban to SALT II are explained, along with what those treaties failed to limit. Chapter 7 deals with the hiatus in arms control during the 1980s, describing the main negotiating proposals made by Washington and Moscow in recent years, the breakdown of talks in 1983 and their resumption in 1985, and the fate of arms control under Ronald Reagan and Mikhail Gorbachev. It concludes with our current policy options—the rival suggestions for arms control agreements of the future—outlining the merits of each possible approach and the grounds for opposition to it.

Clearly this is a book not only about arms control but in favor of it. The aim is to let the reader understand what has happened so far and to provide the basis for intelligent judgment about our best future course. Anyone who reaches the last chapter should be ready to take an informed part in the debates which will shape our next arms control agreements.

NOTES TO INTRODUCTION

1. The same distinction is drawn by Raymond Cohen, *International Politics: The Rules of the Game* (New York: Longman, 1981).

2. Khrushchev's speech was translated in *Current Soviet Policies II*, ed. Leo Gruliow (New York: Praeger, 1957). On peaceful coexistence, see pp. 29–38.

3. Commencement Address at American University in Washington (June 10, 1963), in *Public Papers of the Presidents of the United States: John F. Kennedy, 1963* (Washington: Government Printing Office, 1964), pp. 459–64.

4. "An Ex-Technician Says Israelis Built A-Bombs," *New York Times*, October 6, 1986, p. A7.

5. George F. Will, "Why Arms Control Is Harmful," *Newsweek* (June 18, 1984), reprinted in *The Nuclear Arms Race Debated*, ed. Herbert M. Levine and David Carlton (New York: McGraw-Hill, 1986), pp. 82–83.

6. "Is Arms Control Too Modest a Goal?" *The Guardian*, September 22, 1980, p. 12.

7. Michael Howard, *The Causes of Wars* (Cambridge, Mass.: Harvard University Press, 1984), p. 5.

8. Harold Brown and Lynn E. Davis, "Nuclear Arms Control: Where Do We Stand?" *Foreign Affairs* (Summer 1984), pp. 1145–46.

9. "Brezhnev: Central Committee Report," in *Current Soviet Policies VI* (Columbus, Ohio: American Association for the Advancement of Slavic Studies, 1973), p. 13.

10. Jonathan Schell, *The Fate of the Earth* (New York: Alfred A. Knopf, 1982), pp. 217–19.

11. Kenneth N. Waltz, *Man, the State, and War* (New York: Columbia University Press, 1959), p. 169.

P A R T   I

NUCLEAR WEAPONS AND DELIVERY SYSTEMS

1

NUCLEAR WEAPONS AND THEIR EFFECTS

—

Two basic discoveries of the past ninety years make this the "nuclear" century. The first, made by Albert Einstein at the beginning of the century, was that matter can be converted into energy. A second, more practical discovery, made in the 1930s, was that this conversion can be achieved by the splitting of the nucleus of an atom. We will scrutinize this process of nuclear "fission" more closely in a moment. These revolutionary advances on the part of physicists have been used for two fundamentally different purposes: in a controlled fashion to generate energy without causing an explosion and in a way deliberately calculated to release energy suddenly and explosively. The former is the procedure at nuclear power plants; the latter describes a nuclear weapon.

Granted, we may have every reason to deplore both uses of nuclear physics. Or we may happen to favor both. Nuclear power plants keep the air free of the polluting hydrocarbons that are a by-product when we generate energy by burning things. On the other hand, they produce deadly wastes with life expectancies in the thousands of years. Nuclear weapons, which could destroy most or all human life on the planet, may also be responsible for the past forty years of peace among the great powers.

Whatever the merits of nuclear power plants or nuclear weapons, the two are analytically distinct and need to be evaluated separately. For that reason, this book ignores the "peaceful uses" of nuclear energy and concentrates on nuclear weapons: on their technologies, on strategies for using them, and on the limits that have or might be placed on them. Only when arms control arrangements explicitly involve nonweapons technologies (as in the Nonproliferation Treaty of 1968 or the Peaceful Nuclear Explosions [PNE] Treaty of 1976) will they be discussed. This is not a "nuclear" book. It is a book about arms control.

A second distinction is also useful in understanding nuclear weapons: that between explosive devices (bombs and warheads) and the vehicles used to carry them to their targets. Both are commonly discussed under the rubric of "nuclear weapons." For our purposes, this term will be used strictly to mean only nuclear explosive devices. We will treat them in this chapter and their delivery vehicles in the next.

Only a few current issues of arms control have to do with nuclear weapons in this strict sense, the debate over a proposed comprehensive nuclear test ban being one. Present efforts are largely aimed at ending an arms race in delivery vehicles—bombers, ballistic missiles, and cruise missiles—and at thwarting a potential arms race in defenses against delivery vehicles. The weapons themselves were the subject of earlier arms control agreements, such as the Limited Nuclear Test Ban Treaty (1963) and the Nuclear Nonproliferation Treaty. While those accords worked fairly well, the competition to produce more and better delivery vehicles has been harder to stifle.

THE ATOMIC BOMB (OR FISSION WEAPON)

The early A-bombs the United States dropped on Japan at the end of World War II used a different principle to release their explosive energies from that used for most of the weapons in current superpower nuclear arsenals. They relied purely on the splitting of atomic nuclei (nuclear fission) to do their job. As German scientists discovered in the 1930s, the large nucleus of the uranium atom (92 protons and 143 neutrons bound together by the

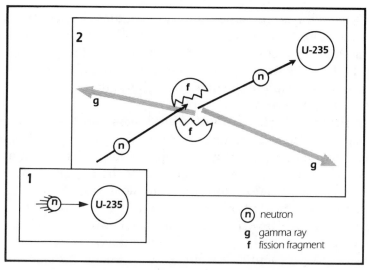

Figure 1-1—Nuclear Fission Chain Reaction

extraordinary energy physicists called the strong force) can be split in two. When this fission occurs, a minuscule amount of mass converts into energy according to Einstein's formula $E = mc^2$. His mathematical expression is a way of reckoning how much energy is derivable from a given amount of mass: Multiply mass by the square of the speed of light—186,000 miles per second squared—to calculate its equivalent in energy.[1]

How can fission of the uranium nucleus be induced? The "trigger" turned out to be bombardment with neutrons, the electrically neutral atomic particles which make up nuclei, along with their positively charged kin, protons. Figure 1-1 shows what happens when a high-speed neutron strikes a uranium (U-235) nucleus. The large uranium nucleus splits into two medium-sized nuclei called fission fragments (for example, krypton and xenon nuclei), freeing more neutrons in turn and emitting energy in the form of gamma rays and the motion of the fission fragments. If one or more of the neutrons released from each split nucleus goes on to strike another uranium nucleus, the nuclear reaction becomes self-sustaining. A "chain reaction" gets under way.

Once scientists understood nuclear fission, it still took them several years and a crash program to construct a fission bomb. In the first place, it is difficult to accumulate the uranium for a bomb. Most naturally occurring uranium takes the form of

U-238, which has the same number of protons in each nucleus but three more neutrons than the U-235 nucleus. (In other words, they are two different isotopes of uranium.) U-238 is less fission-able than U-235, and reactions started in it tend to fizzle out. Anyone who can afford the uranium still has to separate the two isotopes to get a critical mass of U-235.

The next task is also tricky. A critical mass is just large enough to keep a chain reaction going once it is triggered. The fission bomb exploited the properties of a supercritical mass of uranium, one in which the neutrons escaping from the average splitting nucleus go on to cause more than one additional fission. In a fraction of a second, billions upon billions of uranium nuclei (the figure is roughly 10 with twenty-four zeroes after it) split apart in an explosion which vaporizes all surrounding matter.

This is not an event that would be welcome in the laboratory or aboard the planes that carried the early A-bombs. How can the right amount of fissile material be assembled in the right place at exactly the right time? Two techniques were devised initially. One divided the uranium into two parts and kept them separate until the explosion was to be triggered. Then one part was shot into the other, as if down the barrel of a gun, reducing the ratio of surface area to volume of uranium and creating the conditions for an explosion. The United States used this gun-assembly tech-nique to detonate "Little Boy," the bomb which destroyed Hiro-shima in August 1945. A second method, still employed for fission explosions, keeps the fissile mass subcritical by hollowing it out. To achieve explosion, the hollow sphere is suddenly compacted by many conventional explosives arranged around its circumfer-ence and precisely timed to go off together. That was the princi-ple behind "Fat Man," the bomb dropped on Nagasaki three days after Hiroshima. The fissionable material in Fat Man was not uranium, but the man-made element plutonium, currently gen-erated by nuclear power plants.

Figure 1-2 shows these immense early nuclear weapons, so large they could scarcely be carried by the aircraft of their day. When compared with the other weapons used in World War II, their destructive power was phenomenal. Each had roughly the same effect as 15,000 or 20,000 tons of TNT. Nuclear weapons are still measured by comparison with conventional explosives in this fashion. Thus the first fission bombs are described as 15- or 20-

Figure 1-2—Early Nuclear Weapons: "Little Boy" and "Fat Man"
Source: Department of Defense Photo

kiloton weapons. The still more powerful weapons of our own day have damage ratings in *megatons:* A one-megaton explosion causes the same destruction as 1 million tons of TNT.

Luckily for the West, these secrets of turning nuclear fission into a weapon were unraveled first in the United States. Germany's scientists, decreased by the flight of many from Hitler's dictatorship, had taken a wrong turn as they tried to engineer the A-bomb. In America Enrico Fermi, Leo Szilard, and other scientists working on the Manhattan Project achieved a nuclear chain reaction in 1942, and when the war ended in Europe, their fevered efforts had brought the United States to the brink of a nuclear weapons capability.[2] By the summer of 1945, when the first test of a fission weapon at Alamogordo, New Mexico, proved a success, Japan was still refusing to surrender to the advancing Allied forces, even though it was reduced to defending its home islands against invasion. President Truman faced the momentous decision of whether to use the new bomb against a human population.

To this day there are those who think the President made the wrong choice. The U.S. military estimated in 1945 that it would take at least a year and perhaps a million American lives to conquer Japan by conventional means. On the other hand, the entry of Soviet troops into the war against the Japanese that August improved chances of a capitulation by Tokyo. If the Allies had abandoned their insistence on unconditional surrender, some historians believe, Japanese leaders who favored peace might have gained the upper hand.[3]

President Truman considered his alternatives: He might warn the Japanese of the bomb's unprecedented power with a test demonstration over an uninhabited Pacific island or he might identify the targeted Japanese cities in advance, allowing evacuation to cut back the scale of destruction. If Truman chose the first course, he ran the risk of an embarrassing failure. The fission bomb had been tested only once, and the second time might yield a different result. Since the United States had produced only three bombs to begin with, a second test would leave it with just one remaining weapon for actual use against Japan. The option of prior warning also had its risks. The Japanese might move American prisoners of war to the targeted cities, forcing Washington to kill its own people with its nuclear explosions.

When American planes did drop the A-bomb on Hiroshima and Nagasaki, it brought the Second World War to a prompt conclusion. At the same time it made the United States the first (and to date the only) country actually to use its nuclear arsenal. Washington entered the postwar era with a nuclear monopoly which became the envy of every other nation seeking the status of a great power.

NUCLEAR FUSION AND THE HYDROGEN BOMB

The American nuclear monopoly was not to last long. In Moscow Joseph Stalin ordered a crash program to duplicate Washington's achievement. The United States and the USSR made feeble efforts at eliminating nuclear weapons before they could spread, but these came to naught. (The 1946 Baruch Plan and Soviet counterproposals are treated in Chapter 6.) In 1949 the USSR joined the "nuclear club" by exploding its own atomic bomb. That left President Truman with a second decision of monumental dimensions: whether to have American scientists build the vastly more potent hydrogen bomb.

Based on an energy source like the sun's, the hydrogen bomb was estimated to have destructive potential a thousand times greater than the early fission weapons. (Those estimates ultimately proved correct. While the first A-bombs had yields of twenty kilotons or less, the explosive force of hydrogen bombs had to be measured in megatons. At the peak of the race for the biggest bang, the Soviets exploded a fifty-eight-megaton device.) Scientists in the West, foreseeing the human devastation a war with such weapons could wreak, offered conflicting recommendations to the President. Some argued that using the H-bomb would be a form of genocide; it could kill whole nations and races, not just the fractions of populations that had been the victims in previous wars. They urged Truman to content himself with the growing U.S. arsenal of fission weapons. Others, fearing that it was only a matter of time until Moscow had the hydrogen bomb, insisted the United States must get there first.[4]

Wisely or not, Truman again opted for the arms race. The weapon he ordered for his nation derived its power from nuclear fusion, the forcing together of atomic nuclei at very high temperatures. Instead of the large uranium or plutonium nuclei involved in fission, fusion takes place between the smallest nuclei—those of two hydrogen isotopes, deuterium and tritium. These ele-

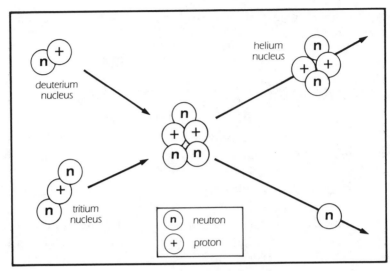

Figure 1-3—Nuclear Fusion

ments, with only one proton in the nucleus of each, can be generated by bombarding the chemical lithium deuteride with neutrons. It takes intense heat to force the positively charged deuterium and lithium nuclei close enough together for fusion to occur, but once it does, the release of energy is enormous. The conversion of a minuscule quantity of matter from each nucleus into energy yields conditions like those at the center of the sun.

Because of the million-degree temperatures required to start nuclear fusion, the hydrogen bomb is sometimes called thermonuclear. Modern weapons use a small fission explosion to produce the necessary initial heat. Once hydrogen nuclei begin fusing, throwing off helium nuclei and high-energy neutrons, they release enough energy of their own to sustain fusion in other nuclei. Figure 1-3 sketches the fusion reaction at the heart of contemporary nuclear weapons.

Since the escaping neutrons have sufficient energy to cause fission in the normally recalcitrant U-238 nucleus, a "shield" of uranium usually encases the fusion chamber, adding the benefits of additional fission to the weapon's explosive force. The hydrogen bomb is thus really a fission-fusion-fission device. If the uranium shield is omitted, the blast effects of the explosion are reduced, and far more neutrons escape. In this configuration—

the neutron bomb—a fusion weapon causes more radiation damage to humans nearby, while the destruction of structures from its blast is confined to a smaller area. Recent American administrations have argued that these characteristics make it ideal for use against attacking Warsaw Pact forces in a European war.

As the timeline in Figure 1-4 indicates, the United States acquired the hydrogen bomb fewer than three years after Truman's decision in its favor. By the end of 1955 Moscow also had the H-bomb. Tests of the new device proliferated rapidly, until the superpowers and Great Britain (whose own nuclear device had first been tested in 1952) were setting off nearly ninety nuclear explosions a year in the atmosphere. Radioactive debris from their tests was entering the stratosphere and falling out on populations around the globe. In the late 1950s American researchers detected in the milk of cows strontium 90, a radioactive element that can replace the calcium content of human bones.

Concern over radioactive fallout from atmospheric tests accounted for the first major success in arms control. After four years of grappling, London, Washington, and Moscow reached agreement in the 1963 Limited Nuclear Test Ban Treaty to confine themselves to underground nuclear testing. All three have observed the treaty ever since, and even though two other nuclear powers (France and China) never signed the treaty, they gradually moved their tests underground as well.

The shift from fission bombs to the incomparably more powerful fusion weapons made possible another, less beneficial trend. The immense early bombs dropped from aircraft were replaced by smaller and smaller warheads which could still do far more damage. New means of delivery thus became feasible; they ranged from land- and sea-based missiles with intercontinental range to miniature nuclear artillery for use on battlefields. By the 1960s the United States was developing multiple-warhead missiles, each capable of carrying several nuclear charges to separate targets. The arms race had shifted from a competition in nuclear weapons per se to a rivalry in nuclear delivery vehicles that continues to the present day. That aspect of the arms race forms the focus of the next chapter. We first need to look, though, at the results produced by nuclear explosions and what they mean for our choices in the era of nuclear warfare.

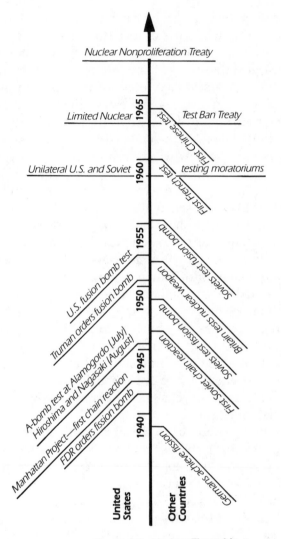

Figure 1-4—Nuclear Timetable

THE PRIMARY EFFECTS OF NUCLEAR WAR

Fission and fusion as processes can be grasped far more readily than the magnitude of destruction they have at their disposal if turned into weapons. The numbers scientists use in describing nuclear explosions—the millions of degrees of heat, the tens of thousands of megatons in modern weapons arsenals, the potential casualties in the hundreds of millions—convey too little to the mind in terms of the human consequences of nuclear war. It is easier to speak of "winning" a nuclear war, for example, if only the number of surviving warheads on each side is calculated than if the fate of human populations is taken into account. The bombing of Hiroshima killed more than 100,000 people, and even more survived with physical and emotional injuries which still cripple them more than forty years later. A modern weapon, if exploded in a populated area, would leave behind it far more human casualties. A one-megaton warhead, common in today's superpower arsenals, has more than fifty times the force of the Hiroshima bomb. And any large city in the United States or the Soviet Union is probably targeted with several of these at the moment.

What, then, would be the results of a nuclear war? We can provide some of the answers with near certainty simply by looking at the effects of earlier explosions and extrapolating them to our current weapons. These are the primary effects, which occur locally and over a short period of time:

- Initial radiation from the fireball of a nuclear explosion takes several forms: gamma rays, X rays, and a shower of escaping neutrons. It is intense enough to kill humans within a mile or two of ground zero (the point on the earth at which or above which a nuclear device is detonated). In practice this radiation effect is of little immediate consequence since the blast and heat following it kill the same people more quickly. But it renders an area around ground zero uninhabitable for months or years afterward.

- An electromagnetic pulse, many times stronger than a bolt of lightning and affecting a much larger area, disables electric and electronic devices near the explosion. These include radio and television, as well as the control circuits in computers. Because of the ban on atmospheric testing, the electromagnetic pulse remains more of a mystery than other primary effects. Many scientists believe, however, that only a few high-altitude explosions over a country's territory would destroy the communications it needs for control of its own nuclear weapons.

• Heat and light account for nearly half the energy from a one-megaton explosion, a flash that is blinding to the unprotected eye and thermal radiation intense enough to set fires at distances of five miles or more from ground zero. In some cases (such as Hiroshima) these conflagrations merge into a continuous fire storm, burning everything in the area it covers. People in shelters under a fire storm are asphyxiated as carbon dioxide replaces oxygen in the air they are trying to breathe.

• The blast wave traveling outward through the air from each explosion is likely to be the most destructive aspect of nuclear war for human habitations. It arrives as a shattering blow, followed by winds as strong as the most powerful hurricane and by atmospheric pressures several times normal for a number of seconds. Reinforced concrete structures within a half mile of ground zero collapse, and frame houses as far as five miles away are destroyed. With ten or a dozen nuclear explosions occurring in any major metropolitan area, even its suburbs would probably be reduced to rubble.

• The shock wave transferred to the ground when nuclear warheads are detonated on the earth's surface is enough to jolt missiles in their hardened underground silos. If the warheads are aimed at missile silos and delivered accurately enough, even the best-protected land-based missiles may be disabled by an incoming nuclear attack.

• Nuclear fallout, a delayed form of radioactive exposure, is likely to harm more people than the initial, direct radiation from nuclear explosions. Especially in the case of ground burst weapons, the fission fragments combine with dirt and other particles as these are carried into the atmosphere by the fireball's intense updrafts. For hours and days after the explosion, this radioactive fallout sifts back down to earth, making areas downwind of ground zero uninhabitable. Radiation sickness then afflicts survivors of the original blast, bringing many of them to less merciful, longer-drawn-out deaths.[5]

GLOBAL EFFECTS OF NUCLEAR WAR: A "NUCLEAR WINTER"?

About these short-term effects of nuclear war a fair amount is known. More problematic, and perhaps more threatening to the human future, are the global effects of nuclear war. The destruction described above resulted from only one or a very few nuclear explosions. In an all-out nuclear exchange between the superpowers, however, thousands of nuclear weapons are likely to be detonated at the same time. Their effects would become cumulative in ways that may put in jeopardy both human civilization and possibly the future of human life itself.

Scientists in the 1980s have been running computer simulations to estimate the global effects of nuclear war. Some studies suggest that a warming of the earth's climate would result. Others point to a nuclear winter severe enough and long enough to kill most or all of the earth's human population.[6] The term "nuclear winter" derives from a projected reduction in the sunlight reaching the earth's surface, causing prolonged sub-freezing temperatures in the main growing areas of the Northern Hemisphere. Those who expect a nuclear winter after a mutual attack by the United States and the USSR argue as follows.

If even a few thousand of the world's 50,000 nuclear warheads were used in a major war, the dust thrown into the upper atmosphere by ground burst weapons and the soot rising from burning cities would soon encircle the globe. Soot in particular is good at absorbing the sun's heat and light, while it lets energy radiated back from the earth escape into space. Temperatures over the United States, Canada, Europe, and the Soviet Union, where the postwar gloom would be deepest, might fall below normal by as much as forty to seventy degrees. In such circumstances groundwater would freeze, and any crops not already destroyed by fire and radiation would perish in the cold. With the breakdown of transportation and distribution networks, most human survivors would probably die of starvation in just a few weeks. Others might remain to fight over dwindling stocks of uncontaminated food and water. Even south of the equator, in countries not targeted with nuclear weapons, the global cloud of debris could be thick enough to stop photosynthesis in plants.

To these possible climatic effects of nuclear war, we have to add at least two more imponderables: depletion of the earth's ozone shield and genetic mutation. The phenomenal heat of the fireball from a one-megaton explosion brings nitrogen in the air to combustion, forming oxides of nitrogen which are swept upward into the stratosphere. There they interact with ozone in the delicate layer that protects organisms on earth from much of the sun's ultraviolet radiation. If the ozone shield suffered major damage in a nuclear war, skin cancer in humans would proliferate. Other effects of ozone depletion may be even more serious. As the globe began recovering from the reduced temperatures and light of the nuclear winter, its impaired food chains could be subjected to overdoses of ultraviolet radiation lasting a year or longer. Aquatic life, which might survive the nuclear winter in better shape than animals or plants on land, may be especially vulnerable to the effects of ozone depletion.

We have little way of guessing the full effects of radiation on human and other organisms in the years following a nuclear war. It is well established that radiation causes genes to mutate, but what kind and number of mutations would several thousand nuclear explosions bring in their wake?[7] We do not know for how many generations a human race weakened by starvation and disease would face disabling genetic mutations. Least of all can we foresee what radiation-induced viral strains would attack the remains of human civilization. Considering many of these anticipated, though so far unverified, effects of nuclear war, one study by Carl Sagan and other scientists reached the following ominous conclusion: "In almost any realistic case involving nuclear exchanges between the superpowers, global environmental changes sufficient to cause an extinction event equal to or more severe than that at the close of the Cretaceous when the dinosaurs and many other species died out are likely. In that event, the possibility of the extinction of *Homo sapiens* cannot be excluded."[8]

EFFECTS OF NUCLEAR WAR: POLICY IMPLICATIONS

If these are the likely effects of nuclear weapons, what conclusions can we draw from them? Are nuclear weapons so destructive that we have to forswear their use under any circumstances? Should we eliminate them from our arsenals entirely? Can their possession have the ironic effect of making nuclear war less likely? Studies of nuclear winter have made those policy implications a matter of lively debate in the 1980s.

In *The Fate of the Earth* Jonathan Schell concludes that only the abolition of war can protect us against nuclear catastrophe. He argues that in the nuclear era national sovereignty must be supplanted by world government, and nuclear arsenals eliminated altogether. By contrast, the Harvard Nuclear Study Group— made up of policy experts as informed and experienced as Albert Carnesale and Joseph Nye—predicted in 1983 that we would have to live with nuclear weapons for the indefinite future. "Since the moral claims for deterrence rest on averting large-scale nuclear war, the truly immoral behavior is to have nuclear force and doctrines that invite pre-emptive attack by one's opponent or by oneself."[9]

Another attempt to sort through the policy issues posed by nuclear weapons and their threat to human society was made by the American bishops of the Roman Catholic Church, working within that church's centuries-long tradition of teachings on the ethics of war. The pastoral letter issued by the bishops in 1983 focused on whether it can ever be right to use nuclear weapons, given their disastrous consequences. It begins by ruling out the first use of nuclear weapons as an ethical choice: "We do not perceive any situation in which the deliberate initiation of nuclear warfare, on however restricted a scale, can be morally justified."[10] On this point they disagree with the recommendations of the Harvard Nuclear Study Group, which argued: "What morality and prudence dictate is 'no early use' of nuclear weapons . . ., and a highly selective and limited use if it should come to that."

The bishops' conclusion also contradicts the foreign policy of the United States, which reserves the right to respond with nuclear weapons if the armed forces led by the Soviet Union in Eastern Europe launch a conventional (that is, nonnuclear) assault on Western Europe. Their pastoral letter goes even further, however, considering the question whether a country should respond with nuclear warfare once it has been attacked with nuclear weapons. The wisdom of the postwar era has nearly always answered this question affirmatively, prescribing retaliation against an enemy's population centers in response to a nuclear first strike. Here, too, the Catholic bishops dissent, deriving support from their church's doctrine against the deliberate taking of noncombatant life in war. In the pastoral letter they quote the Second Vatican Council of 1962: "Any act of war aimed indiscriminately at the destruction of entire cities or of extensive areas along with their populations is a crime against God and man itself." The bishops conclude: "This condemnation, in our judgment, applies even to the retaliatory use of weapons striking enemy cities after our own have already been struck."

To complete this brief sample of the diverse policy conclusions which can be drawn from our current estimates of nuclear destruction, let us consider the advice of Carl Sagan, whose vision of the global effects of nuclear war we examined above. "To me," he reasons, "it seems clear that the species is in grave danger at least until the world arsenals are reduced below the threshold for climatic catastrophe. . . ." Accordingly he offers an estimate of 500 to 2,000 warheads—about 1 to 4 percent of current world totals—as the most the nuclear powers together should have.

How is it possible that a set of prominent, responsible individuals like Schell, Sagan, the Harvard Nuclear Study Group, and the American bishops, informed with the same data on nuclear weapons and their effects, can reach such disparate conclusions on policy? Is there some key to their logic which the reader lacks at this point? In fact, there are probably several. So far we have dealt only with the technology of nuclear explosives, leaving aside the means of delivering nuclear weapons to their targets. These form the subject of the next two chapters. Even more crucially, we have yet to look at the many ways strategists think about using nuclear weapons, at the competing "strategic doctrines" of the postwar nuclear powers. They are considered below in Part II.

Whether we should have nuclear weapons, under what circumstances we should threaten to use them, and which weapons capabilities give the most stability to the military balance among nuclear-armed nations—all these are problems which defy solutions based on the horrors of nuclear war alone. The same is true of arms control. To select among the array of options for reducing nuclear stockpiles, to decide which weapons each side in the arms race can safely get rid of, requires knowledge of more than nuclear weapons and their effects. This chapter, like later ones, ends with a sketch of two sides to a controversial issue, designed to bring the controversy into sharper focus. The reader may be interested to see which side of the argument has the greater initial plausibility. Subsequent materials provide the basis for informed judgment on this and other issues.

Controversy:
MUST WE GET RID OF OUR NUCLEAR WEAPONS?

YES! The more we find out about the effects of nuclear war, the more senseless it becomes to keep nuclear weapons around. Since the days when the United States had only 3 small A-bombs in its arsenal, the total of nuclear weapons worldwide has gone to more than 50,000, most of them far more destructive than those which leveled Hiroshima and Nagasaki. If even a few thousand of these were used in a war, scientists now estimate, deaths would not be limited to the cities of the combatant powers. Radiation overdoses, harmful ultraviolet exposure, and the cold and dark of nuclear winter would overspread the globe. Human extinction, a fate allowing no postwar recovery, may be the logical conclusion of the nuclear era.

This capability of the human race to exterminate itself is something entirely new in war, mandating a new set of political relations on a globe divided into conflicting nation-states for the past several centuries. Now that war is not only inhumane but suicidal, a common human stake in survival should make it possible to overcome national divisions. Since the First World War, statesmen have tried twice to eliminate national arsenals and guarantee world peace by creating an international order. What we are learning about nuclear winter makes it imperative to try again and to succeed.

In the meantime, the sheer national interest of nuclear powers gives them reason to negotiate away their nuclear arsenals, returning to conventional weapons for such defense as they still need. The top priority of arms control—a limited process that can do some interim good—must be the complete elimination of nuclear weapons.

NO! The unprecedented destructive power of nuclear weapons means they must never be used or that they may be used in only a limited fashion, not that it is wrong to possess them. For all their squabbles and anxieties, the past forty years have been the longest period of peace between the great powers in modern history. This has not been the achievement of the United Nations. More likely, the very possession of nuclear weapons by the conflicting powers has kept them from attacking one another.

Policies in the nuclear era must focus on preventing nuclear war. Since no realist can imagine that we will be without the bomb anytime soon, our task is to learn how to live with it, how to threaten credibly that which we do not want to do in actuality. Better control over the nuclear weapons we do have, measures to reduce the chance of war by accident, even negotiated reductions in stockpiles of destabilizing weapons—these are all to the good and feasible in today's world of competing nation-states.

But there is a limit beyond which arms control should not go. Each of the superpowers needs enough survivable nuclear weapons to destroy its enemy's society in retaliation for a first strike. That capacity to retaliate is what keeps the peace. In a world without nuclear weapons, we would be less safe than we are in our current plight.

FOR MORE DETAIL

David P. Barash, *The Arms Race and Nuclear War* (Belmont, Calif.: Wadsworth Publishing Co., 1987). Beautifully illustrated, comprehensive account of nuclear weapons and war, especially appropriate for science students.

Albert Carnesale et al., *Living with Nuclear Weapons* (New York: Bantam Books, 1983). Authored by the Harvard Nuclear Study Group, a useful counterpart to Schell's *The Fate of the Earth.*

The Challenge of Peace: God's Promise and Our Response (Washington, D.C.: United States Catholic Conference, 1983), excerpted in "Nuclear Strategy and the Challenge of Peace," in *The Nuclear Reader: Strategy, Weapons, War,* ed. Charles R. Kegley, Jr., and Eugene R. Wittkopf (New York: St. Martin's Press, 1985). Contains the central arguments about nuclear war made by the American Catholic bishops.

Jack Dennis, ed., *The Nuclear Almanac: Confronting the Atom in War and Peace* (Reading, Mass.: Addison-Wesley Publishing Co., 1984). Several essays edited at MIT offer more detail on nuclear physics and the workings and history of nuclear weapons; very well illustrated.

Paul R. Ehrlich et al., *The Cold and the Dark: The World After Nuclear War* (New

York: W. W. Norton & Co., 1985). Easily readable materials on the possible effects of nuclear war, including Carl Sagan's work.

Lawrence Freedman, *The Evolution of Nuclear Strategy* (New York: St. Martin's Press, 1981); Michael Mandelbaum, *The Nuclear Question* (Cambridge, England: Cambridge University Press, 1979). The first sections of these two standard works on strategic doctrine trace America's entry into the nuclear era and early policy disputes over nuclear weapons within the U.S. government.

Walter M. Miller, *A Canticle for Leibowitz* (New York: Bantam Books, 1976). A classic fiction work, set several hundred years after a hypothetical nuclear war.

Bruce M. Russett and Bruce G. Blair, eds., *Progress in Arms Control?* (San Francisco: W. H. Freeman & Co., 1979). Reprinted articles from *Scientific American*, including pieces on the debates over the hydrogen and neutron bombs.

Carl Sagan, "Nuclear War and Climatic Catastrophe: A Nuclear Winter," in *The Nuclear Reader*, loc. cit. Another presentation of Sagan's findings, here in tandem with essays on many other aspects of the nuclear arms race.

Jonathan Schell, *The Fate of the Earth* (New York: Alfred A. Knopf, 1982). Controversial account of the effects of nuclear war along with Schell's policy recommendations, originally serialized in *The New Yorker*.

Starley L. Thompson and Stephen H. Schneider, "Nuclear Winter Reappraised," *Foreign Affairs* 64, 5 (Summer 1986): 981–1005. Questions conclusions such as Sagan's about the likelihood of nuclear winter.

Unforgettable Fire: Pictures Drawn by Atomic Bomb Survivors (New York: Pantheon Books, 1981). Words and pictures from those who have seen nuclear weapons used on a human population.

U.S. Congress. Office of Technology Assessment. *The Effects of Nuclear War.* (Washington, D.C.: U.S. Government Printing Office, May 1979). Concise, authoritative summary of what is known and unknown about its subject.

NOTES TO CHAPTER 1

1. The physics of nuclear energy are ably described and illustrated in Therese Dennis, "A Little Physics," in *The Nuclear Almanac*, ed. Jack Dennis (Reading, Mass.: Addison-Wesley Publishing Co., 1984). Richard Rhodes's recent book *The Making of the Atomic Bomb* (New York: Simon and Schuster, 1986) details the twentieth-century revolution in physics which made nuclear weapons possible.

2. The drama of the Manhattan Project is captured by Alice Kimball Smith, "Manhattan Project: The Atomic Bomb," in *The Nuclear Almanac*, loc. cit, ch. 1.

3. Lawrence Freedman discusses the American decision to use nuclear weapons against Japan in the first chapter of *The Evolution of Nuclear Strategy* (New York: St. Martin's Press, 1981).

4. See Herbert F. York, "The Debate over the Hydrogen Bomb," in *Progress in Arms Control?*, ed. Bruce M. Russet and Bruce G. Blair (San Francisco: W. H. Freeman & Co., 1979).

5. Most of these effects of nuclear explosions are found in Part 1 of Jonathan Schell's *The Fate of the Earth* (New York: Avon Books, 1982). They are also summarized in Kosta Tsipis's contribution to *The Nuclear Almanac*, loc. cit., entitled "Blast, Heat,

and Radiation." For a U.S. government source, see the Office of Technology Assessment, *The Effects of Nuclear War* (Washington, D.C.: Government Printing Office, May 1979).

6. The bases for these conclusions about nuclear winter are explained in Paul R. Ehrlich et al., *The Cold and the Dark: The World After Nuclear War* (New York: W. W. Norton & Company, 1984). A less pessimistic view is offered by Starley L. Thompson and Stephen H. Schneider, "Nuclear Winter Reappraised," *Foreign Affairs* 64, 5 (Summer 1986), 981–1005.

7. In his science-fiction classic *A Canticle for Leibowitz* (New York: Bantam Books, 1976) Walter Miller populates a neomedieval postnuclear world with miscreants of all sorts, including the two-headed woman who sits at confession as a second nuclear war begins centuries later. Jonathan Schell is less sanguine about the human fate. He describes the result of nuclear war as "A Republic of Insects and Grass."

8. Carl Sagan, "Nuclear War and Climatic Catastrophe: Some Policy Implications," *Foreign Affairs* 62, 2 (Winter 1983/84): 257–92.

9. Albert Carnesale et al., *Living with Nuclear Weapons* (New York: Bantam Books, 1983), p. 247.

10. *The Challenge of Peace: God's Promise and Our Response* (Washington, D.C.: United States Catholic Conference, 1983), excerpted in "Nuclear Strategy and the Challenge of Peace," in *The Nuclear Reader: Strategy, Weapons, War*, ed. Charles R. Kegley, Jr., and Eugene R. Wittkopf (New York: St. Martin's Press, 1985).

2

STRATEGIC DELIVERY SYSTEMS

—

Merely possessing nuclear weapons does not give a nation the ability to destroy an opponent's society with them. To do that requires a set of expensive delivery systems able to convey the weapons to hundreds of targets, often across thousands of miles. Fewer than half the world's nuclear warheads are mounted on *strategic delivery systems*—planes or missiles with ranges long enough to let one nuclear power attack the homeland of the other. The rest are designed for use in regional "theaters" of war (Europe, the Middle East, East Asia) or on particular battlefields. Because intermediate-range nuclear weapons in Europe presented a major arms control dilemma in the 1980s, we consider them separately in the next chapter. Otherwise this book deals only with strategic nuclear warheads, of which the United States has over 12,000 deployed and the Soviet Union nearly 11,000.

THE STRATEGIC TRIAD: BOMBERS, ICBMs, AND SLBMs

Americans and Soviets have been deploying their nuclear arsenals in three basic ways for so long that strategic triad is practically a household phrase. The bomber, the intercontinental ballistic missile *(ICBM)*, and the submarine-launched ballistic missile *(SLBM)* have been with us long enough to become self-perpetuating; they have ironclad constituencies within the institutes, committees, and bureaucracies where our delivery systems are chosen. Each system has its advantages over the others, and as technology changes, each develops its drawbacks. The invulnerability of submarines may be challenged by antisubmarine warfare, for example, just as SLBMs begin to rival the accuracy of their land-based brethren.

Strategic bombers were the first means each side had of conducting a nuclear strike against the other from its own territory. They carried the growing U.S. nuclear arsenal through most of the 1950s. The Soviets used bombers initially, too, while racing to put their weapons on missiles. Even though the United States quickly developed its own missile systems, it kept the bomber, improving it repeatedly over the next thirty years.

Bombers have the great merit of being recallable after they have left ground. They can take off when an attack is suspected, then return to base with their weapons still on board if the warning proves to be a false alarm. American strategic aircraft are prepared to do just this in an alert, flying as far as northern Canada before a decision has to be made that would send them across the North Pole and over Soviet territory. Because bombers can be scrambled in a short time, no enemy will count on destroying all of them in a surprise attack. The United States keeps a substantial part of its B-52 fleet on fifteen-minute alert at all times, and nearly all of it would be on alert during a world crisis.

The strategic bomber helps reassure a nuclear power that it has a survivable retaliatory capability—the ability to destroy an opponent's homeland even after suffering an all-out nuclear blow—while its recallability reduces the risk of war by accident. Compared with other delivery systems, however, it is extremely slow to reach its target. Flying at just less than the speed of sound, a B-52 or a Soviet Bear or Bison needs several hours to make its intercontinental journey. It can still destroy enemy cities, but with so much warning of impending attack that the victim has plenty of time to launch its own missiles and aircraft. The bomber is an excellent delivery vehicle for retaliation, but useless if you want to strike first.

For much the same reason, strategic bombers are easier than missiles to shoot down. As they approach an opponent's borders, bombers come under assault from surface-to-air missiles and other antiaircraft systems. Slower and larger than missiles, bombers are more likely to be hit and would have to fight their way to their targets with heavy losses. The USSR maintains more than 10,000 antiaircraft missiles to protect its territory from incoming bombers, even though it has shown less interest in modernizing its own strategic bomber force than in developing its other offensive systems. The latest U.S. response to the penetrability problems of bombers is to load them with the air-launched cruise missile *(ALCM)*, about which more will be said below. At an earlier stage in the evolution of delivery systems, the answer was the ballistic missile.

Intercontinental ballistic missiles (ICBMs) were developed first by the Soviet Union. Used to boost an earth satellite into orbit in 1957, the ICBM quickly became the mainstay of both Soviet and American nuclear arsenals in the 1960s. Exaggerated reports that Moscow would soon have hundreds deployed gave a crisis atmosphere to the 1960 election campaign, when Democrat John Kennedy used the "missile gap" to help defeat his Republican rival, Richard Nixon. (It is currently believed that Moscow actually had only a handful of ICBMs deployed by the early 1960s.)[1] A crash program then put Washington ahead in the race for strategic land-based missiles, and it was the end of the decade before Moscow caught up again.

Why the rush to a second type of delivery vehicle when strategic bombers could already carry annihilation across the Arctic? Ballistic missiles overcame the slowness of aircraft, speeding through space to cover the distance between the superpowers in thirty minutes or less. They work on the same principle as a tossed ball, traveling in a smooth arc from launch to landing. Boosted from their silos by powerful rocket engines, ICBMs do not depend on the earth's atmosphere; unlike aircraft, they have no wings which need air for lift, and no jet engines, which use air to burn their fuel. ICBMs quickly pierce the atmosphere, moving through space on a ballistic trajectory unaffected by anything but the earth's gravity. As with the tossed ball, when an ICBM gets under way, nothing can be done to call it back or change the targets it will strike.

Figure 2-1—Minuteman III ICBM in Its Silo
Source: Department of Defense photo

The speed of ballistic missiles—many times that of bombers—makes them preferable in more ways than one. It solves the problem of penetrability since the technology to intercept a missile in flight is much more sophisticated than antiaircraft defense. At least for the present, essentially all missiles either superpower fires will reach their targets. Speed is crucial, too, if one side hopes to destroy the other's delivery systems while they are still on the ground. To strike a bomber before it takes off and a missile before it is launched means giving an opponent less warning time than is needed to get them aloft. If a superpower's ICBMs are accurate and plentiful enough, they stand a chance of eliminating nearly all the other's land-based missiles and a fair portion of its strategic bombers in a surprise attack.

The ICBM thus has some important capabilities the bomber lacks. It also has some drawbacks. Chief among them is its vulnerability to attack by an opponent's missiles. As long as they are land-based in fixed silos, ICBMs present an excellent target.

If a superpower waits to launch them until it can verify an incoming attack, it runs the risk of losing them. If it fires them as soon as the first warning of an attack comes, it may start a nuclear war by mistake. The latter policy, called launch on warning, has apparently been avoided so far by both the United States and the Soviet Union; otherwise the many false alarms that take place each year would already have put an end to us. Even so, ICBMs are doubly destabilizing. A nuclear power fearing assault in a crisis may launch them to prevent the destruction of its own weapons, or it may deliberately start a war with a preemptive attack on its enemy's ICBMs, hoping to disarm its opponent. As we will see shortly, MIRVing ICBMs—placing more than one warhead on each—has simply worsened this "crisis instability."

Submarine-launched ballistic missiles (SLBMs) make up the third leg of the traditional strategic triad. The inherent vulnerability of land-based missiles led both Moscow and Washington to place some of their ballistic missiles on submarines. Like ICBMs, they can reach their targets quickly; the shortest strike times, in fact, are afforded by SLBM-carrying submarines (SSBNs) stationed just off an opponent's coasts. The Soviets could destroy Washington in this way in fewer than ten minutes, and an attack on Moscow from the Mediterranean takes only slightly longer. As a platform for strategic attack an American submarine is thus a little like a piece of Wyoming floated in secret up to the shores of the USSR. With ranges of several thousand miles, SLBMs can now be fired from almost any part of the world's oceans, where they cannot be located by an opponent hoping to disable them in a first strike.

SLBMs have disadvantages, too. Submarines cannot launch missiles as accurately as ICBMs since the crew has no way to determine the precise location of the vessel without surfacing and exposing it to attack. If the crew members misjudge the ship's coordinates by even a few hundred feet, any missile fired from it will land that much farther from its target. An error of this magnitude means little in attacking cities, but it greatly reduces one's chances of disabling an ICBM in a hardened silo.

It may also be hard to communicate with submarines in time of war. While ICBMs receive the launch command electronically through wires, signals to commanders of submerged vessels must somehow pass through water. Much of the current effort to

Figure 2-2—Submarine with SLBM Tubes Open
Copyright © 1981 Union of Concerned Scientists. Reprinted with permission.

improve strategic command, control, and communications (often combined with intelligence and written C³I) centers on reliable ways to get SLBMs fired when the national leadership wants them to be and not before.[2] To the submarine's detriment, too, it must spend a good part of its time in port being serviced and changing crews. Only a part of a nation's SSBNs are actually on station at any one time, although the percentage can be increased during a crisis. The Soviets have special problems in this regard since their ports are a longer way from open water than the United States is.

Thus the basic strategic triad: bombers that are recallable and can be scrambled to escape attack but are slow to target and have difficulty penetrating enemy airspace; land-based ICBMs with high accuracy and prompt delivery capability but with tempting vulnerability; and SLBMs, which cannot be targeted when on station but lack the accuracy to destroy the other side's land-based missiles. Soviet and American arsenals have had this three-legged configuration since the mid-1960s. Not surprisingly, considering the imperfections of each system, the superpowers have labored mightily for the past twenty years to improve all three.

THE STATE OF THE ART: UPGRADING THE STRATEGIC BOMBER

The USSR has done relatively little to modernize its archaic fleet of strategic bombers, though rumors of a new Soviet intercontinental bomber in development and about to be deployed have cropped up repeatedly over the past decade. By contrast, the United States has upgraded its B-52s a number of times, making them faster and more likely to penetrate air defenses. Washington is also investing heavily in a new generation of bombers. The controversial B-1, now entering the American fleet, flies at supersonic speed to shorten its time to target and improve its penetrability. A still more advanced aircraft technology, nicknamed Stealth, promises to defeat air defense radar with streamlined profiles and coated wing surfaces, giving the strategic bomber an even better chance of hitting its targets in the 1990s.

The most radical improvement in the air-based U.S. arsenal, however, is the ALCM (air-launched cruise missile). Carried in the body or under the wings of a strategic bomber, it can be fired from outside enemy airspace to strike targets more than 1,000 miles inland. The ALCM lets bombers themselves "stand off" an opponent's shores while attacking, with no need to surmount air defenses. It was this new capability that led President Carter to cancel plans for the penetrating B-1 bomber, later resurrected by the Reagan administration.

Cruise missiles operate on principles different from the ballistic missiles described earlier. They are, in fact, small pilotless aircraft, continuously powered during flight and relying on the atmosphere for lift. Highly advanced computers on board compare the terrain below them with maps inserted into their memories before launch, allowing cruise missiles to correct their paths

Figure 2-3—ALCM in Flight
Source: Department of Defense photo

and strike within perhaps 100 feet of their exact targets. Unlike the much larger bomber, they can travel close to the ground, maneuvering past obstacles while evading ground radars. They thus combine high accuracy with enhanced penetrability.[3]

The ALCM has some interesting implications for crisis stability and for arms control. Accurate enough to threaten ICBMs in hardened silos, it is still too slow for use as part of a first strike. It constitutes an excellent retaliatory weapon but does nothing to create the expectation of a surprise attack. On the other hand, the same small size that helps it penetrate makes it easy to hide and hard for an opponent's satellites to count. Future arms control agreements that seek to limit the numbers of ALCMs on both sides will be difficult to verify unless the superpowers agree to mount them only outside the bodies of bombers. As the United States and the USSR add long-range cruise missiles to their naval fleets (SLCMs, or sea-launched cruise missiles), this problem is compounded further. Since there is no easy way to discover how many of these sea-launched cruise missiles have nuclear warheads, controlling their numbers may now mean banning long-range SLCMs outright.

THE STATE OF THE ART: MORE ACCURATE, MIRVed ICBMs

Much energy on both sides has gone into improving ICBMs. Over the past twenty years, for example, the American Titan missile has been supplanted by the Minuteman, which has in turn been upgraded several times. The latest U.S. ICBM—the MX—has just begun entering the force. Modernization means greater and greater accuracy for land-based missiles. The Minuteman III and MX can, in theory at least, strike within 600 feet of their targets, compared with about 3,000 feet for the Titan. Modern Soviet ICBMs, such as the SS-18, are only slightly less accurate, with *CEPs* of 1,000 feet or so. (*CEP*, or circular error probable, measures the radius of a circle within which fall half the warheads fired at a target. A smaller CEP, therefore, means greater accuracy.) That degree of accuracy makes it likely that only two incoming warheads would be needed to destroy a hardened target such as an opponent's ICBM in its silo.

A second major change in ICBM capabilities came through MIRVing, or putting more than one warhead on each missile. (*MIRV* stands for multiple independently targetable reentry vehicles.) The United States began MIRVing its Minuteman arsenal in the early 1970s, enabling a Minuteman III to fire a different warhead at each of three separate targets. A "bus" in the nose cone of the missile carries the three warheads until, at several points in its trajectory through space, it unloads its warheads in different directions. The Minuteman warheads then reenter the atmosphere separately on their way to three different targets. The warheads themselves are called reentry vehicles (RVs), while the missiles bearing them are now described as delivery vehicles (DVs).

Until recently Washington had put only three warheads on its MIRVed ICBMs. Proponents of the new MX missile argued, though, that an American ten-warhead ICBM was overdue, since the Soviets already had one. The USSR started MIRVing well behind the United States but then proceeded to do a more thor-

Figure 2-4—Multiple Warheads on MX Missile
Source: Department of Defense photo

ough job. Most of Moscow's land-based missiles now carry multiple warheads; the latest version of the SS-18 can deliver ten half-megaton nuclear weapons within 1,000 feet of their separate targets.[4]

Ironically, as accuracy and MIRVing "improve" the land-based missiles of one superpower, the development renders ICBMs on the other side more vulnerable. The "window of vulnerability" for American ICBMs, to use President Reagan's term, derives from this combination of accuracy and MIRVing in the Soviet arsenal. Enough MX missiles deployed by the United States would make Soviet ICBMs equally insecure. A series of diagrams can explain how this works:

The three diagrams depict the land-based leg of the strategic triad for two superpowers, one of which is shown with 11 ICBMs, the other with 14 (in rough proportion to the actual 1,052 and 1,398 land-based launchers the United States and USSR had in the early 1980s). In Diagram 2-1, each ICBM is assumed to carry

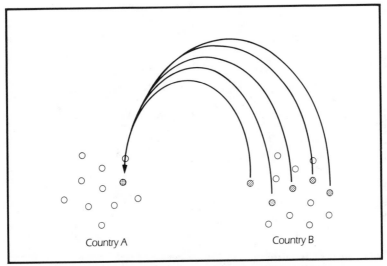

Diagram 2-1—Single-Warhead ICBMs with Low Accuracy

only a single warhead, and each has low accuracy. To stand a 90 percent chance of destroying one enemy missile in its silo, either superpower needs to fire five of its ICBMs at it. Suppose Country B contemplates a disarming first strike to destroy Country A's land-based arsenal in a crisis. *(Only* the *land-based* weapons of each are considered here, as if neither had submarines or bombers. This is an extremely important limitation to keep in mind.) With the 5:1 "crosstargeting" forced on it by the low accuracy of its ICBMs, Country B would have to use all its 14 missiles to kill only 3 missiles on the other side. It would be worse, not better, off after such a strike. For Country A, which is inferior in missile numbers, a disarming first strike against Country B is even more out of the question.

Next observe what happens if accuracy improves. In Diagram 2-2, each country has the same number of ICBMs as before, and each missile still carries only one warhead. Accuracy has been increased in both land-based arsenals, however, so that only 2:1 crosstargeting is needed for a 90 percent probability of kill. Any two missiles launched by Country B can now hope to kill one of Country A's ICBMs in its silo. (The newest land-based missiles deployed by Washington and Moscow have approximately this degree of accuracy.) Still, a first strike makes no sense for either side. Country B would have to aim all 14 of its weapons at just 7

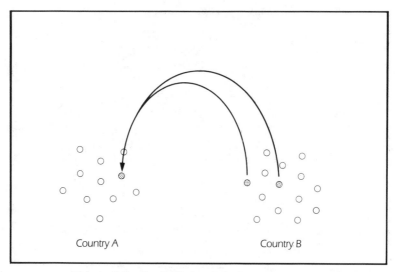

Diagram 2-2—Single-Warhead ICBMs with High Accuracy

of Country A's, and even then, because of the 90 percent kill probability, it would more likely destroy only 6. Country A, of course, has still less incentive to strike first.

Crisis instability results when highly accurate missiles are MIRVed. Suppose each side places five warheads on its average ICBM, as depicted in Diagram 2-3. Country B can now hope to

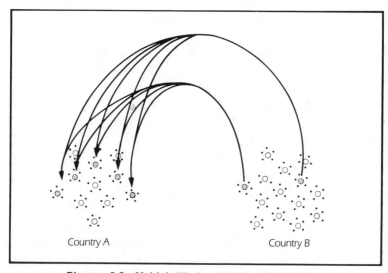

Diagram 2-3—Multiple-Warhead ICBMs with High Accuracy

kill 5 (actually 4.5) of Country A's ICBMs with only 2 of its own. With 4 of its missiles it could count on destroying 9 on the other side, and in an all-out first strike it could destroy all of its opponent's land-based missiles with fewer than half its own. This increased incentive to strike first results from a change in the warhead-to-aimpoint ratio. Originally Country B had only 14 warheads targeted on 11 enemy aimpoints (ICBMs silos). Now the same 11 aimpoints have 70 warheads aimed at them. MIRVing has worsened the warhead-to-aimpoint ratio, while greater accuracy has cut down the crosstargeting requirements. Crisis instability is the result.

Three more points will complete this discussion of state-of-the-art ICBMs. First, notice that if Country A's missiles are highly accurate and MIRVed to 5, it also has a first-strike incentive, even with fewer land-based launchers than its opponent. Any 2 of its ICBMs can destroy 4.5 of Country B's, 4 could kill 9, 6 could kill 13.5, and with only 7 of its 11 weapons it could hope to obliterate its enemy's superior land-based arsenal entirely. Supporters of the highly accurate ten-warhead MX missile would like to give the United States exactly this capability against the Soviets, whose ICBMs can already place the American land-based arsenal in jeopardy.

But remember that all the scenarios just presented make sense only if we ignore the sea-based and air-based parts of the superpower triads. For either side to profit from a first strike, not only must it come out of the exchange with more ICBMs than its victim, but its society must also survive. The global effects of the thousands of warheads it sets off in its own assault may be enough to annihilate the attacking power along with its victim. If not, then the opponent's retaliatory action probably will. Only if it can somehow neutralize the other side's SLBMs and strategic bombers does either of the superpowers stand a chance of "winning" any nuclear war it starts.

Finally, note the appeal of mobile ICBMs in the situation just described. Suppose, for instance, that each of Country A's ICBMs in Diagram 2-3 could rotate undetected and at random through twenty different silos instead of sitting fixed in one. Without knowing the location of its target, Country B would have to aim forty missiles, not two, at each ICBM in a first strike. Its entire land-based force would be exhausted long before it could destroy

Country A's. The incentive to strike first would evaporate, or to use the Reagan idiom, the window of vulnerability for Country A would be closed. The Carter administration proposed roughly this basing mode (multiple protective shelters or the "shell game") for the American MX. Moscow has just begun deploying its first mobile land-based missiles, which are evidently the wave of the future. The Soviets are also experimenting with a second mobile ICBM, while the projected U.S. Midgetman is to be a mobile ICBM with a small single warhead.[5]

THE STATE OF THE ART: COUNTERFORCE-CAPABLE SLBMs?

The third leg of the traditional strategic triad, submarine-launched ballistic missiles, is also being included in the modernization drive. In the 1970s, while Moscow was rushing to MIRV its land-based missiles, Washington was doing the same with its SLBMs. By the mid-1980s about half of all American strategic warheads (more than 5,000 of them) could be found on about 600 SLBMs. These provide an ideal retaliatory force since they are not vulnerable to attack and lack the accuracy to pose a destabilizing first-strike threat against the Soviet Union. (In the jargon of strategic doctrine, they are not yet counterforce-capable. The distinction between counterforce and countervalue targeting is drawn in Chapter 4.) At present, though, the U.S. Navy is bringing the best Western technologies to bear on making its submarine-based warheads more accurate. By the end of this decade the Trident II SLBM with its planned D-5 warhead should be able to determine its exact position on the way up into space, adjust its flight path accordingly, and hit Soviet missile silos as accurately as the latest ICBM.[6]

THE STRATEGIC NUCLEAR BALANCE

These are the main ways the superpowers can deliver nuclear strikes against each other. Little in this chapter so far is contro-

		UNITED STATES	USSR
ICBMs	Launchers	1,000	1,389
	Warheads	2,331	6,400
SLBMs	Launchers	1,624	936
	Warheads	5,472	3,372
LONG-RANGE		350	160
BOMBERS	Warheads	4,948	880
TOTAL	Launchers	1,974	2,485
	Warheads	12,751	10,652

TABLE 2-1—STRATEGIC LAUNCHERS AND WARHEADS (1988)
Source: Arms Control Association

versial. The capabilities ascribed to each delivery system vary somewhat from one account of them to another, but not in any important way. Why, then, is there so much disagreement on the relative strengths of the superpower arsenals, on who is "ahead" in the nuclear arms race? How do some commentators, including official Soviet sources, find rough parity between the strategic weapons of East and West, while others, including many Americans inside and outside government, paint a picture of growing Soviet superiority in the 1970s and 1980s?

Institutional self-interest may explain some of the differences of opinion. Those seeking new weapons allocations in Washington or Moscow are likely to see "woeful inadequacies" in their country's defenses; others, seeking to divert resources from military budgets, will perceive existing defenses as adequate. (Chapter 5 details some of these disagreements over defense policy in the Soviet Union.) But there are also real ambiguities and asymmetries in the East-West strategic equation. Neither side is clearly ahead in all measures of strength: strategic launchers, nuclear warheads, overall megatonnage, accuracy, and a variety of quality considerations. To a great extent, therefore, one's view of the balance depends on the aspects of nuclear weaponry one considers most important.

Looking at delivery vehicles and warheads, Table 2-1 gives current estimates of strategic nuclear forces in each part of the American and Soviet triads. The numbers presented are estimated totals for 1988. The first difficulty with them is that they are only estimates. Actual launcher and warhead numbers change almost daily, as Washington and Moscow gradually take out of service older systems, usually with fewer warheads, replacing them with more up-to-date, more highly MIRVed delivery vehicles. Figures for launchers (numbers of missiles and bombers) can be given with reasonable precision, though the most authoritative sources, such as *The Military Balance,* published annually by the International Institute for Strategic Studies in London, and figures provided by the Arms Control Association in Washington differ slightly even on these. More important is the much wider variation among estimates of Soviet warhead totals. Many of the ICBMs and SLBMs in the Soviet arsenal are being upgraded, making it impossible to say with certainty how many warheads they carry at a given moment. Since warhead estimates for the USSR generally assume that all missiles of a given type are fully MIRVed, they may be somewhat overstated.

Even if there were complete agreement on the figures in Table 2–1, experts would still argue about the balance. As the table shows, the Soviets have roughly a 25 percent lead over the United States in strategic delivery vehicles (launchers), which they have had for more than a decade. Nevertheless, they have never equaled the American arsenal in numbers of strategically deliverable warheads. On the average, U.S. strategic launchers are more highly MIRVed. In terms of delivery vehicles, the advantage is with the East; in terms of reentry vehicles, the West holds the lead.

This discrepancy only hints at a larger problem in evaluating the two forces. The balance depends on which delivery systems seem most important to a particular analyst. Look at the warhead subtotals for various types of launchers in Table 2-1. In strategic bombers the U.S. lead is commanding, and it has grown of late, as more ALCMs have been deployed. But bombers are slow and vulnerable to air defenses. Considering only warheads on ballistic missiles (ICBMs and SLBMs), the two sides drew even in the early 1980s, and the Soviets have recently pulled ahead.

When we break down the missile totals into their two main components, the difference between ICBMs and SLBMs is enormous. The USSR keeps nearly three times the U.S. number of warheads on land-based missiles. Soviet ICBMs are on average more highly MIRVed than American ones, with at least the theoretical ability to destroy the U.S. ICBM force in a surprise first strike. Critics of U.S. defenses consider this asymmetry alarming

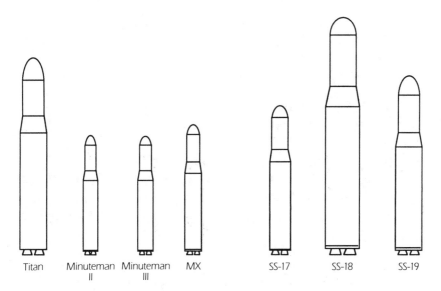

Titan   Minuteman Minuteman   MX   SS-17   SS-18   SS-19
              II   III

Figure 2-5—U.S. and Soviet Land-Based Ballistic Missiles

since, as we saw above, ICBMs have capabilities no other strategic delivery system possesses. If Washington wants fast, accurate strikes against hardened targets in the Soviet Union, it currently has too few ICBMs.

ICBMs have their drawbacks, however. Critics of Soviet defense planning point out that nearly two-thirds of their strategic warheads are potentially vulnerable to attack because they are land-based, while the United States could lose all its ICBMs and still have four-fifths of its force intact. They like the American decision to put half the West's warheads on submarines, where they would survive a first strike by the other side. Some, persuaded that stability requires each superpower to be confident of its retaliatory capability, wish the Soviets had gone the same route. To a certain extent the USSR is moving its forces "out to sea," putting more warheads on SLBMs. But for the foreseeable future the preponderance of Soviet weapons will be on land, while most American warheads will remain underwater.

This basic asymmetry of strategic force structure is compounded by two further considerations: the larger size of Soviet ICBMs and the superior quality of U.S. submarines. The scaled representation in Figure 2-5, showing the U.S. Titan, Minuteman II, Minuteman III, and MX next to the Soviet SS-17, SS-18, and

SS-19 suggests the magnitude of the first problem. By virtue of their larger size Moscow's ICBMs have greater *throw weight* than Washington's—that is, they can deliver more and larger warheads. The newest Minuteman III warheads (three to a missile) carry 335 kilotons of destructive power each, while the modernized SS-18 delivers ten 550-kiloton warheads. (Only thirty-three ten-warhead MX missiles had been deployed by the United States by 1988). This makes the overall ICBM imbalance seem just that much more troubling. But many specialists consider this a fictitious advantage. The United States deliberately moved to smaller ICBMs from its much larger, earlier Titan missiles; accuracy improvements had made the old blockbusters obsolete. The closer a warhead comes to its precise target, the less explosive force it needs to destroy it. In fact, the inverse relationship between accuracy and required megatonnage is dramatic, such that one warhead an eighth the size of another can do the same damage if it is twice as accurate. For this reason, some of the megatonnage on Soviet ICBMs may be excess—a compensation for earlier, much less accurate weapons.

A second consideration magnifies the U.S. advantage in SLBMs. The vessels carrying them are generally quieter and faster and spend less time in port for maintenance than Soviet submarines. As a result, more can be kept on station at a given time, and they are less susceptible to antisubmarine warfare (ASW) in an era of superpower competition in ASW technologies. Unlike American subs, the Soviet fleet coming out of Murmansk or Vladivostok must pass through narrow "choke points" formed by Greenland, Iceland, and the Faeroe Islands in the first case and by the islands of Japan in the second. There Western underwater sonar equipment monitors their movements, letting Washington know how many are at their deepwater posts at any time.

Which side is ahead, then, in the nuclear arms race? The mix of strategic weapons for the two superpowers is sufficiently different to give grounds for almost any opinion. Which of the two forces just described would a commander in chief in Washington or Moscow prefer to have? If he is more impressed with ICBMs, chances are he will want the Soviet arsenal, with its abundant highly MIRVed land-based missiles. If the invulnerability of SLBMs appeals to him more, he will be drawn to the American force, which deploys more of its warheads on advanced missile-carrying submarines.[7]

But one more consideration may be essential in deciding the issue. What is it we want to do with our weapons? Is it important to be able to attack an opponent's ICBMs in their silos? If so, the U.S. arsenal is less adequate, at least until its submarines are equipped with more accurate warheads. Or is the principal mission of our strategic forces to threaten a would-be attacker with the destruction of its society in a retaliatory strike? In that case Washington's capabilities appear in a better light, and it may be that each strategic force has more than enough for that purpose. The complicated issues of *strategic doctrine*—guidelines for the use or threatened use of weapons in a nuclear war—come into play when this kind of choice has to be made. Chapters 4 and 5 explore competing doctrines from the standpoints of Washington and Moscow and should make the comparison of superpower arsenals meaningful.

STRATEGIC DEFENSE: IS THE BEST OFFENSE A GOOD DEFENSE?

Our discussion of strategic weapon systems so far has dealt with only half an equation. Bombers, ALCMs, ICBMs, and SLBMs constitute the main strategic offensive forces of the two superpowers. We have ignored strategic defense—devices to block incoming strategic delivery systems—because for the most part they do not yet exist. The only major exception is air defense against bombers, a form of defense grown less critical with the switch of offensive weapons to ballistic and cruise missiles. Defense against ballistic missiles, while it would revolutionize our thinking about nuclear war, has so far been avoided on any major scale by both the United States and the Soviet Union.

The idea of strategic defense is not a new one. In the early 1960s each superpower watched the other start deploying silo-based ICBMs and submarine-launched ballistic missiles that could not be destroyed reliably in a nuclear first strike. Rather than leave their populations open to attack from these sources, political leaders in Washington and Moscow began contemplating ballistic missile defense, or *BMD*. (The original abbreviation was ABM, for antiballistic missile system. Note that BMD is an ambiguous term; it should be taken to mean defense *against* ballistic missiles, not necessarily defense *of* ballistic missiles or *by* ballistic missiles.) For several years both superpowers experimented with weapons designed to protect their territories from incoming missiles before reaching agreement in 1972 to put a lid on the competition.

What was this first-generation BMD like, and why the decision to give it up? Until the "Star Wars" visions of the 1980s, ballistic missile defense was basically a matter of shooting down missile warheads with other missiles. In the grandest view it might be possible to protect the whole territory of a country from ICBMs and SLBMs with enough interceptor rockets of sufficient precision to blunt the entire incoming strike. This failing, a more modest approach would ring the principal cities of either side with clusters of interceptors, hoping to minimize damage in a nuclear strike. A third, perhaps more realistic goal would be to defend one's own ICBM installations against attack. Soviet and American experiments of the 1960s sought to determine which of these defensive missions was feasible.

In the United States, at least, complete agreement about the potential of BMD was never reached. As debate raged in the Pentagon, in Congress, and in the press, several arguments began to tell against the plan.[8] First, a leakproof defense seemed unattainable. Heavily populated areas, targeted with several nuclear weapons in an attack, would not be much better off if struck with only two or three. That tended to force proponents of BMD back to the defense of silos, where destroying half of an enemy strike might double the number of surviving ICBMs. A second consideration though, was cost. An interceptor rocket aimed at a ballistic missile warhead in flight has a relatively small, extraordinarily fast target to hit. Even if one that would succeed half the time could be devised, it might cost several times as much to produce as the warhead it destroyed. In the parlance of nuclear exchange, it would not be a "cost-effective" weapon. That realization led to a third and probably the most telling argument against BMD: It was likely to induce an opponent to deploy more offensive weapons. If the Soviet leadership, for example, expected

American ballistic missile defense to disable half its ballistic missile warheads in a nuclear exchange, it could simply double the number of its missiles or put twice as many warheads on existing missiles.

By 1967 Lyndon Johnson and his advisers had begun to see this connection between East-West competition in strategic defenses and the ongoing race to deploy more and more offensive weapons. They suggested to Soviet Premier Aleksei Kosygin an agreement to limit the arms race in both forms. The Soviets had been working on BMD, too, and any or all of the above debate may also have taken place in Moscow. One further drawback to a defensive arms race probably troubled defense planners there: Western technological superiority might mean that American BMD would do the job better, if it could be done at all.[9]

For their own reasons, then, Soviet leaders agreed to negotiate. The result was SALT I, whose terms and subsequent revision we review in a later chapter. Its main effect on ballistic missile defense was to limit each superpower to one cluster of land-based interceptors totaling not more than 100 units—far too few to make a dent in an assault by thousands of ballistic missile warheads. The USSR constructed a BMD force of 64 interceptors around Moscow, while the United States decided to deploy none at all.

There, one might suppose, the tale would rest. But the imperative of the arms race seems to be, What is not prohibited is required. Prohibited by SALT I were the development, testing, and deployment of interceptors in excess of 100. Not prohibited was research—research to improve the allowed interceptors and research toward new BMD technologies, for use if the treaty was ever abrogated. Moscow has been refining its few interceptors ever since, as the U.S. Army and Air Force struggle to generate credible options for ballistic missile defense.

In June 1984 an American interceptor rocket struck a ballistic missile for the first time—an American missile, of course, and without a live warhead. The event, which took place at the Kwajalein testing range in the Pacific, encouraged defense scientists trying to build a working "layered defense" of ICBM silos. As it had evolved since the 1970s, the technology now included several elements: high-altitude interceptors to destroy ballistic missile warheads in space, before they reenter the atmosphere; long-range radar to help the interceptors find their targets; a set of low-altitude interceptors (LOADS, for low-altitude defense system) around each missile silo to attack warheads that get through the first shield; and local radar to guide them.[10] The overall goal is to screen out most of the warheads the Soviets would aim at American ICBMs in a first strike. It is another possible way to close the window of vulnerability, and to the extent that it did that, it would be a healthy development.

Notice two problems with layered defense, though. First, as with any form of strategic defense, it may just lead to more missiles on the other side. More subtly, even if intended only to protect silos, layered defense would look suspicious in Moscow. The LOADS portion is capable of nothing but silo defense (point defense), but high-altitude interception has other implications. It could potentially defend American cities against second-strike retaliation from the USSR (area defense), allowing Washington to contemplate a first strike with impunity. From the standpoint of an opponent, the other side's ability to defend its own territory may look like the perfect offense.

In any case, ballistic missile defense by land-based interceptor rocket is now being upstaged by other, more exotic alternatives. A year before the successful interception of a missile by a missile at Kwajalein, President Reagan stirred the nation with a vision of space-based BMD that would make "nuclear weapons impotent and obsolete."[11] His speech of March 1983 committed the resources of the United States to a decades-long quest for the perfect defense against ballistic missiles. This time the interceptor technologies of earlier efforts would be replaced by missile-destroying beams or projectiles hurled from space. A new generation of scientists, stimulated by a chance to end the dread of nuclear attack, leaped to the task of undoing the harm caused by their predecessors.

Research on the Strategic Defense Initiative (SDI, or "Star Wars," as the media instantly dubbed it) is at a very early stage, too early to judge whether it will get anywhere or what form BMD of the future might take. One potential technology can give some of the flavor of the enterprise.[12] It envisions several space stations using an energy source of some kind—possibly chemical, possibly nuclear—to generate laser beams that would destroy missiles during their boost phase. Lasers (for "light amplification by stimulated emission of radiation") are vastly more intense than most light beams because the energy in them is better organized, its waves traveling in lockstep together. A space defense station might use a giant, nearly perfect mirror to focus energy into a laser beam and direct it earthward against missiles in flight. Warheads which escape this boost phase attack might then be subjected to other, more traditional forms of interception as they approach their targets.

As with any futuristic technology, space-based ballistic missile defense attracts both enthusiasts and skeptics. For the enthusiasts it offers hope of safety from nuclear attack: high-energy lasers, guided by the latest generation of computers, destroying thousands of warheads in just the few minutes between launching and reentry over a victim's territory. To the skeptics BMD from space suffers from the same limitations which characterized earlier forms of strategic defense. If the United States began deploying a laser defense network, the Soviet Union would undoubtedly take countermeasures against it. By spinning its ICBMs in flight, for example, it could lengthen the time needed for a laser to destroy each one, forcing the West to deploy more and more laser stations. By shortening the boost phase, it could achieve the same result. The countermeasures might easily cost less than the defensive weapons. Or the USSR might simply proliferate missiles, hoping to saturate American BMD.

Technological questions aside, the Strategic Defense Initiative has become one of the hottest issues of arms control today. It is criticized for holding up negotiations to reduce strategic offensive weapons. And since space stations may be easy to attack, they could invite a war in space that would then lead to war back home on earth. We review the logic of arguments for and against the concept after a brief look at another controversial weapon, the MX missile.

Controversy 1:
DOES THE UNITED STATES NEED THE MX?

A new ten-warhead ICBM for the U.S. arsenal has been under consideration for more than a decade and has recently begun deployment. In an earlier version it was to be mobile, with twenty or more silos per missile, but current plans are to put it in existing superhardened fixed silos. Is the MX necessary?

YES! The latest Soviet ICBMs, their SS-18s and SS-19s and their new SS-24s, have from six to ten warheads apiece. Even without using all of them, Moscow could destroy the entire American ICBM force in a first strike. If the United States had mobile ICBMs, such as the MX in its original form, this result would be unattainable. Even after a Soviet attack, the United States would have some of its highly accurate MIRVed ICBMs left and could destroy any missiles the USSR might have "held back" in its silos. The mobile MX is stabilizing since it reduces the first-strike incentive for the other side.

Even if not mobile, the MX is an important asset. Given the delicate global balance of power, the West cannot afford to fall behind in any part of the strategic triad. American land-based missiles are currently inferior to Moscow's, giving the East the appearance of greater strength in the ongoing struggle for influence. Especially since ICBMs have prompt hard-target kill capabilities no other weapons can offer at present, the United States must keep its land-based missiles up-to-date.

If strategic arms control negotiations are ever to get anywhere, Moscow will have to give up a large part of its most destabilizing weapons, its heavy MIRVed ICBMs. We can never expect the Soviets to do that unless Washington has equivalent systems to bargain away. The MX, because it counterbalances the SS-18, will give the Soviets a reason to strike a bargain.

NO! The MX is a destabilizing first-strike weapon, just like the newest Soviet ICBMs. It will create the same insecurity in Moscow that the SS-18 causes in Washington. The most likely result of deployment will be new weapons on the Soviet side, probably mobile ICBMs which can get out from under the attacking MX. There is such a thing in the arms race as "enough," and the United States has it already in its SLBM force and its new ALCMs, most of which would survive any first strike by an opponent. The ability to retaliate with these two legs of the triad can deter attack without threatening the kind of silo-busting damage the West would need for a first strike.

The history of arms control negotiations shows that weapons

deployed as bargaining chips simply get added to arsenals on both sides, driving higher and higher the totals we are trying to reduce. This was the case with MIRVing in the 1970s. In the next arms control agreement the West should trade reductions in Soviet ICBMs for cuts in its superior submarine- and air-based forces.

Controversy 2:
SHOULD THE STRATEGIC DEFENSE INITIATIVE GO AHEAD?

Advanced technologies and a resurgence of interest in defense spending have renewed the arguments of the 1960s about strategic defenses. In 1972 both sides decided against building them. Does the possibility of ballistic missile defense from space mean that we should reverse that decision?

YES! For forty years the world has lived with the nightmare of nuclear holocaust. The superpowers both have what it takes to destroy each other several times over, but neither can defend itself against annihilation. The logic of nuclear exchange is "offense-dominated" because of a commitment to *mutual assured destruction* (MAD), the vulnerability of each side to the other's retaliation. We need no longer be satisfied with this unstable form of deterrence.

The United States, with its advanced space technology, can eventually have the means to protect its society from ballistic missile attack. We do not yet know the exact techniques since American physicists have just begun directing their attention to the challenge of space-based defense. But with the commitment of enough resources the job can be done. Once the West learns how to destroy missiles and warheads in flight, the arms race will grind to a halt since any new offensive weapons will be obsolete before they are built. In the nuclear era the only safe world is a "defense-dominated" world.

NO! The Strategic Defense Initiative differs from earlier concepts of ballistic missile defense only in its technology. It is open to the same objections, and the logic for banning it by mutual consent is just as strong. Since perfect defenses are too much to hope for, the most SDI can do is to limit the damage suffered in a nuclear attack. If either side seems able to do that, it will only encourage the other to expand its offensive forces. Both sides would then be back where they started, but with more weapons all around. At worst, whichever nuclear power found itself lagging in strategic defenses might try to close the gap with a preemptive attack on its opponent's new defenses while they were still being built.

Space-based BMD just makes matters worse. Because its laser stations or projectile sources would be located in space, not on the territory of the nuclear adversaries, the Strategic Defense Initiative encourages both superpowers to contemplate a preemptive attack of the sort just described. Each might hope to disable the other's defenses with little risk of retaliation since no damage to civilian populations would be involved. What started as "Star Wars" could quickly spread to earth, however, as the United States or the Soviet Union found itself suddenly undefended and rushed to strike its opponent's missiles on the ground. Strategic defenses sound comforting, but the risk of nuclear war will actually increase as we try to build them. Washington and Moscow should adhere to the provisions of SALT I, which prohibited the development, testing, or deployment of space-based BMD.

FOR MORE DETAIL

Bruce G. Blair, *Strategic Command and Control: Redefining the Nuclear Threat* (Washington, D.C.: Brookings Institution, 1985). Describes recent efforts by the United States to improve command, control, and communications with its strategic forces.

Ashton B. Carter and David Schwartz, eds., *Ballistic Missile Defense* (Washington, D.C.: Brookings Institution, 1984). Several essays by prominent authors discuss the technology, history, and logic of ballistic missile defense.

Bernard T. Feld and Kosta Tsipis, "Land-Based Intercontinental Ballistic Missiles," *Scientific American* (November 1979): 55–61. Explains the workings of MIRVed ICBMs.

Jack Dennis, ed., *The Nuclear Almanac* (Reading, Mass.: Addison-Wesley Publishing House, 1984). Part III presents the technology and strategies of nuclear warfare.

Thomas Karas, *The New High Ground: Systems and Weapons of Space Age War* (New York: Simon and Schuster, 1983). Seminal work by a leader of the movement for SDI.

Franklin A. Long, Donald Hafner, and Jeffrey Boutwell, eds., *Weapons in Space,* (New York: W. W. Norton & Co., 1986). Essays on space-based BMD and antisatellite weapons. David Holloway's contribution presents the Soviet view of strategic defense.

The Military Balance (London: International Institute for Strategic Studies, annual). Comprehensive information, published each fall, on the latest additions to the armed forces of the United States, the Soviet Union, and their allies.

Michael Nacht, "ABM ABCs," *Foreign Policy* (Spring 1982): 155–74. Analyzes BMD technologies of the 1970s, before the advent of "Star Wars" scenarios.

Keith Payne and Colin S. Gray, "Nuclear Policy and the Defensive Transition," *Foreign Affairs* (Spring 1984): 820–42. Two forceful advocates of SDI make the case for defense-dominated strategies.

Kosta Tsipis, "Cruise Missiles," *Scientific American* (February 1977): 20–29. How cruise missiles work and the problems they pose for arms control.

Joel Wit, "American SLBM: Counterforce Options and Strategic Implications," *Survival* (July/August 1982): 163–74. Technologies for improving the accuracy of the U.S. SLBM force.

NOTES TO CHAPTER 2

1. On the fiction and reality of the missile gap, see Richard Smoke, *National Security and the Nuclear Dilemma,* 2d ed. (New York: Random House, 1987), pp. 99–109.

2. Lawrence Meyer discusses the control of SLBM launches in "Fail-Safe and Subs," *Washington Post Magazine,* September 30, 1984, p. 7ff.

3. Kosta Tsipis explains ALCM technology in "Cruise Missiles," *Scientific American* (February 1977): 20–29.

4. Bernard T. Feld and Kosta Tsipis, "Land-Based Intercontinental Ballistic Missiles," *Scientific American* (November 1979): 55–61.

5. According to figures supplied by the Arms Control Association in March 1988, at least 100 single-warhead SS-11 warheads had been replaced by mobile single-warhead SS-25s. The new ten warhead SS-24 was not yet operational.

6. Joel S. Wit, "American SLBM: Counterforce Options and Strategic Implications," *Survival* (July/August 1982): 163–74.

7. For further discussion of the strategic balance, see Albert Carnesale et al., *Living with Nuclear Weapons* (New York: Bantam Books, 1983), ch. 6. Footnote 2 to that chapter gives the formula for deriving equivalent megatonnage (EMT), a frequently used measure of the destructive power of nuclear weapons, which takes into account the fact that ten 100-kiloton warheads can do more damage than a single 1-megaton warhead.

8. John Newhouse details the ABM debates of the 1960s in *Cold Dawn: The Story of SALT* (New York: Holt, Rinehart and Winston, 1973), ch. 2.

9. For Soviet attitudes toward the proposed ban on ABM systems, see David Holloway, *The Soviet Union and the Arms Race* (New Haven: Yale University Press, 1983), ch. 3., and his essay "The Strategic Defense Initiative and the Soviet Union," in *Weapons in Space,* ed. Franklin H. Long, Donald Hafner, and Jeffrey Boutwell (New York: W. W. Norton & Co., 1986).

10. Michael Nacht describes the BMD technologies of the 1970s in "ABM ABCs," *Foreign Policy* (Spring 1982): 155–74.

11. Address to the Nation, March 23, 1983, in the *Weekly Compilation of Presidential Documents*, vol. 19 (Washington, D.C.: General Services Administration, 1983), pp. 442–8.

12. A detailed account of current BMD alternatives can be found in the first four chapters of *Ballistic Missile Defense*, ed. Ashton B. Carter and David N. Schwartz (Washington, D.C.: Brookings Institution, 1984). See also the essays on strategic defense technologies in *Weapons in Space*, loc. cit, Part 1.

3

NUCLEAR WEAPONS
IN THE EUROPEAN
THEATER

—

By most accounts the world's nuclear powers now possess more than 50,000 nuclear weapons, all but a few hundred of them in the arsenals of the two superpowers. Of this total, fewer than half are strategically deliverable—that is, mounted on delivery vehicles with sufficient range to travel from the territory or submarines of one nuclear power to the homeland of another. Most of the others are battlefield weapons, miniaturized for short-range use in naval, air, or land confrontations in locations like Europe's "Central Front," West Germany's border with Communist East Germany and Czechoslovakia.

Between the two extremes—battlefield and intercontinental delivery vehicles—lurks a perplexing middle category: nuclear weapons positioned in such a way that they can reach targets in Western and Eastern Europe, China, and the USSR without crossing intercontinental distances. The nuclear forces of Great Britain, France, and China fall into this category. So does a portion of Soviet and U.S. arsenals. Intermediate-range weapons have vexed arms controllers since the 1950s, and all negotiations concerning strategic delivery vehicles have had to deal with them in some way.

At the heart of the issue is the definition of "strategic." The Soviet Union considers a nuclear delivery system strategic if one nuclear power can use it to attack the homeland of another. The United States insists on a definition in terms of range: A system is strategic if it can cross the intercontinental distance between North America and Eurasia—about 3,400 miles. By the Soviet definition, American aircraft and missiles "forward based" in Europe fall into the strategic category; by the U.S. definition, they do not.

Arms control negotiators seeking a superpower accord on strategic arms generally toss these weapons into a separate basket: intermediate-range nuclear forces *(INF)*. The round of East-West talks which began in Geneva early in 1985 thus had three arenas with different negotiating teams involved in each: space weapons, strategic offensive arms, and INF. What does this last category include, how did it come into being, and what does it mean for the future of arms control?

THE LESSER NUCLEAR POWERS: BRITAIN, FRANCE, AND CHINA

Shortly after the USSR had exploded its first atomic bomb, a third country entered the nuclear arms race. With U.S. help, Great Britain acquired nuclear weapons in the early 1950s and, again with help from the United States, began deploying them in the 1960s on submarines and aircraft where they could reach Moscow. After a lag of about a decade France achieved the same capabilities independently, including in its force a small number of IRBMs, (land-based intermediate-range ballistic missiles). Finally, by the end of the 1960s, the Chinese, who initially had Soviet assistance, also started mounting nuclear weapons on ballistic missiles of intermediate range—anywhere from about 600 to 3,400 miles.

At the beginning of the 1980s, when arms control negotiations between Moscow and Washington resumed after SALT II, British and French INF included:

TABLE 3-1—British and French INF[1]

MISSILES		AIRCRAFT	
British on subs	64	British bombers	48
French on subs	80		
French land-based	18		
Total missiles	162		

These weapons are currently being upgraded, so that British and French missiles which now carry one warhead each will soon be MIRVed. Missile warheads deliverable by the two countries against the Soviet Union will then total several hundred. Chinese delivery systems are less precisely accounted for, but they probably include about 100 single-warhead IRBMs and about the same number of intermediate-range aircraft.

What difference have these weapons made to arms control? They form a small fraction of world arsenals, but they have loomed large in discussions on the issue. At each stage in the history of East-West negotiations, Moscow has proposed counting European INF in the strategic totals for the West. After all, no one has much doubt that their targets are in the socialist camp. Add to them the several hundred aircraft armed with nuclear weapons the United States maintains in Europe, within fighting range of the USSR, plus the intermediate-range missiles newly deployed in Europe by the United States in the 1980s, and one finds 1,000 or more nuclear delivery vehicles aimed at Soviet territory, with no equivalent threat to the United States.

Each time Moscow and Washington have reached an agreement on strategic delivery vehicles—in SALT I, SALT II, and the Vladivostok accords of the mid-1970s—the United States has insisted on leaving its forward-based systems *(FBS)* out of the equation. SALT set them aside to be considered in a separate negotiation that the Soviets maintained should treat British, French, and Chinese INF, American FBS, and Soviet intermediate-range weapons as one package. East-West bargaining on a framework for such an accord formed the focus of arms control efforts through most of the 1980s. But radical disagreements about whose weapons to include and how many each side had long prevented any positive outcome.

EQUAL SECURITY: THE SOVIET VIEW OF INF

Ballistic missiles began upstaging bombers as a nuclear delivery system in the late 1950s. Since intermediate-range missiles became operational sooner than ICBMs, the emerging superpowers initially relied on them to enhance their arsenals. The Soviets developed the SS-4 IRBM and, slightly later, the SS-5, stationing them in the western part of the USSR, where they could attack America's European allies. America, in turn, put its Thor and Jupiter missiles into Western Europe and Turkey, where they could strike the Soviet Union. Within a few years, though, the two nations each had several hundred missiles of intercontinental range, able to destroy a rival in the opposite hemisphere even if based at home. The Kennedy administration decided to pull Washington's IRBMs out of Europe and Turkey, where they made easy targets for Moscow's new weapons, and for the next two decades the United States relied on a land-based nuclear force made up entirely of ICBMs.

Not so the Soviets. They kept 450 of their SS-4 and SS-5 missiles in place, posing a threat to America's NATO allies for which the United States had no counterpart. These they justified with the logic of *equal security*. Usually coupled in Soviet utterances with the concept of parity, equal security formed a second Soviet premise for nuclear arms limitation. Parity, according to Moscow, describes the current relationship between superpower strategic arsenals. Its existence at the end of the 1960s was what made SALT possible. Equal security required something more: a Soviet counterpart for the weapons of opponents other than the United States. In terms of conventional arms this meant Japan, China, and the NATO countries; in nuclear terms it referred to British, French, and Chinese INF.

Thus Moscow kept a second nuclear missile arsenal apart from the strategic offensive weapons of SALT I, aimed at American allies in Europe. And just as the 1970s saw a modernization of Soviet intercontinental missiles to more accurate MIRVed forms, the same decade brought a new generation of Soviet intermediate-range nuclear forces, alarming the West and complicating the next rounds of arms control negotiations. Compared with the newest ICBMs, Soviet SS-4s and SS-5s were out of date. Most of them were based on the surface rather than in silos, they had less accuracy than newer land-based missiles and carried only one warhead each, and it took nearly twenty-four hours to prepare them for firing. If a nuclear war broke out in Europe, they would virtually invite a Western preemptive strike.

The East-West agreement to exclude INF from SALT I probably made inevitable a new generation of intermediate-range weapons on both sides. Just as the decision not to limit warhead totals in SALT I drove the strategic arms race in the direction of MIRVing, cutting INF out of the deal practically dictated that more of them would be built. David Holloway, a leading British expert on Soviet strategic thought, expresses the political logic in Moscow this way: "By [the early 1970s] it was clear that medium-range systems would not be covered by SALT I. The old systems were obsolescent. The case for deployment must have seemed overwhelming."[2]

So it was that the *SS-20* came into being. The new Soviet IRBM, deployment of which began in 1977, had all the advantages of the latest Soviet technology. It was mobile and could be launched on short warning, reducing the chances of losing it before it could be used. It carried three warheads and could deliver them accurately enough to take out hard targets. And its range, at the upper limit for the INF category, allowed it to strike anywhere in Western Europe from European Russia and to cover all of China from Soviet Asia. By 1985 American sources counted more than 400 SS-20s, fitted with more than 1,200 warheads, in Soviet arsenals. About two-thirds of this total were said to be within range of Western Europe.

The characteristics of the SS-20 look ideal from the standpoint of the Soviet defense planner. In the event of war it can achieve a wider variety of objectives than the older models it was replacing. But for Europeans it established a new imbalance in nuclear weapons, dwarfing British and French arsenals with their scant 162 missile warheads. Even if those two European nations modernized their nuclear forces, bringing their weapons totals closer to comparable Soviet figures, they would still be relying largely on inaccurate submarine-based missiles lacking the first-strike capabilities of the SS-20. The inequality was conceptually parallel to the strategic U.S.-Soviet balance, outlined in the last chapter, in which highly accurate Soviet ICBMs, able to destroy hard targets, faced less accurate American SLBMs designed largely for use against population and industry.

The war-fighting qualities of the upgraded Soviet INF seemed to many Europeans like an attempt at nuclear blackmail, a threat to destroy West Germany, for example, without involving the United States in their attack. Could Washington be counted on to respond with its strategic arsenal when the United States could escape destruction by accepting the defeat of its allies?

As the first SS-20s were being deployed in 1977, West Germany's Social Democratic chancellor, Helmut Schmidt, warned that NATO's deterrence strategy for Europe was in jeopardy. The SALT process, he pointed out, codified strategic parity between the superpowers without assuring a balance in their nuclear and conventional forces in Europe. "[S]trategic arms limitations confined to the United States and the Soviet Union," Schmidt argued, "will inevitably impair the security of the West European members of the Alliance *vis-à-vis* Soviet military superiority in Europe if we do not succeed in removing the disparities of military power in Europe parallel to the SALT negotiations. . . . The Alliance must, therefore, be ready to make available the means to support its present strategy. . . ."[3] NATO would have either to match Soviet intermediate-range forces or to persuade Moscow to reduce them.

At the urging of the Europeans and with the consent of the Carter administration, NATO endorsed Schmidt's logic in its 1979 dual-track decision. Washington would base several hundred missiles of intermediate range on the ground in five European countries (West Germany, Great Britain, Belgium, the Netherlands, and Italy), while negotiating with Moscow to cut back INF on both sides. The Reagan administration, by contrast with Carter's reluctant support for the decision, came to office enthusiastically committed to carry out this policy.

EXTENDED DETERRENCE AND THE U.S. NUCLEAR UMBRELLA

America's new INF deployments, which got under way late in 1983, bring us back to the logical currency of the early nuclear era. As the next chapter explains, the initial postwar rationale for nuclear weapons was to stop Soviet aggression by threatening to do to Moscow what had just been done to Hiroshima and Nagasaki. In particular, they were thought of as a deterrent to an attack by the USSR on Western Europe.

The end of the Second World War found Soviet troops in most of Eastern Europe, where Stalin was setting up Communist-dominated regimes he could control. With Germany and Italy defeated and France and Great Britain exhausted by the war, two factors implied a Soviet conventional military preponderance in Europe for the foreseeable future: (1) West European economies were too feeble to support a military force equal to Stalin's, and (2) the American public was eager to bring U.S. troops back home. What was to stop the Red Army from sweeping westward across the rest of the European continent?

President Truman's answer was the atomic bomb. As long as the United States enjoyed a monopoly on this fearsome new weapon, it could hold a nuclear umbrella over the endangered countries of Western Europe. If Moscow's troops marched westward, Stalin faced the nuclear destruction of his own cities. As a result, no Soviet attack would occur.

This is an early example of nuclear *deterrence*, a concept to be explored more fully in a later chapter. It involves dissuading an opponent from an action it would otherwise take by making a credible threat to do unacceptable damage in return. In this case the action deterred is Soviet aggression by conventional (i.e., nonnuclear) means in Europe, and the threatened response is an American nuclear strike against targets in Russia. Deterrence more commonly involves blocking an enemy attack on one's *own* territory, and it often seeks to prevent a *nuclear* assault by threatening nuclear retaliation. When one country (the United States) sets out to deter attack by a second country (the USSR) against a *third* party (Western Europe), its logic is called *extended deterrence*, a more exalted name for a nuclear umbrella.

Extended deterrence sounds like a simple enough concept, and it was relatively simple to practice in the days of the American nuclear monopoly. It has two traits, though, that make it trickier to accomplish than simple deterrence of an attack against one's own country:

1. Extended deterrence involves persuading an enemy that another nation's territory means as much to you as does your own. By seek-

ing to protect Western Europe in this way, Truman was telling Stalin that West Germany counted as if it were the state next to Maine. For the strategy to work, this equation of another nation's assets with one's own has to be believable.

2. Where deterrence of a conventional onslaught is the objective, extended deterrence means the threat to use nuclear weapons *first*. It is therefore unlike a deterrence strategy that says, "If you strike me with nuclear weapons, I will retaliate in the same way." In the latter case the onus of starting a nuclear war weighs on the opponent. Under the logic of extended deterrence, the United States must make credible its willingness to go nuclear first.

During the 1950s Washington and Moscow set up formal alliance networks in Europe: the North Atlantic Treaty Organization linked most West European nations to Washington, while the Warsaw Pact made Moscow responsible for defending Eastern Europe north of the Balkans. The East's conventional superiority—more men under more arms, more tanks and other battlefield weapons—forestalled any Western effort to "liberate" Poland or Hungary. On its side, NATO relied on extended deterrence to keep the superior armies of the Warsaw Pact from marching westward or from possible political intimidation of a weakened West on issues such as Berlin.

But then something critical to NATO's logic changed. The Soviet Union came up with nuclear weapons of its own. At first these were deployed on delivery vehicles that did little to undercut extended deterrence: intercontinental bombers which could be destroyed as part of an American nuclear strike and intermediate-range ballistic missiles incapable of reaching the United States. With the silo-based ICBMs and submarine-launched ballistic missiles of the 1960s, however, Moscow developed a secure means of retaliation against the United States, means that could survive any NATO attack on the USSR and respond with an attack on American cities.

What would become of extended deterrence now? Could the United States still credibly threaten to make first use of nuclear weapons against Moscow if Warsaw Pact forces launched a conventional weapons attack on West Germany? Or would the growing Soviet capacity to bring nuclear war to the American mainland neutralize the threat behind extended deterrence? Were U.S. nuclear weapons now useful only to deter a direct Soviet attack on the United States?

For twenty years these questions have nagged at NATO strategists, who worry about the decoupling of Western European and American defenses. A variety of answers have been offered, none of them entirely satisfying. For example:

• Strengthen NATO's conventional forces enough to deter a Warsaw Pact assault without threatening the first use of nuclear weapons. This is a more expensive option than a nuclear umbrella, and while European nations have long since recovered from the postwar economic weakness that initially ruled it out, they remain unwilling to pay the price. Some strategists argue that no feasible additions to the conventional capabilities of NATO would suffice to offset Moscow's advantage if the first use of nuclear weapons by the West were excluded.[4] Furthermore, if the conventional buildup were entirely European, it might signal a declining U.S. interest in defending Western Europe.

• Put a European finger on the nuclear "trigger," involving American allies such as West Germany in the decision to go nuclear. A plan of this sort (a multilateral nuclear force, or MLF) was endorsed by President Kennedy in the early 1960s. Because a nuclear war in Europe would be fought on German soil, at least in the beginning, it was hoped that an expanded role for West Germany would keep extended deterrence credible. The plan fizzled, however, because other Europeans were generally averse to giving the Germans any control over nuclear weapons. Furthermore, any command arrangements requiring approval by several nations, not just the United States, to initiate the use of nuclear weapons in Europe might easily fail in a crisis.[5]

• Rely on the U.S. strategic arsenal, based outside Europe, to threaten Soviet targets in the event of Warsaw Pact aggression. This was, in fact, the strategy of the 1960s, after the primitive Thors and Jupiters had been withdrawn and while American strategic superiority over the Soviets was still clear-cut. Even then, though, there was reason to question whether any degree of superiority could let one superpower credibly threaten to start a nuclear war, given a survivable retaliatory force on the other side.

• Place U.S. intermediate-range missiles on the ground in Europe once again. Although the new weapons could have no targets not already "covered" by American ICBMs, SLBMs, and bombers, Moscow might believe Washington would actually use them in a limited nuclear first strike, holding its "central systems" in reserve in the hope of averting all-out war. This was Schmidt's solution. It depends heavily on the assumption that a U.S. threat to attack the USSR from Europe is more credible than extended deterrence by means of intercontinental ballistic missiles.

• Decide that Western Europe is already sufficiently defended against the threat of Warsaw Pact aggression. The unreliability of Soviet allies in Eastern Europe has been amply demonstrated by uprisings in Hungary, Czechoslovakia, and Poland over three decades. If Soviet generals deliberately launched their country into a European war, Moscow would have to count on East European troops to fight on its side and would find itself supplying its forces across a possibly hostile Poland. It would need to move Soviet troops westward out of volatile areas of the USSR, like the Baltic republics and the Ukraine. And it would open itself up to the only scenario—a two-front war—in which China might realistically think of attacking dwindling Soviet forces in the Far East. The relative political reliability of NATO and Warsaw Pact armies is one of the West's greatest advantages, but it is generally ignored in NATO's war plans.

THE PERSHING II IRBM AND THE TOMAHAWK GROUND-LAUNCHED CRUISE MISSILE

NATO's dual track decision went into effect early in the 1980s, with the White House occupied by a President more skeptical of arms control than any of his predecessors and the Kremlin experiencing a succession of four leaderships in just over two years. Not surprisingly, the policy's deployment track saw swifter action than its arms control track. Though negotiations to limit INF started in late 1981, they produced no result and were overtaken at the end of 1983 by U.S. deployment of two new systems in Europe. Another two years and all 108 Pershing II missiles were in place, while about one-quarter of the scheduled 464 Tomahawk cruise missiles had gone in.

What could these missiles do that could not already be accomplished by American aircraft and shorter-range missiles based in

Europe? The *Pershing II* was, in fact, a second cousin to the earlier Pershing I, a short-range ballistic missile based in West Germany since the 1960s. The range of the earlier version kept it from reaching the USSR and also from being considered a form of INF, until a change in the parameters of that term occurred late in the negotiations. The Pershing II, by contrast, is a ballistic missile of range sufficient to strike much of European Russia. It is accurate enough for use against Soviet missiles, for example, or to destroy hardened command posts between Moscow and the front lines of any European war. And it is mobile, less susceptible than its predecessor to being destroyed before it can be used.

In all these ways the Pershing II component of American INF mimicked earlier Soviet moves to upgrade its intermediate-range ballistic missiles in Europe; the trend is toward longer range, greater accuracy, and mobility. The Pershing II is un-Mirved and at least in that way less destabilizing than the SS-20. From the Soviet standpoint it nonetheless poses an exceptional threat: Its flight time to the Soviet Union is fewer than ten minutes. That combined with extraordinary accuracy (an estimated CEP of about 100 feet) would make it highly useful as part of a U.S. first strike. If, as the Soviets claim, it can reach Moscow from its launch sites in West Germany, the Pershing II is the perfect "decapitating" weapon, capable of destroying the Kremlin's control over its own forces in the first act of a nuclear war.

America's second new system in Europe, the *Tomahawk ground-launched cruise missile (GLCM),* could serve best as a retaliatory weapon. Like all cruise missiles, it travels at much slower speeds than ballistic missiles, penetrating enemy territory at low altitudes and hugging the terrain to avoid detection by radar that could guide Soviet air-defense interceptors. Based on the ground in several West European locations, GLCMs are mounted four to a launcher, though each cruise missile itself carries only one warhead. They are mobile, like the Pershing II and the Soviet SS-20, and have at least the accuracy of those two IRBMs. But because of their smaller size, they posed problems for arms controllers. If their deployment mode were redesigned, they could be hidden from Soviet reconnaissance satellites, which would have to be able to count them if verifiable limits on INF were to be set.

THE INF BALANCE, A STICKING POINT FOR ARMS CONTROL

These, then, were the items for negotiation in the INF arena: British, French, and sometimes Chinese missiles based on land and at sea, Soviet SS-20s along with some remaining SS-4s, the U.S. Pershing II and GLCMs, and a bewildering array of aircraft deployed by each of these nations, armed with nuclear weapons and stationed so as to be useful in a European or Asian war.

Why did it take nearly a decade to reach an agreement limiting these weapons, whose modernization was making them ever more dangerous? Part of the answer lies in the conflicting attitudes of the superpowers concerning the intermediate-range forces they needed. As we have seen, Moscow maintained that it needed weapons to offset the burgeoning nuclear delivery systems of three opponents besides the United States. The Soviet search for equal security led to a demand for totals in excess of the American equivalents. Washington rejoined that British, French, and Chinese nuclear forces were not under its command and that they could not be counted on for the defense of countries like West Germany or Japan. The United States, for its part, seemed determined to keep nuclear missiles as well as aircraft in Europe for a mission the USSR did not have: extended deterrence of an enemy attack on its allies. It sought a nuclear offset for superior Soviet conventional capabilities. The Kremlin claimed that the Europeans could manage their own defense and that the United States had no business in Europe.

Apart from these disagreements over doctrine, radically differing counts of intermediate-range weapons by the two sides stood in the way of arms control. Especially if aircraft in the European theater were counted, the numbers could be juggled to produce almost any result desired by a particular observer. In the early 1980s, for example, the Reagan administration announced that the Soviets had a six-to-one lead over the United States in intermediate-range launchers in Europe. It supported that ratio with a count including about 700 nuclear missiles and more than 3,000 aircraft for the USSR, compared with 560 U.S. aircraft in Europe:

TABLE 3-2—U.S. INF Count[6]

UNITED STATES		SOVIET UNION	
Missiles	0	SS-20s	250
F-111 fighter-bombers	164	SS-4s and SS-5s	350
F-4s	265	SS-12s and SS-22s	100
A-6s and A-7s	68	SS-N-5 SLBMs	30
FB-111s	63	Backfire bombers	45
		Badgers and Blinders	350
Total U.S. INF	560	Su-17, Su-24, and	
		Mig-27 bombers	2,700
		Total Soviet INF	3,825

The figures here have been "cooked" in a number of ways to minimize U.S. totals while maximizing Soviet totals. Short-range missiles not normally counted as INF have been included for the USSR (SS-12s and SS-22s) but not for the West (the Pershing I). Submarine-based missiles dedicated to the European theater appear in estimates for the Soviet Union but not as a part of U.S. forces. But the most significant addition by far comprises 2,700 aircraft of disputed range, which Moscow excludes from its account of the INF balance.

With sleight of hand to match Washington's, the Kremlin produced figures to show a rough balance of INF forces in 1982, before U.S. deployment of any Pershing II or Tomahawk missiles:

TABLE 3-3—Soviet INF Count[7]

UNITED STATES		SOVIET	
Pershing I missiles	108	SS-20s, SS-4s,	
Fighter-bombers	555	and SS-5s	496
		SS-N-5s	18
BRITISH		Backfire, Badger, and	
Polaris SLBMs	64	Blinder bombers	461
Vulcan bombers	56		
		Total Soviet INF	975
FRENCH			
Land-based missiles	18		
SLBMs	80		
Bombers	33		
WEST GERMAN			
Pershing I	72		
Total Western INF	986		

Here the Soviets were playing some numerical tricks of their own. Reversing the U.S. procedure, they counted short-range

Pershing I missiles, under West German control and with nuclear warheads held separately by the United States, but left out their own weapons of the same range. They added about 250 British and French missiles and bombers ignored in Washington's count. But easily the greatest difference between the two versions resulted from Moscow's exclusion of Soviet aircraft which, presumably, were considered too short-range to be INF.

A FINAL CATEGORY IN EUROPE: SHORT-RANGE INF

As will be related below in Chapter 7, a series of dramatic shifts in the Soviet position by Mikhail Gorbachev made possible an agreement on intermediate-range nuclear forces in the late 1980s. The complications entailed in counting theater nuclear aircraft were removed when both sides consented to limit only missile INF. Moscow dropped its demand that third-party weapons be included, and verification was simplified by a decision to eliminate all U.S. and Soviet missiles of intermediate range worldwide.

As the prospects for eliminating the entire category of intermediate-range missiles grew brighter, however, many within the Reagan administration became anxious about Soviet superiority in a further class of nuclear missiles in Europe which would remain after an INF treaty. These they described as short-range INF. The weapons we have been discussing were called long-range INF in Washington, and they were defined by a range of between 600 and 3,400 miles. Beneath the bottom of that range was a variety of shorter-range and battlefield nuclear weapons maintained in Europe by NATO and the Warsaw Pact, many mounted on missiles and accounting in total for more warheads than were included in the category of long-range INF.[8] While some were usable only along the immediate line of battle, others could cover distances of from 300 to 600 miles, allowing either side to attack supply lines and command posts well behind the front.

It was the shorter-range nuclear missiles in this last category that became the final hurdle to an INF treaty in 1987. NATO's 72 Pershing I short-range missiles belonged to West Germany, although warheads for them were controlled by U.S. forces. Washington maintained that they could not be considered in a treaty governing U.S. and Soviet weapons, just as it had refused to include longer-range British and French INF. The United States reserved the right, then, to match about 130 Soviet short-range missiles in Europe after an INF agreement was signed, possibly by removing one stage from the Pershing II missiles it would be dismantling, thereby converting them to shorter ranges. We shall see in Chapter 7 how the issue of short-range INF was resolved.

WEAPONS AND STRATEGY

Our review of nuclear weapons, strategic and intermediate-range, is now complete. But the principal question facing the student of arms control—which of these weapons should be reduced or eliminated by negotiated agreements—remains unanswered. We have not yet given ourselves a way of deciding how many and what kinds of nuclear weapons are actually needed by East and West for their security in a world of superpower antagonism. How crucial are U.S. intermediate-range forces to overall Western strategies of deterrence? Does Washington need more ICBMs to forestall an attack by Moscow? Should the Soviets be allowed to make their ICBMs mobile? To answer these and similar questions is the job of strategic doctrine, the subject of the next two chapters.

We have already encountered one instance of this complex nuclear logic, however, in the discussion of extended deterrence above. Before we go on to examine the many other puzzles involved in strategic doctrine, the following controversy section points up the critical issues surrounding the nuclear defense of Western Europe and an arms control treaty to abolish INF.

Controversy:
DOES THE UNITED STATES NEED INTERMEDIATE-RANGE MISSILES IN EUROPE?

YES! Unlike the Soviet Union, the United States has a set of allies in Europe which could be overrun by the superior conventional forces of the Eastern bloc. It would be too expensive to match the Warsaw Pact soldier for soldier and tank for tank. Instead, the nuclear forces of NATO must be able to defend Western Europe by threatening a direct attack on the Soviet Union, should Communist-bloc ground forces mount an assault westward.

At an earlier point in the nuclear era this mission of extended deterrence could be carried out by the nuclear weapons in America's strategic arsenal. The threat to go nuclear in a European war was credible, however, only as long as U.S. strategic superiority lasted. SALT brought that superiority to an end, codifying parity between the central systems of the superpowers. To keep the West's nuclear umbrella over Western Europe viable, NATO needs intermediate-range missiles that can bring destruction to Soviet territory, even if American ICBMs and SLBMs are held back to preserve the United States from attack.

The USSR upgraded its threat to Western Europe in the 1970s, when it introduced SS-20 IRBMs in large numbers. To keep extended deterrence credible, the West urgently needs the Pershing II and cruise missiles Washington has been deploying. They should not be traded away in an arms control agreement since they are essential to extended deterrence, whether or not the Soviet Union keeps its SS-20s.

NO! It is true that extended deterrence is now an empty doctrine. Once the Soviet Union deployed a secure retaliatory force in the 1960s, NATO's threat to start a nuclear war in defense of Western Europe lost its credibility. But the Pershing II and Tomahawk GLCM do nothing to restore it. Why would an American nuclear strike on Russia from Europe seem any different to the Kremlin from the use of our home-based strategic arsenal? Both would elicit the same response: retaliatory destruction against the United States.

If anything, new U.S. INF in Europe increases the danger of war there, just as Soviet SS-20s do. Because their flight time is so short compared with ICBMs, the Pershing II and SS-20 give an opponent too little chance to evaluate false warnings of an impending attack. Each side has a heightened incentive to get its missiles off the ground, if a crisis seems about to usher in a war. This "trigger-happy" effect of intermediate-range missiles makes them a worse threat to Europe than any deliberate onslaught by the East.

Even in the nuclear era a conventional threat to Western Europe has to be countered by conventional means. Given the superior technology of NATO's weapons, the unreliability of Moscow's "allies" in the Warsaw Pact, and the presence of U.S. ground forces to "couple" American and European defenses, any Soviet attack along the Central Front is already deterred. The American nuclear umbrella collapsed long ago, but luckily for everyone, it isn't raining.

FOR MORE DETAIL

David Holloway, *The Soviet Union and the Arms Race* (New Haven and London: Yale University Press, 1983). Chapter 4 gives the Soviet point of view on theater nuclear weapons in Europe.

William G. Hyland, "The Struggle for Europe: An American View," in *Nuclear Weapons in Europe*, ed. Andrew J. Pierre (New York: Council on Foreign Relations, 1984). The editor of the widely read journal *Foreign Affairs* presents the same forces as seen from Washington.

Edward Luttwak, "How to Think About Nuclear War," *Commentary* (August 1982): 21–28. An outspoken conservative evaluates the Soviet threat to Western Europe and possible NATO responses.

Helmut Schmidt, "The Alistair Buchan Memorial Lecture," *Survival* (January–February 1978): 2–10. This speech by the former West German chancellor formed the basis for NATO's dual track decision on INF.

David N. Schwartz, *NATO's Nuclear Dilemmas* (Washington, D.C.: Brookings Institution, 1983). Leon V. Sigal, *Nuclear Forces in Europe: Enduring Dilemmas, Present Prospects* (Washington, D.C.: Brookings Institution, 1984). Two creditable attempts to sort through the puzzle of extended deterrence.

Gregory Treverton, *Nuclear Weapons in Europe*, Adelphi Paper No. 168 (London: International Institute for Strategic Studies, 1981). A detailed evaluation of conflicting arguments concerning INF.

Karsten D. Voigt, "Nuclear Weapons in Europe: A German Social Democrat's Perspective," in *Nuclear Weapons in Europe*, ed. Andrew J. Pierre (New York: Council on Foreign Relations, 1984). A leader of the West German Bundestag questions the logic of the dual-track decision.

NOTES TO CHAPTER 3

1. Adapted from Gregory Treverton, *Nuclear Weapons in Europe*, Adelphi Paper No. 168 (London: International Institute for Strategic Studies, 1981), p. 33. The figures are for 1979.

2. David Holloway, *The Soviet Union and the Arms Race* (New Haven and London: Yale University Press, 1983), p. 70.

3. Helmut Schmidt, "The Alistair Buchan Memorial Lecture," *Survival* (January–February 1978): 2–10.

4. For example, see Edward Luttwak, "How to Think About Nuclear War," *Commentary* (August 1982): 21–28.

5. A brief description of the MLF can be found in Lawrence Freedman, *The Evolution of Nuclear Strategy* (New York: St. Martin's Press, 1983), pp. 327–29.

6. Adapted from Jane M. O. Sharp, "Four Approaches to an INF Agreement," *Arms Control Today* (March 1982): 1–3, and the *New York Times*, June 29, 1982, p. A6.

7. *New York Times*, June 29, 1982, p. A6.

8. Exact figures and weapons types in the short-range INF category are given by the *New York Times*, September 15, 1987, p. A6.

PART II

THINKING ABOUT NUCLEAR WAR

4

―――――
―――――

STRATEGIC DOCTRINE
IN THE WEST

—

Indispensable to any evaluation of arms control is an understanding of the strategies which account for weapons acquisition. What are the different things we might want to do with our nuclear weapons? What are their likely missions, and which weapons have the capabilities to achieve those missions? How do the scenarios of nuclear war look from the standpoint of our opponents? Which weapons might they reasonably want to keep in their arsenals?

The next two chapters deal with these questions. Like any argument of logic, this one can drive our reasoning powers around in circles. Each line of argumentation usually begins with a "What if" question. What if the other side should do this? What would we need in order to stop them or to dissuade them from that line of attack? Then what if they should do something else? Would we need something different to thwart that course of action? Such considerations generate a long list of nuclear "needs" for each side. But they also raise an alarming question: What if our own mounting weapons arsenals lead our opponent into a course more harmful still than the ones we have been imagining?

Over the past four decades some of the world's most prominent defense specialists, and most political leaders of both East and West, have been driven mercilessly through this cycle of questions, coming down first at one point, then at another. As eminent a thinker as Robert McNamara (defense secretary to two American Presidents) reasoned first through the need for more military options and then back to the need for fewer. As powerful a leader as Leonid Brezhnev (general secretary of the Soviet Communist party for eighteen years) demanded first a furious military buildup for his nation and then a series of negotiated arms restraints.

Strategic doctrine—the principles we use in thinking about nuclear war—may well be the most difficult aspect of arms control. It is also one no thoughtful student of the subject can avoid. To unravel its logic, we use a historical approach here, outlining in sequence the main concepts of nuclear exchange common among governments over the past forty years. Stripped of their intricacies, these doctrines divide roughly into two sorts: those with a single, main use for nuclear weapons in mind—assured destruction, for example—and doctrines which demand more options in the case of nuclear war, such as the countervailing strategy. As we proceed historically, I emphasize this distinction between single-purpose and multiple-options doctrines, indicating at the same time the differing economic philosophies closely connected with them.

Some oversimplification is bound to occur with this approach; there has rarely been a theory that envisioned one and only one possible use for nuclear weapons. Still, we can profitably concentrate on the dichotomy between more demanding and less demanding doctrines since they differ greatly in their implications for the arms race and for arms control. To add to the complexity of the subject, governments rarely follow one single doctrine at a time. Any government includes civilian and military leaders, who often disagree, and any modern military establishment breaks down into rival services pursuing conflicting ends. This is as true of Soviet leaderships, whose views we discuss in the next chapter, as of American governments. As we go along, then, we will have to look at the official doctrine of a given era and also at the competing theories of its critics, who often went on to overturn one doctrine and replace it with another.

STRATEGIC DOCTRINE IN AN AGE OF NUCLEAR SCARCITY

The nuclear age began in the summer of 1945, when the United States exploded the world's first fission device and went on to drop the atomic bomb on two Japanese cities. At the end of that year the American stockpile contained only two nuclear weapons; by 1946, nine; by 1947, thirteen; and by July 1948, fifty. Even then the United States had only about thirty aircraft capable of delivering the immense early A-bomb.[1] Not surprisingly, little attention was given in these first years to strategies for using nuclear weapons in case of war. Military analysts thought of them simply as more potent versions of the conventional bombs dropped on Germany and Japan in the last war, when "strategic bombing" of cities sought to destroy the enemy's industrial assets and weaken the will of its population.

Note that "strategic" is being used in two ways here. As defined earlier, the term describes attacks on the homeland of an opponent and the weapons employed in such attacks. In this sense we speak of "strategic delivery systems" for nuclear weapons and of the "strategic bombing" of Dresden and Tokyo in World War II. But the word has a second, more fundamental meaning, from which the phrase "strategic doctrine" derives. The concepts of the current chapter are "strategic" in that they refer to *strategies* for achieving various ends in warfare. Strategy here means simply the process of matching means to ends, of relating objectives to resources.[2] The objective might be to destroy an enemy's cities, but it might just as easily be to kill its troops on a distant battlefield. The means, then, could be nuclear bombs in some cases, but in other cases it might be land mines or submarine torpedoes. In this chapter we examine the ways people imagine using nuclear weapons to achieve military objectives.

Strategic doctrine governing the use of nuclear weapons was at first a simple matter because the resources involved were so few. Early bombs were weak compared with our present warheads, and until the end of the 1940s they added up to less than 1 percent of what either superpower has now. The Truman administration accordingly chose a limited objective for them: Its Trojan war plan, approved in 1948, identified seventy Soviet cities for attack with 133 fission bombs. The plan simply extended the strategic bombing concept of the Second World War to the new technologies of the nuclear age.[3] If ever the United States had a true single-purpose strategic doctrine, this was it.

But events soon conspired against the simplicity of early doctrine. In 1949 the USSR exploded its own nuclear device. Even though it would take the Soviets several years to find a way of delivering their bombs to the Western Hemisphere, the American nuclear monopoly was over. Thinkers in Washington had to face the prospect of nuclear assault on their own country in any war with Moscow. American capabilities were developing quickly, too. At the beginning of 1950 President Truman overruled the objections of some of his advisers and authorized work toward the H-bomb, whose radically greater destructive potential would put an end to nuclear scarcity on the Western side. With these new threats and capabilities in the offing, strategic doctrine began to change.

AMERICA ENTERS THE AGE OF NUCLEAR ABUNDANCE

By 1950 the mentality of the Cold War held the United States in its grip. American strategic thinkers started from the axiom that the Soviets might launch a major war in Europe at any time, overrunning U.S. allies there and taking control of a continent divided between East and West since the end of World War II. In the early postwar years merely the possession of nuclear weapons by the United States—its ability to devastate Russia in the first hours of any new war—had seemed enough to keep Moscow in check. The West built down its conventional forces in Europe until they were undeniably inferior to the ground troops of the Communist nations. "Containment" relied on the U.S. nuclear monopoly until suddenly the Soviet Union turned up with nuclear means of its own. With that development, critics of Truman's strategic doctrine came to the fore, and the administration began to shift its policy.

Two new lines of thinking about war emerged. The first, which demanded a rapid buildup of Western conventional forces, was embodied in a lengthy National Security Council document dating from early 1950 and designated *NSC-68*. Its twin premises were: (1) that Communist Russia was innately aggressive and without sufficient military resistance from the United States would achieve world domination, and (2) that nuclear weapons had now to be thought of primarily as a deterrent to war, not as a means of fighting one. Bernard Brodie, an eminent postwar strategist, had pointed out this paradox of the nuclear revolution in warfare. Soon, he noted, each superpower would be capable of destroying the society of the other, a capability against which no adequate defense was likely to develop. "Thus far the chief purpose of our military establishment has been to win wars," Brodie observed. "From now on its chief purpose must be to avert them."[4]

NSC-68, accepting Brodie's wisdom, argued that American defenses were insufficient for the requirements of the nuclear age because U.S. strategy called for the early, devastating use of nuclear weapons in any war with the Soviet Union (and, by 1950, Communist China). "The only deterrent we can [now] present to the Kremlin," it warned, "is the evidence we give that we may make any of the critical points which we cannot hold the occasion for a global war of annihilation." The alternative recommended by the National Security Council was "to increase as rapidly as possible our general air, ground, and sea strength and that of our allies to a point where we are militarily not so heavily dependent on atomic weapons."[5]

Did this imply, then, that U.S. nuclear capabilities were adequate as they were? Here a second new direction in strategic doctrine clearly answered, "No!" Hand in hand with a conventional buildup must go a strengthening of nuclear forces so the West could win a nuclear war if one broke out. NSC-68 urged "greatly increased air warning systems, air defenses, and vigorous development and implementation of a civilian defense program" to limit damage to the United States from a Soviet nuclear assault. But finally, since some of America's retaliatory forces might well be destroyed in a strike from the East, NSC-68 proposed "a further increase in the number and power of our atomic weapons. . . ."

What would henceforth be the targets for the American nuclear arsenal? Here NSC-68 was oddly vague, mentioning "strategic and tactical targets" without specifically identifying them. A proliferation of targets was becoming possible, though, because the American nuclear stockpile was growing rapidly. By the middle of 1950 the Strategic Air Command had more than 250 nuclear-capable aircraft. In August the Joint Chiefs of Staff added to the list of nuclear missions "the destruction of known targets affecting the Soviet capability to deliver atomic bombs."[6] Presumably this meant that airfields in the USSR were now targeted along with cities.

As nuclear weapons got more numerous and more powerful, they were also getting smaller. This made it feasible to think about using them on the battlefields of Europe against troops, tanks, and supply lines. Between 1950 and 1952 the first NATO supreme allied commander, Dwight Eisenhower, as it happened, advocated planning for the tactical nuclear defense of Europe. By the time Harry Truman left office, the number of U.S. nuclear bombs was approaching 1,000, and with their growing numbers went a growing set of ideas about how to use them.

It was in this way that the United States got its first multiple-options doctrine: accidentally, increment by increment, with additions from various government agencies and military commands. Unlike later doctrines, it had no particular name, but most elements of the more elaborate doctrines of the 1960s and 1970s were already there in rudimentary form:

- Nuclear weapons capable of strategic retaliation against Soviet cities, even after a first strike against the United States

- Additional nuclear weapons to strike at the growing Soviet strategic forces before they could be used in an attack

- Air defenses to limit the damage those forces could do to the United States

- Larger conventional forces on the ground, at sea, and in the air, to postpone the moment when the West would have to go nuclear in a war with the Soviet Union

- The introduction of nuclear weapons into plans for limited theater war

One may wonder whether these multiple objectives form a coherent set or whether some conflict with others. If conventional forces are built up to keep nuclear ones in reserve as a deterrent, does it make sense to proliferate atomic (later hydrogen) bombs with nuclear war-fighting scenarios in mind? Some see a contradiction here, an overabundance of objectives generated by growing nuclear resources. To others, nothing short of the total package seems enough to deter Communist attack. The same differences of opinion crop up regarding later doctrine, too, for the competition among theories governing nuclear weapons has never ended.

Of one thing there could be no doubt: This first multiple-options doctrine was an expensive one, with its demands for more of everything in the way of weapons. NSC-68 took pains to point out that the U.S. peacetime economy was operating far below capacity, its plants underutilized and its labor force partly unemployed. Adopting the economic philosophy expounded earlier by British economist John Maynard Keynes, advocates of a rapid defensive buildup argued that it could be sustained without reducing American living standards. It would actually be healthy for an economy in recession, they maintained, putting money into the hands of people who would in turn spend it and create additional jobs.

NSC-68, along with the Korean War, which followed close on its heels, justified a deliberate program of deficit spending in the United States. During the last three years of Truman's presidency, defense budgets skyrocketed, and Americans went back to work. But as a new defense-based prosperity developed, the country began using its resources to full capacity, and the worry of unemployment was replaced by the specter of excess demand with its resulting inflation.

REPUBLICANS AND THE "NEW LOOK" IN STRATEGIC DOCTRINE

Styles change. With the crew cuts and sack dresses of the mid-1950s came a new fashion in defense policy. Dwight Eisenhower was President, and he intended to wring inflation out of the American economy by balancing the federal budget. His first year in office brought an end to the Korean War and its irresistible demands for more troops and more weapons. Once again U.S.

conventional forces were pared back, as they had been after World War II, and once again a simpler strategic doctrine put strategic nuclear retaliation front and center.

At the core of Eisenhower's defense planning was the concept of *massive retaliation*. Never set forth in a single document, it grew from the anti-Communist rhetoric of his secretary of state, John Foster Dulles, and from positions taken by the National Security Council. Dulles regarded the Korean War as a signal that Truman's strategy had failed. The Democratic policy of blocking all enemy moves when and where they occurred meant prolonged, large-scale conflicts, like that in Korea, entailing "military expenditures so vast that they lead to 'practical bankruptcy' " for the United States.[7] Especially with the new hydrogen bomb, carrying destructive power hundreds of times greater than the early A-bombs, America could count on containing Soviet power by simpler means. Washington would not abandon regional defenses entirely, but it would "depend primarily upon a great capacity to retaliate, instantly, by means and places of our choosing."

Like most American doctrine in the postwar era, massive retaliation was a theory of deterrence. It aimed at preventing an opponent from taking actions it otherwise would take by threatening to do unacceptable damage in return. It did not contemplate an unprovoked assault on an enemy, and if successful, it would mean that no military action was taken by either side. It was, like NSC-68 before it and nearly all strategic doctrine after it, a theory about averting war.

To be coherent, any strategy of deterrence needs to specify two things: what actions an opponent would likely take if not deterred, and what threat is both credible and sufficient to stop the opponent from taking those actions. Modest as these requirements sound, they seem to defeat most strategists, who either cannot or will not be specific on these two counts. The thinkers of the Eisenhower administration were no exception. Dulles apparently believed the fighting in Korea had come to an end because of a threat by the Eisenhower administration to use nuclear weapons there. How, then, to extend this experience to the broader international environment? If the answer was massive retaliation, its terms were extremely vague. The National Security Council in 1953 proposed to defend against the "Soviet threat" by emphasizing "massive retaliatory damage by offensive striking power."[8] A major assault on Western Europe, "brush fires" in the Middle or Far East, possibly even the overthrow of conservative governments by revolutionary movements—seemingly any of these could occasion a response of massive retaliation.

To be fair to Eisenhower and his strategists, their ambiguity may have been deliberate. Dulles argued that deterrence worked best if the enemy was kept guessing about U.S. responses to its actions. "It should not be stated in advance," he reasoned, "precisely what would be the scope of military action if new aggression occurred."[9] There was no need to specify what forms of misconduct by the Russians (Chinese, North Koreans, etc.) Washington hoped to deter. The same was true for the nature of Western retaliation: "[B]y means and at places of our choosing" meant rejecting the idea of local actions proportionate to the Kremlin's aggression in each case, but it declined to say what was threatened instead. Most observers took Dulles to mean an all-out nuclear assault on the Soviet Union.

They may have been wrong. Dulles denied that the United States "intended to rely wholly on large-scale strategic bombing as the sole means to deter and counter aggression." Early in the Eisenhower years, as American conventional manpower was being scaled back, the administration sent tactical nuclear weapons of miniature size to its forces in Europe. Part of the threat intended by massive retaliation was thus probably not massive at all but a willingness to go nuclear on the battlefield if necessary to stop superior Communist troops in Europe.

One aspect of massive retaliation was clear to everyone: It saved money. A smaller army with its firepower enhanced by nuclear means costs less than a larger army with purely conventional weapons. During Eisenhower's first years the only service whose budget grew was the Air Force, which controlled American nuclear weapons. As these took a larger role in deterrence, the other services suffered reduced appropriations, though not without a struggle.

Recently declassified national security documents of the 1950s depict the Eisenhower era as a time of turmoil in defense policy.[10] From the start Army commanders demanded more attention to conventional forces and the problems of limited conflicts.

Their pleas fell victim to the economic priority of cutting the federal budget. The Navy, watching the Air Force come up with more and more targeting requirements against the Soviet Union and envying the Strategic Air Command's expanding hoard of nuclear weapons, devised a nuclear role for itself. While the Air Force developed plans for a land-based missile force under its command, the Navy argued for ballistic missiles on submarines, where they would be safe from a Soviet first strike.

By the end of his term Eisenhower was presiding over a feuding set of defense chiefs and advisers, each wanting to dethrone massive retaliation in favor of one or another more expensive strategy. Even John Foster Dulles was admitting that his original strategy had outlived its usefulness. The beleaguered President left office with a warning to the nation against the power of the "military-industrial complex," a rapidly expanding set of government agencies and their supporting industries which relied on growing defense budgets for their institutional prosperity.[11]

Outside the government, criticism of Eisenhower's single-minded approach to strategic doctrine grew shrill. Massive retaliation meant the United States would have to start a nuclear war if its conventional forces got into a losing battle for some vital world asset. It mandated exactly that overreliance on the "bomb" which NSC-68 had warned against. Even worse, if nuclear war did break out, the doctrine left the country undefended against annihilation by the Soviets, who were installing nuclear weapons on their first ICBMs.[12] Eisenhower's vice president, Richard Nixon, fell prey to these attacks on his mentor's defense policy, as his opponent in the 1960 elections blamed the Republicans for letting the USSR get ahead of the United States in nuclear delivery systems.

By the end of the 1950s massive retaliation had been overtaken by the surging technology of nuclear delivery systems. As intercontinental ballistic missiles came on line, the United States grew more vulnerable and at the same time more capable. Its nuclear stockpile had grown from about 1,000 in 1953 to nearly 18,000 by the end of Eisenhower's presidency. These weapons could be carried by aircraft, delivered against the Soviet Union by ICBMs, used on the battlefield, or, very soon, stationed underwater. As with the Truman administration in 1950, a new configuration of threat and capability induced new ways of thinking about war in the nuclear age.

ALTERNATIVES TO MASSIVE RETALIATION

Before we look at the next official strategic doctrine—Kennedy's flexible response—a short exercise in logic may be useful. We have examined the criticisms of Eisenhower's massive retaliation. Now consider some of the logical alternatives from the standpoint of Washington at the start of the 1960s:

1. A rarely mentioned option for the United States at the dawn of the missile era was *preventive war,* an unprovoked nuclear strike at Soviet delivery vehicles on the ground. The first Soviet ICBMs were not sheltered in hardened silos and could probably have been destroyed by hydrogen bombs dropped from aircraft. Since these primitive missiles required a long preparation time before launch, several hours' warning of an incoming attack would probably not have let Moscow get them off their pads. If airfields in the USSR were attacked at the same time, the United States might hope to escape nuclear retaliation, and if Soviet industry were also targeted, it might take years before Moscow had deliverable nuclear weapons again.

   When the Gaither Committee reported to Eisenhower in 1957 on "Deterrence and Survival in the Nuclear Age," the President was told that three committee members had advised considering the option of preventive war.[13] Washington contemplated a preventive strike against China's young nuclear forces in the 1960s, and it is believed that Moscow gave some thought to the same option. Still, neither superpower has actually used its nuclear weapons in this unprovoked fashion. It is a striking fact of the modern era that no nuclear power has ever used its nuclear forces against another nuclear power.

2. A second strategy would take the United States in the opposite direction, away from the early use of nuclear weapons in a war with the Soviet Union. From this viewpoint, the first line of defense in Europe, for example, should be more and better-armed conventional forces, sufficient in themselves to keep Moscow from launching an

assault with its ground troops. As a fallback position, the West should be prepared for limited nuclear war, using nuclear weapons only on the battlefield. American strategic capabilities would be held in reserve to respond to a direct attack on the United States.[14] This is an expensive option, requiring a large draft army, costly conventional armaments, and a proliferation of nuclear weapons with different yields and ranges.

3. A third possibility—actually a set of several coordinated strategies—provides for *damage limitation* in the event of nuclear war involving the United States. In this version of strategic doctrine, the question being asked is no longer just, "How can we stop our enemies from attacking us?" Damage-limiting strategies accept that deterrence might fail and pose the dilemma, "What then?" Sometimes referred to as war-fighting strategies, they specify a variety of targets for American nuclear weapons, seek ways to destroy Soviet weapons before they reach their targets, and try to minimize damage to Western populations and other assets in the course of a nuclear war. The aim of damage limitation is to be able to "win" a nuclear war and, by demonstrating that you can win, to make one less likely to occur.

How might this be done? Strategies of damage limitation are more elaborate and more demanding than those we have seen so far. As a first cut, consider just four of their many aspects:

a. Civil defense. Acknowledging that American cities may be attacked with nuclear weapons, the United States could prepare shelters for its citizens in advance or arrange for them to flee the most likely target areas in times of international crisis. Efforts along these lines began in the 1950s and have been revived sporadically since then, always accompanied by controversy about their effectiveness.

b. Ballistic missile defense. If strategic bombers can be tracked and shot down before they reach their destinations, why not ballistic missiles? A perfect ballistic missile defense would restore the United States to the security it felt in the mid-1950s. Even partially successful BMD would limit the damage from a Soviet onslaught.

c. A *preemptive strike* against Soviet weapons to destroy them before launch. If Washington knew an attack by Moscow was imminent, it could defend itself by striking first. Only a thin line separates this strategy from preventive warfare, discussed above, and the difference is in the eye of the Pentagon. While preventive war involves a "bolt from the blue" which could be undertaken at any time, preemption is advocated only when an enemy assault is expected immediately. Both are first-strike strategies, and in the missile age both require fast, highly accurate weapons in large numbers.

Like preventive war, preemption involves nuclear *counterforce capabilities,* the ability to attack and destroy an opponent's weapons. Unlike the simpler threat to hit Soviet cities in retaliation (*countervalue* retaliation), a strategy of preemption is credible only if a nuclear power has enough ICBMs to eliminate all or most of its opponent's nuclear weapons wherever they may be found. Bombers and cruise missiles are too slow for first-strike purposes, and SLBMs are too inaccurate for use as counterforce weapons.

d. Limited strategic use of nuclear weapons. Here we mean something different from limited nuclear war in the usual sense that the weapons are used only in a limited battlefield outside U.S. or Soviet territory. Instead, a nuclear strike inside the Soviet Union is contemplated, but against a limited set of targets. Washington might want to warn Moscow that a war in, say, the Middle East was getting out of hand by striking a few missile silos in remote areas of the USSR. Or if the United States had already been attacked in a nuclear war, it might need to get at any weapons Moscow had "held back" in its first strike. In either case, counterforce nuclear capabilities are again essential.

Which of these many conflicting approaches to nuclear war, with the vast array of weapons they mandate, makes the most sense? To choose one strategy, thus rejecting others, means leaving the West undefended in one way or another. The best answer may seem to be "all of the above," if the price can be afforded. That was the initial reaction of the Kennedy-Johnson administrations of the 1960s. By the end of that decade, though, American leaders were left trying to avoid some of the costs imposed by a new multiple-options doctrine.

DEMOCRATS IN THE WHITE HOUSE: PRESIDENT KENNEDY'S FLEXIBLE RESPONSE

The election of a Democratic President in 1960 reflected a mood of national dissatisfaction. Eight years of Republican rule had produced three economic recessions, the last of them still under way at election time. Americans had the impression, encouraged by Democratic campaign rhetoric, that their defenses had stagnated along with the economy under Eisenhower, letting the Russians catch up to what had been a militarily superior America. The voters wanted growth, and they wanted security.

President John Kennedy brought into his administration many of Eisenhower's most vocal critics. Impatient with the Republicans' fetish for balanced budgets, which Eisenhower had failed to achieve anyway in the absence of rapid economic growth, they turned to the Keynesian economics familiar to Democrats since the New Deal. They would reduce taxes and spend more on domestic programs and defense, bringing America's military strength up to muster while stimulating its sluggish economy at the same time. When Kennedy presented his program to Congress in 1961, he proclaimed, "Our arms must be adequate to meet our commitments and ensure our security, without being bound by arbitrary budget ceilings."[15] Lyndon Johnson, taking over the presidency after JFK's assassination, exuberantly declared, "We are the richest nation in the history of the world. We can afford to spend whatever is needed to keep this country safe and to keep our freedom secure."[16]

More was to be spent for defense, then, but on what? The basic strategy was to give Kennedy more options than Eisenhower had left him, to permit a *flexible response* to Communist aggression. As Kennedy had put it before his death, "We intend to have a wider choice than humiliation or allout nuclear action."[17] If this sounds like the principle of NSC-68, that is exactly what it is. Given the opportunity of expanding defense budgets, military strategists come up with remarkably familiar ideas. The technologies of the 1960s made for some new wrinkles, but the underlying strategic options were the same.

As in 1950, the initial thrust was toward more conventional arms, especially in Europe. Oddly enough, the Pentagon's argument for more American ground troops there derived from a favorable reassessment of the existing East-West balance. The Warsaw Pact had several times the number of divisions NATO maintained in Europe, and Eisenhower (like Truman before NSC-68) had taken that to mean the West could not conceivably win a purely conventional war. It would have to go nuclear. New intelligence estimates showed, however, that Soviet divisions were only about one-third the size of U.S. divisions. Consequently, a credible deterrent might be mounted without the early use of nuclear weapons if Washington increased its troop strength in Europe and kept its forces better armed than Moscow's.[18]

A second form of conventional buildup also interested Kennedy. The United States had taken on commitments to smaller countries in a great arc around the USSR from the Mediterranean to the Pacific, forming defensive alliances with such countries as Turkey and Iraq in the Middle East and South Vietnam in Asia. Since none of these countries could withstand a Communist onslaught on its own, the United States needed air, naval, and ground forces adequate to intervene in their defense. Noting that communism threatened these nations with internal subversion more often than with attack from without, JFK proposed to add counterinsurgency to the conventional operations U.S. forces could carry out. Vietnam would prove a test of this new strategy.

What, then, of nuclear weapons? Flexible response so far seems to minimize their role. Did Washington already have a large enough nuclear arsenal? It did not. Kennedy's new secretary of defense, Robert McNamara (who served through most of the Johnson years as well), had a dazzlingly inventive mind. His "whiz kids"—the strategists McNamara brought with him to the Pentagon—devised new roles for nuclear warheads that required whole new generations of delivery vehicles. Under their leadership the United States doubled the number of tactical nuclear weapons it kept in Europe, and the strategic triad took on its contemporary form, adding ICBMs and SLBMs by the thousand to a modernized intercontinental bomber force. Why?

In Europe stronger conventional forces gave the West a better chance of staving off an attack by the Warsaw Pact on the ground and thereby reduced the likelihood that Moscow would try such an attack. But what if one did occur? And what if NATO found itself losing? Better to prepare for the limited use of nuclear weapons in Europe than to rely on all-out U.S. strategic retaliation, which would bring destruction on the American homeland in response. To make this option credible, Kennedy proposed a multilateral nuclear force (MLF) for Europe, intermediate-range nuclear weapons based at sea and under the joint control of American Western European commanders. He ordered U.S. land-based missiles out of Europe, where they were becoming vulnerable to attack by Soviet missiles. In the end, nothing came of the MLF since Europeans were divided over its utility. But the logic of limited nuclear retaliation from within Europe attracted the Carter and Reagan administrations nearly twenty years later, when the same rationale was advanced for putting mobile U.S. IRBMs there.

At the same time McNamara's strategists developed new uses for the American strategic arsenal. As one of his colleagues put it, the secretary thought "the best strategy was to let the circumstances determine the choice of weapons and make sure that there was a plentiful supply in each major category."[19] First of all, a secure second-strike force permitting retaliatory destruction of enemy cities had to be maintained in the circumstances of the missile age. SLBMs could do that, and they were ordered by the hundreds. But missiles launched from submarines could serve only the purposes of countervalue retaliation. What if Moscow struck the United States first, targeting just its missile silos and air bases, not its cities? If Washington retaliated against the Soviet population, that would certainly bring forth a Soviet third strike, raining destruction on the American people. It might be important to mount counterforce-only retaliation, equivalent to the first strike by the Soviet Union.

So evolved what became known as McNamara's strategy of city avoidance, a precursor of contemporary nuclear war-fighting concepts. City avoidance demanded accurate land-based ballistic missiles which could survive a first strike by Moscow, whether they were sheltered in hardened silos, clustered tightly together, or mobile. A U.S. strategic force including these weapons could then retaliate against Soviet nuclear delivery vehicles still on the ground without attacking the cities where most Russians live. Unfortunately, from the Soviet standpoint these retaliatory counterforce weapons look just like the beginnings of a Western first-strike capability.

With city avoidance, the Kennedy administration had half a damage-limiting strategy. It could dig out any ICBMs held back by the Soviets in a first strike, destroy any aircraft that might return to bases in the USSR, and neutralize a potential Soviet capability to "reload" its empty silos. It was only the shortest logical step to the second half of damage limitation: strategic defense. In 1961 McNamara asked Congress to fund "a practical and effective system of active defense against the ICBM."[20] Research on what was then called an ABM system proceeded throughout the 1960s. It was justified first by the hope of protecting American cities from Soviet attack, then by the less challenging threat of Chinese attack, and ultimately with the even more modest aim of limiting damage to U.S. missiles in a nuclear war. When Congress finally approved the Safeguard ABM system in 1970, it was with this last goal in mind. Again unfortunately, there was no way for Moscow to distinguish Safeguard from the first steps toward a full area defense of the United States. If Washington could defend American cities against Soviet attack, then the United States might contemplate a nuclear first strike against the USSR with impunity, counting on strategic defense to neutralize Soviet retaliation.

RETREAT TO ASSURED DESTRUCTION

In flexible response the Democrats had generated a multiple-options doctrine par excellence. It allowed the United States, at least in theory, to counter almost any military threat anyone could imagine, from local insurgencies to large-scale conventional war in Europe, from tactical nuclear war in individual "theaters" to all-out strategic attack. As the 1960s rolled on, though, its logic began to erode.

The first reality to overtake flexible response was economic. As Kennedy's advisers had predicted, the rapid growth of defense spending gradually returned American industry to full employment. By the second half of the decade, military expenditures had come to be seen as taking away limited resources from civilian purposes: the government's war on poverty and the consumer and capital needs of the private economy. And as the Vietnam War heated up, its demands for manpower and equipment made strategic weapons harder and harder to afford. Ballistic missile defense and a proposed new generation of ICBMs began to look too expensive. Lyndon Johnson's interest in arms control toward the end of his term arose in part from these tough economic choices.

A second objection to flexible response, particularly to its nuclear war-fighting scenarios, was purely logical. From Washington's standpoint, the entire program was intended as a deterrent, to ward off attack in various forms by showing an enemy it would lose any war it might initiate. Nuclear counterforce capabilities, such as highly accurate land-based missiles, were thought of as retaliatory, and strategic defense was a way to limit damage in a war started by someone else. But consider the same weapons from the vantage point of Moscow. They are exactly the ones American planners would want if they intended to attack the Soviet Union: counterforce-capable missiles to destroy Soviet weapons in a first strike and ballistic missile defense to render Moscow's retaliatory blow ineffective. Just as Americans find it hard to see accurate Soviet ICBMs as part of a deterrent strategy, defense planners in Moscow have no way of telling retaliatory counterforce from first-strike weapons on the Western side. In fact, the two are indistinguishable.

McNamara was among the first to notice this dilemma of strategic logic. He began arguing that there was such a thing as enough for the U.S. nuclear arsenal, that more and better nuclear war-fighting capabilities in the West would just draw forth new generations of Soviet ICBMs. If American cities were protected with ballistic missile defense, cities in the USSR would be, too; then Washington would need more and better missiles to overwhelm Soviet defenses and keep its retaliatory threat credible. The efforts of both sides to prevent defeat in nuclear war would mean only a faster and more costly arms race, not improved security for either superpower.[21]

In this way McNamara arrived at the last of the single-purpose strategic doctrines, one advocated by many arms controllers to the present day, the doctrine of *assured destruction*. It ascribes to the U.S. strategic arsenal only one goal: to threaten the retaliatory destruction of an opponent's society in response to a nuclear attack on the United States. To the question "How do you win a nuclear war if one breaks out?" the doctrine answers, "You can't." To the question "When should the United States be prepared to use nuclear weapons first?" it replies, "Never." The main characteristic it looks for in strategic nuclear weapons is survivability—SLBMs are ideal for assured destruction—and those weapons need be neither highly accurate nor very plentiful. Washington has only to explode a few hundred nuclear warheads over Soviet cities to destroy most of the Soviet Union's population and industry. For the strategy to work, though, those warheads must be sure of reaching their targets. In the logic of assured destruction, ballistic missile defense is worse than useless.

To do justice to McNamara, it is not clear whether his version of assured destruction was as single-minded as this full-blown theory of minimum deterrence, to use the name sometimes given it by its proponents. The doctrine logically provides no way for the United States to defend its allies with the American strategic arsenal. Unless Washington is willing to initiate nuclear war—in which case all the requirements of damage limitation come back into play—the defense of Europe must be provided in Europe. Few U.S. officials are willing to swallow a logic that blunt, with its alliance-busting corollary that the defense of Europe might have to be provided *by* Europe. In fact, all American administrations since the 1960s have built elements of strategic counterforce and damage limitation into their official doctrine.

STRATEGIC DOCTRINE IN THE 1970S: THE REPUBLICAN YEARS

The decade which followed Richard Nixon's inauguration in 1969 saw three Presidents at the helm in Washington: Republicans Nixon and Gerald Ford and Democrat Jimmy Carter. Surprisingly, in the light of this quick turnover in leadership, the 1970s added little new to the concepts of strategic doctrine already in place. It was a time when strategic arsenals continued to grow despite the first arms control limits imposed by SALT I. The United States MIRVed its Minuteman ICBMs and multiplied the warheads on its SLBMs. The USSR, after achieving equality with the United States in numbers of strategic launchers, moved ahead with new generations of MIRVed, increasingly accurate ICBMs. American strategic doctrine became more and more an exercise in matching Soviet counterforce capabilities.

Two important reverses in military planning characterized the 1970s, though neither related directly to strategic offensive weapons. Picking up the logic of the late Johnson years, President

Nixon reached an agreement with the Soviets to halt the development of ballistic missile defense on both sides. The defensive element of damage limitation was thus put on ice. In a second major change, conscription of men into the American military came to an end, forcing Washington to rely on smaller, all-volunteer conventional forces in the post-Vietnam era. As if in compensation for these restrictions, however, the U.S. strategic offensive arsenal continued to grow, and each new presidential term produced a new attempt to justify its growth.

The result is a bewildering array of doctrines: the sufficiency criteria of Nixon's early years, the essential equivalence of his second term, and Carter's countervailing strategy. All rely on nuclear weapons as the foundations of deterrence, and all assume that nuclear weapons are usable in fighting wars. In one way or another, all are multiple-options approaches combining various elements of flexible response. They appear so interwoven and indistinguishable in retrospect that Warner Schilling calls the strategic nuclear concepts of the 1970s "The Search for Sufficiently Equivalent Countervailing Parity."[22]

One explanation for the continuity of doctrine under Nixon, Ford, and Carter may be the unyielding economic realities they all faced. Fiscal 1969, the last budget year under Lyndon Johnson, was also the last time the U.S. federal budget actually balanced. After the recession which began late in 1969, the American economy ceased operating at full employment, leaving each new leader to cope with a puzzling combination of inflation, unemployment, and budget deficits. Each committed himself to reduce government spending, but each had to respond to ever-increasing Soviet military capabilities. Although Moscow began to scale back the growth in its own defense expenditures in the mid-1970s, that trend was not noticed in Washington until several years later. Hesitantly and fitfully all three Presidents fell back on the U.S. strategic nuclear arsenal, a relatively cheap element of American defenses, as the bottom line of a credible deterrent.

Richard Nixon's first attempt at strategic doctrine came in 1971, when he was still deeply mired in Vietnam. It began, as all American strategy does, with a basic assured destruction capability. This countervalue force, though, must now meet the second aim of "preventing the Soviet Union from gaining the ability to cause considerably greater urban / industrial destruction than the United

States could inflict on the Soviets in a nuclear war." Ballistic missile defense was still in this early version, "defending against damage from small attacks or accidental launches." Nuclear counterforce requirements crept into the doctrine, too, as the administration made clear that nuclear deterrence extended to U.S. allies as well as to the United States.[23]

By 1973, with the expenses of Vietnam behind it, Nixon's second administration was staking out a grander strategic position. Essential equivalence, as it was called by Defense Secretary James Schlesinger, required: (1) "the ability to withhold an assured destruction reserve for an extended period of time," (2) "the forces to execute a wide range of options in response to potential actions by an enemy, including a capability for precise attacks on both soft and hard targets," and (3) "an offensive capability of such size and composition that all will perceive it as in overall balance with the strategic forces of any potential opponent." U.S. hard-target kill capability was to "match" that of the Russians.

In honor of arms control, Schlesinger's doctrine sought "the avoidance of any combination of forces that could be taken as an effort to acquire the ability to execute a first disarming strike against the USSR." How the United States could attain this objective while meeting the offensive counterforce requirements of "essential equivalence" is difficult to say. The Soviet capabilities Washington was seeking to match already looked like the beginnings of a first-strike force in the eyes of Americans.

THE COUNTERVAILING STRATEGY

The very name the Carter administration used for its strategic doctrine in the late 1970s—the countervailing strategy—suggests a similar effort to match what Moscow was building. It called for the modernization of all three elements of the U.S. strategic triad: air-launched cruise missiles for the bomber force, the longer-range Trident SLBM for submarines, and the *MX* missile, a highly accurate, highly MIRVed ICBM that could do to Soviet land-based missiles what the new SS-18s could do to American ICBMs. In the Carter version the MX was to be mobile, reducing the vulnerability of Washington's land-based forces as it increased the vulnerability of Moscow's.

Central to the countervailing strategy was a concept sometimes called escalation dominance, an attempt to deter a whole range of possible Soviet wartime actions by showing the Kremlin it could not win by escalating to a higher level of nuclear exchange. As one Carter aide phrased this, "[I]t enhances deterrence to have options available that are more differentiated than a massive attack on the full set of economic, military, and control targets."[24] Thus a limited Soviet launch against a few Western military targets had to be met with a limited counterforce response, an all-out counterforce onslaught with all-out counterforce, and so on. Carter's secretary of defense, Harold Brown, declared the countervailing strategy to be "a natural evolution of the conceptual foundation built over a generation by men like Robert McNamara and James Schlesinger."[25] In Carter's final year the President signed Presidential Directive 59 (PD-59) enshrining his strategy, gave up on balancing the federal budget, and set the nation on a course of rapidly growing military appropriations. The logic of the countervailing strategy required the United States to keep up with the Soviets in every major aspect of nuclear capabilities even if it was ahead in some.

The countervailing strategy also meant new American weapons in Europe, although they were not actually deployed before Carter's term ended. If the Warsaw Pact attacked westward through Germany, NATO might need more than ground troops and battlefield nuclear weapons to stop them. To achieve extended deterrence (explained in Chapter 3), Washington would have to threaten the Soviet Union itself with nuclear destruction, while holding its entire strategic arsenal in reserve to deter attacks on the United States. For the first time since the 1960s, NATO agreed to put American intermediate-range nuclear weapons on the ground in Europe.

THE REAGAN YEARS: DAMAGE LIMITATION BOUNCES BACK

Ronald Reagan interpreted his landslide victories over Jimmy Carter in 1980 and Walter Mondale in 1984 as a mandate for radical change. The new President sought a sizable reduction in federal taxes and cutbacks in spending on domestic programs, accompanied by the fastest military buildup since the Vietnam War. While the conservative Republican administration spoke in traditional terms of balancing the budget, it soon exhibited a willingness to see the federal deficit quadruple if necessary to achieve its other objectives. For the first time since the early 1960s, defense spending would be allowed to grow without fear of damage to the civilian economy.

The Reagan presidency produced no new strategic doctrine that can be identified with a particular name. It simply picked up the war-fighting strategies of Reagan's predecessors and carried them to their logical conclusion. The President asked Congress for more and better weapons in all the categories needed if the United States was to prevail in what was referred to as a "protracted nuclear war."[26] The B-1 bomber went into production, along with the development of the more advanced radar-foiling bomber using a technology nicknamed Stealth. ALCMs in large number were added to the bomber leg of the triad. Trident II SLBMs augmented the submarine fleet, and by the end of the decade the more accurate D-5 warhead was expected to make American SLBMs counterforce capable. President Reagan established a commission headed by Brent Scowcroft, arms control adviser to the three previous Presidents, to examine options for American land-based missiles. The Scowcroft Commission recommended building the MX as a stopgap measure until a new single-warhead mobile ICBM (the Midgetman) could be developed and tested. For political reasons, mobile basing schemes for the MX were given up.

In late 1983 the United States began carrying out NATO's two-track decision, deploying ground-launched cruise missiles and the highly accurate Pershing II in Western Europe. The latter could reach targets in Eastern Europe and the western parts of Russia in under ten minutes. Both were intended to make extended deterrence—the threat to use American nuclear weapons against the USSR if it attacked U.S. allies—more credible. The President commented that with these weapons it might be possible to keep a nuclear war limited to Europe: Washington could attack the Soviet Union from West Germany without making a retaliatory strike against U.S. territory inevitable. From the standpoint of Europeans, the prospect of nuclear war limited to their continent was unpalatable; hundreds of thousands took to the streets to protest the new U.S. weapons. From Moscow, of course, the fast, counterforce-capable Pershing II looked like an ideal first-strike weapon.

The great innovation of the Reagan era was the reintroduction of strategic defense against ballistic missiles into American military planning. Some of the possible technologies for space-based BMD are described in Chapter 2. Whether these work or not, the United States is resuming an effort abandoned in the early 1970s as too expensive and too destabilizing. The President advocated ballistic missile defense "to achieve our ultimate goal of eliminating the threat posed by strategic nuclear missiles."[27] His advisers more often explained the project as a way to limit damage to U.S. ICBMs in the course of a nuclear war. A similar war-fighting rationale justified acquiring antisatellite weapons, to destroy the reconnaissance satellites Moscow would need for the conduct of a prolonged nuclear war.

Was there an underlying rationale to the Reagan defense buildup? From one standpoint, Reagan was only implementing the war-fighting doctrines of earlier Presidents. While his predecessors let their concern over expenditures, and over Moscow's perceptions of U.S. nuclear intentions, keep them from building what their own doctrine dictated, President Reagan showed fewer inhibitions of this sort. On the other hand, the more-of-everything quality about the buildup suggests that military scenarios were not its driving force. The United States would need three or four times the 100 MX missiles Reagan requested from Congress, for example, to match the hard-target kill capability of the Soviet SS-18. And neither Moscow's weapons buildup nor the logic of counterforce retaliation makes necessary two new penetrating bombers. The thinking behind the Reagan program may have been more one of simple political instinct: that Washington would get its way in the world more often if it appeared militarily stronger.

Whatever the reason, U.S. strategic doctrine approached the end of the 1980s with all its nuclear options flying. As a result, Moscow now faces some critical choices of its own about the sufficiency of the Soviet nuclear arsenal, the weapons it needs to offset new American capabilities, and the costs it will pay to have them. If we remove from our assumptions the conviction that the United States is interested only in deterrence, not in aggression, the war-fighting arsenal Washington is building looks increasingly threatening. Counterforce-capable SLBMs, the MX missile, the Pershing II with its short warning time, and a shield against Soviet missiles: put these elements together and a U.S. first strike against the Soviet Union becomes more and more credible. The next chapter takes a look at the logic of nuclear capabilities from Moscow's perspective.

Controversy 1:
WHAT DRIVES THE ARMS RACE?

In the United States at least, decisions on what weapons to buy vary a good deal according to who is in the White House. One administration slows the growth in defense spending; the next increases it. One orders the B-1 bomber; the next cancels it. Is this because of the different strategic philosophies of different Presidents? Or does strategic doctrine change to justify weapons American leaders want to acquire for other reasons?

Those who take strategic doctrine most seriously believe Washington simply responds to the external realities facing it when it decides what weapons to buy. The Soviet Union initiates each round of the arms race by developing new technologies into new military capabilities. The logic of strategic doctrine then dictates what countermeasures the United States needs to take. Strategic nuclear bombing became an inadequate basis for defense in the 1950s, for example, once the Russians had begun putting nuclear weapons on ICBMs. More recently a new generation of MIRVed, highly accurate Soviet ICBMs required a counter-buildup in the West. The United States needed to make its own ICBMs mobile and to give them enough accuracy and enough warheads to match Moscow's growing hard-target kill capability. America's military leap into space with BMD and antisatellite weapons is another way to offset Moscow's offensive nuclear capability.

In this side's view, new defense systems have to be acquired whatever the cost since domestic prosperity based on declining international strength is false prosperity. We cannot allow our opponents to gain superiority in any meaningful aspect of the arms race. Strategic logic tells us what we need; our job is to build it.

A different viewpoint is more critical of Washington's contributions to the arms race. U.S. military technology is at least as innovative as Moscow's in driving the arms spiral. After all, the United States was first to have atomic weapons, first to build the hydrogen bomb, and first to deploy the destabilizing MIRVed ICBM. A weapons complex of research institutes, defense contractors, labor unions involved in defense industry, and the armed services has so much clout in American politics that virtually any weapon it comes up with eventually gets built. In the view of these critics of the Pentagon, strategic doctrine serves only to justify what the military wants to build anyway. The demand for multiple options or flexible response is another way of saying that instead of choosing the most cost-effective systems and discarding others, a President or a defense secretary wants more of everything. The innocent-sounding theory of damage limitation is especially culpable in this regard: Once you start thinking of how to fight a prolonged nuclear war, almost any weapon you can produce becomes necessary. When the U.S. economy is in recession, the demands of the military are reinforced by the shortsighted philosophy that "What's good for General Dynamics is good for the USA."

Opponents of the arms race claim that a better logic is the logic of arms control. The endless buildup of arsenals can be reversed by identifying weapons both sides can do without and agreeing to eliminate them. The best place to start is with the weapons each side could use in a first strike against the other.

Controversy 2:
DOES THE UNITED STATES NEED PROMPT COUNTERFORCE CAPABILITIES?

YES! Over the past decade Moscow has upgraded its land-based missile force, MIRVing its ICBMs and improving their accuracy. In a crisis the Soviets could now attack U.S. ICBMs out of the blue, destroying nearly all of them with only a part of the Soviet arsenal. If they do, the American President faces an excruciating dilemma: Either surrender or launch a retaliatory strike against Russian cities. The latter choice would bring on a Soviet third strike against cities in the United States.

It is long since time for Washington to develop its own strategic counterforce options, adding the MX missile to its ICBM arsenal and raising the accuracy of its SLBMs until they, too, are counterforce-capable. American missiles could then threaten the same damage to Soviet weapons that they can do to ours. Prompt counterforce capabilities multiply Washington's options in the event of nuclear war: It can attack all or part of Russia's ICBMs, while holding countervalue retaliation against its cities in reserve.

Arms control agreements that prevent the United States from doing this must be avoided unless they force cutbacks in Soviet ICBMs down to the current U.S. level. The very process of expanding Western counterforce options may make the Soviets more willing to bargain reasonably in arms control negotiations, giving up the weapons that are most threatening to American security.

NO! Americans have been wise to keep most of our strategic nuclear weapons on submarines, where they are invulnerable to attack and present no threat of a first strike against our opponents. Just as the Soviet SS-18, with its prompt hard-target kill capability, evoked hysteria in Washington, so a buildup in American war-fighting options will only drive Moscow to deploy new weapons. Moscow could make its ICBMs mobile, for example, or add to its own invulnerable SLBMs, or set up ballistic missile defenses to defeat the new U.S. systems. It might well do all of these.

It has made no sense to talk about fighting and "winning" a nuclear war since the superpowers first put nuclear weapons on submarines over twenty years ago. With an assured destruction capability on both sides, neither the White House nor the Kremlin can start a nuclear war without risking the destruction of its own society. Pressures for counterforce options in Moscow and Washington simply lead to an escalating arms race that improves security for no one.

The arms spiral will not be stopped by the building of more weapons. The rational course is to call a halt where both sides are now and build down from there. Arms control should focus on reducing the superpowers' counterforce capabilities, leading to smaller, less threatening arsenals for both Washington and Moscow. Replacement of current SLBMs with more accurate ones must be prohibited, and ICBM forces must be restructured in the direction of mobile single-warhead missiles. Improved security requires fewer counterforce options, not more.

FOR MORE DETAIL

Louis Rene Beres, "Tilting Toward Thanatos: America's 'Countervailing' Nuclear Strategy," *World Politics* (October 1981): 25–46. A critique of war-fighting strategies.

Bernard Brodie, *Strategy in the Missile Age* (Princeton: Princeton University Press, 1959). Seminal work by an early advocate of flexible response.

Barry E. Carter, "Nuclear Strategy and Nuclear Weapons," *Scientific American* (May 1974): 20–31. Details the Nixon administration's sufficiency criteria and the Schlesinger doctrine.

Lawrence Freedman, *The Evolution of Nuclear Strategy* (New York: St. Martin's Press, 1981). Michael Mandelbaum, *The Nuclear Question* (Cambridge: Cambridge University Press, 1979). Two excellent histories of U.S. strategic doctrine through the 1970s.

John Lewis Gaddis, *Strategies of Containment* (Oxford: Oxford University Press, 1982). Cogent analysis of strategic thought in the broader context of Cold War politics.

William W. Kaufmann, *The McNamara Strategy* (New York: Harper & Row, 1964). An insider presents the strategic thinking of the Kennedy administration.

"NSC-68: A Report to the National Security Council," *Naval War College Review* (May–June 1975): 51–108. A public version of the NSC document which gave the United States its first multiple-options strategy.

President of the United States, *Report of the President's Commission on Strategic Forces (Scowcroft Report)*, 1983. A commission appointed by President Reagan gives its recommendations for upgrading U.S. nuclear forces.

David Alan Rosenberg, "The Origins of Overkill," in *Strategy and Nuclear Deterrence*, ed. Steven E. Miller (Princeton: Princeton University Press, 1984). This lengthy essay represents the latest research on strategic doctrine in the Truman and Eisenhower years.

Warner R. Schilling, "U.S. Strategic Nuclear Concepts in the 1970s," in *Strategy and Nuclear Deterrence*, ed. Steven E. Miller (Princeton: Princeton University Press, 1984). Continuity and confusion in strategic thought from flexible response through the countervailing strategy.

Walter Slocombe, "The Countervailing Strategy," *International Security* (Spring 1981): 18–27. A defense of the Carter administration's strategic doctrine.

Richard Smoke, *National Security and the Nuclear Dilemma*, 2d ed. (New York: Random House, 1987). A first-rate account of strategic thought and nuclear forces from Truman to Reagan.

Albert Wohlstetter, "The Delicate Balance of Terror," *Foreign Affairs* 37 (1959): 211–34. A classic indictment of Eisenhower's strategic doctrine.

NOTES TO CHAPTER 4

1. David Alan Rosenberg, "The Origins of Overkill: Nuclear Weapons and American Strategy, 1945–1960," in *Strategy and Nuclear Deterrence*, ed. Steven E. Miller (Princeton: Princeton University Press, 1984).

2. John Lewis Gaddis offers this definition in the Preface to his *Strategies of Containment* (New York: Oxford University Press, 1982).

3. Rosenberg, op. cit., p. 126.

4. Bernard Brodie, *The Absolute Weapon* (New York: Harcourt Brace, 1946), p. 76.

5. "NSC-68: A Report to the National Security Council," *Naval War College Review* (May–June 1975): 51–108.

6. Rosenberg, op. cit., p. 127.

7. See Dulles's January 1954 address to the Council on Foreign Relations, reprinted in the *Department of State Bulletin* 30, 761 (January 25, 1954): 107–10.

8. NSC 162/2, "Review of Basic National Security Policy," reprinted in the Senator Gravel Edition of the *Pentagon Papers*, vol. I (Boston: Beacon Press, 1971), pp. 412–29.

9. John Foster Dulles, "Policy for Security and Peace," *Foreign Affairs* 32, 3 (April 1954): 353–64.

10. Rosenberg, op. cit.

11. Farewell address, January 17, 1961.

12. A classic objection to Eisenhower's strategy was offered by Albert Wohlstetter, "The Delicate Balance of Terror," *Foreign Affairs* 37 (1959): 211–34.

13. Rosenberg, op. cit., p. 157.

14. Bernard Brodie argued along these lines in his *Strategy in the Missile Age* (Princeton: Princeton University Press, 1959).

15. Special Message to the Congress on the Defense Budget, March 28, 1961, *Public Papers of the Presidents: John F. Kennedy, 1961* (Washington, D.C.: U.S. Government Printing Office, 1962), pp. 230–31.

16. Remarks at the Defense Department Cost Reduction Week Ceremony, July 21, 1964, *Public Papers of the Presidents: Lyndon B. Johnson, 1963–64* (Washington, D.C.: Government Printing Office, 1965) p. 875.

17. Radio and Television Report to the American People on the Berlin Crisis, July 25, 1961, *Public Papers of the Presidents: John F. Kennedy, 1961*, loc. cit., p. 535.

18. Gaddis, op. cit., p. 207. Chapter 7, "Kennedy, Johnson, and Flexible Response," provides a fine elucidation of this strategy.

19. William W. Kaufmann, *The McNamara Strategy* (New York: Harper & Row, 1964), p. 88.

20. Quoted in Michael Mandelbaum, *The Nuclear Question* (Cambridge: Cambridge University Press, 1979), p. 116.

21. McNamara's logic is explored by Lawrence Freedman, *The Evolution of Nuclear Strategy* (New York: St. Martin's Press, 1981), ch. 16.

22. The subtitle of his essay "U.S. Strategic Nuclear Concepts in the 1970s," in *Strategy and Nuclear Deterrence*, loc. cit.

23. On the sufficiency criteria and essential equivalence, see Barry E. Carter, "Nuclear Strategy and Nuclear Weapons," *Scientific American* (May 1974): 20–31.

24. Walter Slocombe, "The Countervailing Strategy," *International Security* 5, 4 (Spring 1981): 18–27.

25. In testimony before the U.S. Senate Committee on Foreign Relations, September 16, 1980.

26. Richard Smoke emphasizes this continuity between Reagan's doctrine and the earlier flexible response, flexible targeting, and countervailing strategy" in Chapters 11 and 12 of *National Security and the Nuclear Dilemma*, 2d ed. (New York: Random House, 1987).

27. In his televised address of March 23, 1983.

5

SOVIET THINKING ABOUT NUCLEAR WAR AND THE ARMS RACE

—

Military strategists in the USSR entertain almost as many different concepts of nuclear war as their Western counterparts. Virtually every Soviet treatise on the subject, however, contains a reference to a dictum of Karl von Clausewitz, which was also a favorite of Lenin's: "War is not an independent phenomenon, but the continuation of politics by other means."[1] Accordingly, the Communist party, whose task it is to discern the underlying laws of politics, has held the keys of Soviet strategic doctrine tightly in its hands since the days of the Bolshevik Revolution. While the professional military studies the science of war, the party leadership chooses the basic strategies for defending the Soviet Union and determines which weapons are needed to accomplish them.

The common supposition in the West is that the Soviets acquire a particular set of weapons because they believe certain things about nuclear war: that war could be won by their side, for example, or that in war the offensive is preferable to the defensive. In fact, however, Soviet weapons choices are made by a leadership with issues besides war in mind, and changing military doctrine may be formulated more to justify its choices of weapons than to guide them. Soviet strategic thinking, in other words, is more often a dependent variable reflecting Soviet politics at a given moment than an independent variable accounting for what Soviet leaders do.

Our examination of U.S. strategic doctrine in the last chapter revolved around a connection between economic priorities and strategic thinking. An administration like Kennedy's or Reagan's, wishing to increase defense spending, embraces doctrines like flexible response that demand more weapons. Administrations like Eisenhower's or Nixon's at an early point, wanting a way to cut spending on defense, turn to massive retaliation or sufficiency criteria—doctrines that justify reduced expenditures. In the Soviet Union, too, the politics of resource allocation come into play, as the leaders decide what line to take on nuclear war and which weapons to acquire.

In two important ways, though, the politics that affect strategic doctrine in Moscow are different from those at work in Washington, and these differences form the centerpiece of this chapter. First, resource allocation is even more critical in the Soviet Union than in the West because Communist economies rarely have the unemployed labor and unused industrial capacity which typify capitalist economies at most times. Labor may be inefficiently used under socialism, but there are seldom any large number of workers without jobs. Industrial plant and equipment are even more tightly stretched, so that a decision to build more tanks is in effect a decision to build fewer cars, trucks, and buses. A decision by the Communist party leadership to mount a major defense buildup cannot be taken in the hope of spurring other sectors of the economy as well, as the NSC recommended to Truman in 1950 and as John Kennedy expected in the 1960s. For the Soviets, spending more on defense invariably means sacrifices in agriculture, housing, and other needs of the consumer economy.

We can, nonetheless, find a cycle of faster growth alternating with slower growth in Soviet defense spending much like that in the United States and often tied to changing statements about nuclear war that justify the leadership's changing policies. To understand this cycle, we need to pay attention to a second difference between Soviet and American political realities: the different mechanisms of leadership succession. The general secretary of the Communist party and his top colleagues in the Soviet political elite are not elected, as most political leaders are in the

United States, or chosen from a parliamentary majority, as is common in other Western democracies. They are selected by a system of co-optation. Existing members of the party's Politburo, or inner circle, choose new members periodically to add to their numbers and decide which of them will serve as general secretary.

Thus, when a leader dies, his successor is chosen by bargaining within the remaining elite in the Politburo, where competing politicians back candidates they think may be favorable to their own interests. It is at this point that a successful aspirant is likely to seek support from the defense establishment by proposing an ambitious military buildup. As we shall see below, however, once the succession crisis has ended and a new general secretary has become dominant, he may take a different attitude toward defense interests, arms control may seem more appealing, and strategic doctrine usually evolves toward the view that existing Soviet armaments are sufficient.

Competing formulations of Soviet strategic thought may seem to lack the clear-cut quality of the Western positions presented in the last chapter. To the outside observer, Soviet leaders make their differences over doctrine less visible than Washington's, giving them no obvious markers like "massive retaliation" or "flexible response." The politics of the arms race in Moscow must be discerned from nuances in public statements about defense, which are couched in code phrases intelligible within the Soviet elite but less evident to the broader public. The purpose of this chapter is to show how these different phrases signal rival Soviet defense policies and how arms control has been affected by the shifting positions of the Soviet leadership on its country's defense needs through the nuclear age.

LENIN AND THE SOURCES OF INTERNATIONAL CONFLICT

Whatever the changes in Soviet strategic thinking over time, it all must be ritually grounded in the wisdom of the country's revolutionary hero and the first leader of the Soviet Communist party, V. I. Lenin. It was Lenin who gave the USSR its basic philosophy of international relations, derived from the earlier work of Karl Marx; it was Lenin who first formulated the Marxist principles of war; and it is to Lenin that current military theorists of all stripes in Moscow still turn for validation of their arguments. With Lenin's thinking we, too, begin our inquiry into the Soviet view of nuclear war.

V. I. Lenin launched the Bolshevik (later Communist) party in Russia at the beginning of the twentieth century, basing his ideology on the revolutionary theory of his German predecessors, Karl Marx and Friedrich Engels. Marx analyzed the populations of modern industrial countries and concluded they consisted of two hostile classes. He predicted that conflict between them would lead to the overthrow of one class by the other. The ruling class, according to Marx, was the capitalists, whose power was based on their ownership of the factories, equipment, land, and other raw materials (the means of production) society uses to produce goods. The underclass in industrial societies Marx called the proletariat, and he looked to it to make the socialist revolution. Because of the extreme inequalities inherent in capitalism, the workers would get few of the benefits of a constantly improving industrial technology. A growing class consciousness among the proletariat would lead it to seize power and create a socialist state.[2]

By the time of the First World War, when Lenin was seeking a Bolshevik overthrow of the czar in St. Petersburg, some of Marx's predictions were clearly not working out. The most advanced capitalist countries, like Great Britain, the United States, and Germany, had flourishing economies despite the occasional financial jolts Marxists took comfort in. Their working classes, which Marx had depicted as the shock troops of socialist revolution, were materially better off than ever before. Worst of all, from Lenin's standpoint, workers' movements under capitalism were taking the form of trade unions and Social Democratic parties, not of revolutionary activism.

It was Lenin's genius to see that backward Russia, only peeking into the capitalist stage of development at the start of the twentieth century, was riper for revolution than its neighbors to the West. To explain why this was so, he offered the theory of *imperialism,* a theory that has formed the underpinnings of Soviet thinking about international relations ever since. Capitalism, according to Lenin, enjoyed a heyday just before its final collapse, when the tentacles of its power extended around the world. In this "highest stage of capitalism,"[3] the monopolists of the most powerful industrial nations turned abroad, to the less developed world, for cheaper resources, cheaper labor, and larger markets for their products than they could find at home. The power of capitalists to exploit the proletariats within their own countries was transformed into the exploitation of backward countries by the most advanced. And the class conflict Marx had located *within* capitalist societies became an international conflict *between* imperialist nations and their colonial victims.

From this theory of imperialism Lenin drew two conclusions. The first was that socialist revolution would begin at the "weakest link in the chain" of nations, spreading from the less developed back to the most advanced capitalist societies. His second deduction was that the capitalist nations must inevitably go to war with one another. As their power penetrated eastward and southward into Africa, Eastern Europe, and Asia, imperialist governments would soon find themselves trying to colonize the same places. Once the precapitalist world offered no more resources just for the taking, Berlin would have to fight London, or Paris, or Washington to extend its colonial empire. Without an ever-expanding network of colonies, capitalist economies would begin the collapse Marx had envisioned for them. But to improve its access to the less developed world, each imperialist country would have to fight the others.

According to Lenin, in other words, there is something inherent in the very nature of capitalism which makes it aggressive. Current Soviet military thinkers begin with this premise of Lenin's, deriving from it the postulate that the next war will be started by the West. This assumption, which forms the starting point of every thesis on military strategy in the USSR, is a mirror image of the belief in Communist aggressiveness common to most Western thinking about nuclear war. Like the latter premise, it can be taken in many different directions by politically savvy commentators with different axes to grind.

STALIN AND THE INEVITABILITY OF WAR

Lenin's claim that capitalism is innately aggressive tells us nothing directly about East-West relations in our current sense of the term since he proclaimed it before the first Communist government had come to power. Lenin had in mind not wars between capitalist and socialist states but the tendency of one imperialist nation to fight another. The task of discerning the principles which govern relations between capitalism and socialism fell to Joseph Stalin.

As Lenin's successor at the helm of the Communist party in the 1920s, Stalin set in motion a series of radical transformations in the economy and society of the newly created Union of Soviet Socialist Republics. In the process he imposed a repression of individual expression and a reign of terror among his subordinates. Stalin justified his tyranny with a theory of international relations depicting the Soviet Union as an endangered socialist pariah in a world of hostile capitalist states. Just as he saw enemies everywhere within his own country, Stalin spoke of the "encirclement" of socialism by a ring of imperialist aggressors. The military adventurism of Japan in the 1930s and the startling buildup of armaments in a resurgent Germany served as evidence that the Soviet Union would soon be attacked. Stalin regarded the United States and Great Britain as natural allies of the Fascists, all ganging up to destroy socialism in Russia.

In this way Stalin converted Lenin's belief in the aggressiveness of capitalist nations into a theory of the inevitability of war between capitalism and socialism. Germany did attack eastward in 1941, giving partial confirmation to the concept, but London and eventually Washington took part in the war as allies of the Soviet Union. Stalin regarded the split among his "enemies" as temporary, however, remaining true to the ideas of capitalist encirclement and the inevitability of imperialist attack even after the Second World War had come to an end.

It was in this frame of mind that Moscow entered the nuclear era. Its traditional enemy to the west, Germany, lay in ruins, while the nascent power of Japan to the east had also been shattered. But the Soviet Union's new rival for international power, the United States, had the atomic bomb. Later Soviet leaders were to claim that nuclear weapons entirely changed the nature of war. Stalin disagreed. He was committed to the "permanently operating factors" which, he asserted, determined the outcome of any war, including a nuclear one. Denying the importance of nuclear weapons was one thing, however, and doing without them quite another. Stalin raced to build first the atomic bomb and then the hydrogen bomb. By the time of his death in 1953 nuclear weapons had become part of the Soviet arsenal.[4]

A second aspect of the international environment altered at the end of World War II: The USSR ceased being the only socialist state (excepting Outer Mongolia) in a capitalist world. Using the troops it had left in Eastern Europe after the defeat of Germany, Moscow created a series of Communist regimes in the countries immediately to its west. Poland, East Germany, Czechoslovakia, Hungary, Romania, and Bulgaria entered the socialist camp in close alliance with the Soviet Union. By 1949 China also had a Communist government. Did this strengthening of the socialists' world position mean they were less subject to attack by the capitalists?

Apparently some of Stalin's colleagues in the postwar years tried to argue that it did. We have inklings of reform tendencies of various sorts from 1946 onward in the Soviet Union: an impatience with rule by the personal whim of a dictator, concern about the future of an overcentralized economy, and a corresponding interest in improved relations with the capitalist West. But here, too, Stalin insisted nothing had changed. A comment by the dictator just a few months before he died indicates both the pressure for a rethinking of Soviet doctrine on war and Stalin's response: "It is said that Lenin's thesis that imperialism inevitably generates war must now be regarded as obsolete, since powerful popular forces have come forward today in defense of peace and against another world war. That is not true. . . . To eliminate the inevitability of war, it is necessary to abolish imperialism."[5]

By 1953 Stalin seems to have been preparing another of his frequent purges, this time to stem the impetus for change in Moscow's policies. His death in March of that year ushered in the "thaw" of the mid-1950s, in which a new leadership adjusted Soviet thinking about war and international relations to fit the realities of a nuclear world.

KHRUSHCHEV INTRODUCES PEACEFUL COEXISTENCE

Stalin's death marked such a dramatic transformation of Soviet politics that many political scientists think of the post-Stalin political system as an entirely different one. The last execution of a Soviet leader occurred in June 1953, as Stalin's competing successors eliminated the head of the secret police, Lavrenti Beria. For their own well-being and for the sake of stability in Soviet society, the new chiefs of the Communist party agreed to end the arbitrary terror of the Stalin era, establishing a collective leadership that denied domination to any single official. The pathetic condition of the Soviet consumer, forced into decades of sacrifice for Stalin's industrial and military buildup, finally got some attention. In the post-Stalin era the USSR began an ambitious housing construction program that was soon producing more new units each year than any other nation in the world. A series of ill-conceived experiments sought to improve a notoriously short food supply. And light industries, such as pharmaceuticals and textiles, began a meager growth.

These domestic reforms were accompanied by a set of new initiatives in foreign policy. Watching the colonial empires of Great Britain and France dissolve, Moscow decided to step out of its Stalinist introversion and begin competing with the United States for influence globally, though in ways that would not lead to the catastrophe of nuclear war. Nikita Khrushchev, who as general secretary of the Communist party gradually developed more power than his rivals in the Kremlin, gave the new policy its doctrinal baptism under the name of *peaceful coexistence.*

The setting was the Twentieth Congress of the Communist party of the Soviet Union (CPSU), meeting in 1956, just three years after Stalin's death. In a "secret speech" which soon became public, Khrushchev did the hitherto unthinkable: He denounced his predecessor for the purges of the 1930s and for his policy mistakes. Speaking for the record, Khrushchev welcomed a new epoch in international relations. The Soviet Union's success in building a mighty socialist camp, he said, meant that war with capitalism was no longer "fatalistically inevitable." The certain rebuff facing any aggressor might keep the imperialists at bay despite their warring inclinations. The competition between capitalist and socialist systems would continue, but with the right foreign policy, war could be avoided.[6]

Peaceful coexistence was thus a doctrine of both coexistence and competition. On the one hand, Khrushchev was arguing that the capitalist/socialist struggle could be seen to a successful conclusion without the destruction of either in nuclear war. On the other, no letup in the rivalry was planned. Competition would continue in several forms:

- In ideological terms the superiority of "socialist democracy" over "bourgeois democracy" would ultimately be proved for all to see. The Soviet propaganda machine would carry on.

- Socialist and capitalist economies would continue to compete. While the latter would suffer graver and graver crises, socialism would go on generating higher and higher living standards.

- In the third world, where revolutionary insurgencies were trying to overthrow Western-dominated governments, the Soviet Union would step up its support for "wars of national liberation."

For thirty years Soviet leaders have embraced peaceful coexistence as the cornerstone of East-West relations. Subsequent party congresses reiterated support for it, and it continues to be the framework within which Moscow's policy makers work. For our purposes, two of its implications need emphasis. First, peaceful coexistence does not endow capitalism with immortality. Marxists have always expected and continue to expect the ultimate triumph of socialism over capitalism. Khrushchev's comment that the Soviets would "bury" the West—meaning that they would live to see capitalism dead—is entirely compatible with peaceful coexistence as he used the term. The struggle with capitalism goes on, sometimes in violent form, as when Soviet troops or surrogates fight with American forces or U.S.-backed armies in Asia, Africa, and Latin America. Peaceful coexistence rules out only direct, all-out war between the capitalist and socialist camps, a war the Soviets insist would go nuclear. At the same time it requires socialist economies to stay dynamic, demonstating their superiority over the capitalist alternative.

The other aspect of the doctrine worth underlining is that it rules out only the inevitability of nuclear war, not its possibility. The innate aggressiveness of imperialism remains an item of faith for Marxists. Khrushchev was suggesting that the capitalists could be deterred from a frontal assault on his country and its allies. But with what policy? Debate on that point has never ceased to vex Soviet leaders, both civilian and military. If we accept that nuclear deterrence is possible, what does it take to do the job?

Just as American deterrence theories have gone in radically differing directions, from assured destruction to nuclear warfighting scenarios, so have Soviet arguments on the same subject. Some of the more militaristic in Moscow argue that only Soviet superiority in nuclear weapons can ward off a Western attack; only if Washington knows it would lose a nuclear war can it be dissuaded from starting one. At the other extreme, Soviet moderates maintain that the USSR has all the weapons it needs for the defense of socialism. The best hope for peace, they reason, lies in a negotiated end to the arms race. Between the ends of the hawk–dove spectrum lies a variety of more complex opinions.

Because there is no single unanimous opinion on the best defense policy for Moscow, Soviet leaders from Khrushchev forward have been free to adopt a variety of stands on defense preparedness and on arms control. When several leaders are vying for control of the Communist party, defense politics become crucial to the outcome of the leadership struggle. Once a general secretary is firmly entrenched, his statements on foreign policy may change remarkably to reflect his real priorities.

SUCCESSION POLITICS AND DEFENSE POLICY

The post-Stalin political system in the USSR is one of the world's most stable, characterized by institutions which work in predictable ways and by long terms in office for its top leaders. It does have an Achilles' heel, though: The system lacks any reliable way to replace one leader with another. Excepting only Nikita Khrushchev, who was removed by his colleagues in 1964, every general secretary of the CPSU has remained in office until his death. The party's rules make no provision for the choice of a successor before a leader dies, and that event invariably brings on a political crisis, one would-be headman jousting with others to take control of the party organization.

Three succession crises have occurred in Moscow since the nuclear era began, if we take as one case the lengthy transition from Leonid Brezhnev to Mikhail Gorbachev, by way of Yuri Andropov and Konstantin Chernenko (1982–85). Each crisis involved defense policy—the relative priority of military spending compared with other allocations—as a decisive weapon in the contest. Each led to competing formulations of strategic doctrine. In the first two cases victory went to the more hawklike of two major rivals, the one who stressed the threat from capitalism and held fast, at least initially, to the customary Soviet preference for rapid growth in defense spending. That was also the outcome in the most recent transition, until Andropov's early death and Gorbachev's ultimate triumph altered the pattern.

Stalin's death in 1953 brought on the first postwar succession crisis. Out of a collective leadership involving several personalities, Nikita Khrushchev and Georgi Malenkov emerged as the principal opponents. At first Malenkov seemed to be the leading contender, but he announced a radical reorientation of Soviet defense policy in directions that must have enraged the long-favored defense establishment. In a 1954 speech Malenkov asserted that the Soviet armed forces had "everything they need" to ensure the defense of socialism and argued for a reorientation of budgetary priorities away from defense. His formulation would later be adopted by other Soviet politicians wanting to justify restraint in defense spending.

Malenkov took the same occasion to refute Stalin's claim that nuclear weapons changed nothing fundamental to the nature of war. In the nuclear era, he proclaimed, war between imperialism and communism "means the destruction of world civilization." Subsequent opponents of the arms race in the USSR picked up this once-heretical phrase, too, as they urged Moscow not to squander too many of its resources on unusable weapons.

While Malenkov's position undoubtedly pleased the frustrated reformers in Soviet politics, it ran contrary to the interests of two vital constituencies: the Soviet military and the huge industries Stalin had built up to supply it. Khrushchev apparently recognized the influence these institutions had within the Communist party more clearly than his rival did. Aligning himself with a coalition of party leaders who favored "further strengthening" of the Soviet armed forces, Khrushchev had Malenkov removed from the Soviet premiership in 1955 and subsequently sent to direct a power station in Central Asia. A senior representative of the military responded to Malenkov's comments on nuclear war shortly after the latter's ouster by saying, "We cannot be intimi-dated by fables that in the event of a new world war civilization will perish."[7]

Khrushchev's grasp on the helm of the CPSU was still weak even after Malenkov's elimination. A series of economic reforms he instituted offended the same conservatives on the Politburo (the collective ruling body of the Communist party) who had objected to Malenkov's reformist line on foreign policy. After Khrushchev denounced Stalin and proclaimed an era of peaceful coexistence in 1956, his colleagues attempted to depose him as well. He was saved only when Marshal Georgi Zhukov, in charge of the armed forces, flew pro-Khrushchev members of the party elite into Moscow from the provinces. In the end it was Khrush-chev's rivals who fell from power, leaving him in charge of a Politburo packed with his supporters.

A curiously similar series of events occurred in the succession crisis of the mid-1960s. This time the crisis was precipitated by Khrushchev's removal as general secretary, owing in part to the antidefense policies of his final years in office, an about-face we consider below. Again, as in the earlier crisis, a collective lead-ership took over, and again issues of resource allocation and defense policy served as pawns in the maneuverings of rival lead-ers. This time, too, the rivalry boiled down to two personalities: the new Soviet premier, Aleksei Kosygin, and the new party gen-eral secretary, Leonid Brezhnev.

Kosygin, like Malenkov before him, appealed to the interests of the Soviet consumer, advocating a shift in emphasis from defense and its related industries to the lighter industries in which the USSR remained far behind the West. He was outflanked, as Malenkov had been, by the Communist party general secretary, Brezhnev, who espoused the cause of the Soviet military during his first few years in office, bestowing on it defense budgets that have sometimes been called lavish.[8] The highly accurate MIRVed ICBMs which gave Soviet arsenals a more threatening posture in the 1970s were authorized at this time. While placating the mil-itary in this way, however, Brezhnev skillfully used the appoint-ment powers of the general secretary to create a civilian support base within the party. By the end of the 1960s Brezhnev had emerged triumphant, keeping Kosygin in the leadership as a sort of junior partner. Once in command, he changed his tune on defense spending, turning to arms control as a way of restraining the demands of the Soviet military.

The politics of the latest multistage succession seem less transparent, if only because the transition is too recent to be viewed with the full clarity of hindsight. This time the choice was between rival candidates for general secretary, the post vacated when Brezhnev died in 1982. Conflicts over defense policy played a role in the struggle between Andropov and Chernenko that year, as they did a year or two later, when Grigory Romanov and Gorbachev locked horns. The first time around Andropov came out on top with the apparent blessing of the defense establishment. Gorbachev's 1985 victory, by contrast, came at the expense of a more hard-line opponent, and it seems clear that the military was skeptical of him. In view of Gorbachev's emphasis on improving the Soviet economy, his willingness to sacrifice civilian productivity to the military's demands for ever new generations of weapons was in doubt from the start. Gorbachev's daring innovations in foreign policy and substantial concessions on arms control have probably not allayed the fears of the defense establishment.

The history of political succession in the USSR reveals an ongoing conflict among Soviet leaders over how many new weapons the country needs in its stockpile. With the Soviet economy always operating at full capacity, any leadership has to give up something important to support a more rapid defense buildup. During a succession crisis the victorious candidate has usually proposed to do this, thereby assuring himself the military's support against his antagonist. Once firmly ensconced, though, Soviet general secretaries have veered to an entirely different course.

GENERAL SECRETARIES IN POWER: KHRUSHCHEV ALIENATES THE SOVIET MILITARY

All general secretaries since Stalin have found themselves in basically the same position: None has had the power to impose his personal whims on society without regard for the competing interests that now form the Soviet political system. The top leader must be a skillful manipulator of these interests, arbitrating the rival claims for resources placed on the leadership from below. Extravagant spending on one kind of investment—in agriculture, for example, or in capital construction—means shirking other urgent needs, like energy extraction, transportation, or consumer standards of living. By the same token, if the defense sector is allowed to grow faster than the economy overall, many of the leadership's civilian goals will be frustrated. The astute politicians who have become general secretary in the Soviet Union eventually build support bases independent of the military. They then begin a balancing act that limits spending on defense to free funds for other purposes.

Khrushchev was the first to follow this now well-trodden path. When he thought he had the political durability to get away with it, he cut manpower in the Soviet armed forces by more than a third. The increased strength of world socialism, he argued, reduced the threat of conventional attack on the Soviet homeland. He further claimed that in the nuclear era the USSR could make do with fewer surface ships in its navy and fewer aircraft with conventional missions. Instead of these, Khrushchev (like Eisenhower in the United States) invested heavily in the relatively less expensive nuclear weapons that were just coming of age. His memoirs, written a decade later, justified these painful choices. Itemizing the costs of a defense buildup in terms of housing and agriculture, Khrushchev concludes: "If we try to compete with America in any but the most essential areas of military preparedness, we will be doing two harmful things. First, we will be further enriching wealthy aggressive capitalistic circles in the United States who use our own military buildups as a pretext for overloading their own country's arms budget. Second, we will be exhausting our material resources without raising the living standard of our people."[9]

At the end of the 1950s Moscow's armed forces were restructured into the present five services: Strategic Rocket Forces, Air Defense Forces, and a Navy, Air Force, and Army. Of these, the first was Khrushchev's brainchild and the main beneficiary of his defense policies. The last three, by contrast, stood to lose a great deal, and they fought back. In response to the general secretary's efforts the imperiled services turned to new strategic doctrines to justify more weapons, just as the U.S. Army and Navy did in the late 1950s. Consider, for example, the wisdom of Admiral

Sergei Gorshkov, who took command of the Soviet Navy in the 1960s. He argued, first, that the Soviet Navy provided Moscow with a strategic nuclear offensive force superior to land-based missiles, since SLBMs could attack an enemy's homeland with less warning time. But in a second self-serving doctrine Gorshkov demanded a "balanced navy," one whose conventional might equaled its nuclear capabilities. It was onward and upward with the naval forces, whose drive for growth Khrushchev never succeeded in blunting.[10]

Toward the end of his term in office Khrushchev became increasingly hostile to the arms race. At the January 1961 Central Committee Plenum he proposed reducing growth rates in heavy industry and defense spending, criticizing those who "have now developed an appetite for giving the country as much metal as possible." In 1963 Khrushchev spoke out against waste in heavy industry and defense, bluntly commenting that the Soviet economy could not produce "nothing but rockets." In the same year the United States and the USSR reached their first major agreement on nuclear arms control.[11]

Khrushchev thus made political enemies among the professional military and the industrial ministries engaged in defense contracting. In 1962 he rashly tried placing Soviet intermediate-range missiles in Cuba, apparently hoping to compensate cheaply for his country's inferiority in strategic nuclear weapons. His humiliating rebuff by the Kennedy administration further weakened the support for Khrushchev among his Politburo colleagues. When he alienated the regional party leadership with "harebrained schemes" for restructuring the Communist party organization, a coalition of offended interests removed Khrushchev from power, installing Leonid Brezhnev in his place.

GENERAL SECRETARIES IN POWER: BREZHNEV TURNS TO ARMS CONTROL

Brezhnev's initial sympathy for the interests of the Soviet defense establishment has been outlined above. But like Khrushchev before him and Gorbachev after, Brezhnev knew that international power depends on economic as well as military strength. If Soviet defense

budgets grow faster than the overall economy, they stunt progress in civilian sectors, keeping the country behind the West
technologically and lowering the morale of the Soviet work force.
By the time Brezhnev had the upper hand in the Politburo—probably about 1968—economic growth in the USSR was already
beginning to decline. Increasingly the new leader spoke in terms
of the "economic burden of the arms race."

Brezhnev's response found expression in the "peace program"
he announced at the 1971 Communist Party Congress, incorpo-
rating freer trade with advanced Western economies and arms
control to hold down the growth in Soviet military spending.
Strategic parity with the United States, Brezhnev asserted, permitted an end to the rapid defense buildup of his early years in
office. Using the same words as Malenkov two decades earlier—
and to the same end—the general secretary commented, "We have
everything necessary—an honest policy of peace, military might,
the solidarity of the Soviet people—to ensure the inviolability of
our borders against any encroachments and to defend the gains
of socialism." He advocated arms control for its economic benefits: "We are conducting negotiations with the USA on the limitation of strategic armaments. The favorable outcome of these
talks would make it possible to avoid another round in the missile arms race and to free substantial resources for constructive
purposes."[12]

For several years after 1971 Brezhnev battled with other party
leaders and his own defense chiefs to win acceptance for arms
control and a reduced priority for defense in Soviet economic
planning, the SALT I treaty of 1972 represented a major victory,
but it did not sit well with everyone in Moscow. As the party
weekly *Kommunist* reported, some circles found the swift
improvement in relations with the West "difficult to get used
to." The professional soldier who was serving as defense minister, Marshal Andrei A. Grechko, demanded that Moscow's military buildup go on. If capitalism were to be deterred from attacking
the socialist homeland, Grechko urged, the Soviets had to show
they could fight and win any nuclear war the West might start.
Just as war-fighting strategies were popular among defense specialists in the United States, so they were espoused by Soviet
generals to keep the flow of new weapons coming. Brezhnev

retorted, again in the words of Malenkov, that a nuclear war "could have no winners."[13]

From about 1976 onward Brezhnev seems to have had his way. In that year Grechko died and was replaced by a civilian, Dimitri Ustinov, as defense minister. A Grechko ally was supplanted as chief of the general staff by Marshal Nikolai Ogarkov, who supported strategic arms control. And according to Central Intelligence Agency figures, the growth rate in Soviet defense spending began to slow at about the same time. In the late 1960s annual growth rates in the Soviet economy had averaged about 6 percent, with military spending growing at about 4 to 5 percent each year. By the late 1970s overall economic growth annually was only in the 2 to 3 percent range, and the CIA tells us defense budgets in the USSR were growing by only about 2 percent per year as well.[14]

By embracing arms control. Brezhnev had achieved two aims:

1. He had suppressed the rapid growth in defense budgets which characterized his first years in office, limiting the damage they would have caused in the civilian economy if they had gone on gobbling up resources at the same rate in the low-growth 1970s. Weapons procurement continued, but not as fast as military officials demanded.

2. He could justify the restraints of arms control because they applied equally to weapons acquisitions in the United States. After SALT I American defense budgets grew very slowly, too. Thus the relative power of the Soviet Union suffered little. U.S. and Soviet leaders had in effect done a deal that let both sides keep the lid on their respective defense establishments.

RESPONDING TO THE REAGAN BUILDUP: THE SOVIET MILITARY VERSUS SOVIET MODERATES

The last four years of his leadership (1978–82) were difficult ones for Brezhnev's "peace program." Shortly before Moscow and Washington reached agreement on SALT II in 1979, President Carter reversed his original emphasis on curtailing defense budgets and announced a new era of growth in U.S. military spending. The menacing SS-18, entering Soviet arsenals in the 1970s, and the new intermediate-range SS-20 were seen as requiring a Western response in kind. Within a few months of its signing ceremonies, SALT II lay moribund in the Senate, to be dropped entirely after the Soviets had invaded Afghanistan. The next year saw Ronald Reagan's election on a platform of military strength, and in October 1981 the new President announced his defense modernization program, entailing major new investments in all parts of the American strategic triad and a revived interest in ballistic missile defense.

Brezhnev spent his final year fighting Soviet military officials over the best way to respond to the Western buildup. The Defense Ministry's newspaper, *Red Star*, gave lengthy accounts of proposed new weapons systems in the United States, deploring the "insatiable appetite of the Pentagon."[15] Editorials in *Red Star* and speeches by military officials demanded the "further strengthening of Soviet defense capabilities." The general secretary's continuing pursuit of arms control after the failure of SALT II also came under fire. Despite treaty terms that guaranteed the right of both sides to satellite reconnaissance and other "national technical means of verification," the Soviet military went on decrying American reconnaissance as "espionage." According to a 1982 article in *Red Star*, "The U.S. leaders' repudiation of prior accords and violation of their own solemn statements and pledges not only cast doubt on Washington's interest in any arms limitation agreements but also undermine trust in the United States as a partner in negotiations."[16]

Many aspects of the American modernization program—the MX missile and the Trident D-5 warhead, for example—were designed to enhance Western counterforce capabilities, as defense experts in Moscow quickly pointed out. If combined with ballistic missile defense, they might allow Washington to contemplate a first strike against Soviet weapons, hoping to keep retaliatory damage limited. Military officials urged the Kremlin "to take countermeasures in order to guarantee that the nuclear missile weapons of the USSR remain intact."[17] Just what they had in mind was not specified publicly; the logical alternatives included proliferating ICBMs, making them mobile, and building ballistic missile defenses of their own.

What sense did a Soviet counterbuildup make, in the light of Brezhnev's oft-repeated dictum that "a nuclear war would have no winners"? Strategic thinkers in the West justified war-fighting plans with the argument that deterrence might fail unless Moscow knew the United States could prevail in a nuclear war. The Soviet military espoused a similar logic, relying on the shop-worn maxim that "the best defense is a good offense." If war did break out, they reasoned, Moscow would need to destroy American (and possibly British, French, and Chinese) nuclear weapons in the shortest possible time. Once they knew an attack was imminent, their best option would be a massive, preemptive assault on the enemy's forces. With those forces scheduled to grow rapidly in the 1980s, the Soviet military, in its own version of a countervailing strategy, demanded major new additions to Soviet arsenals.

While the Soviet military took a hard line in the face of the Reagan buildup, a coalition of Soviet moderates continued to support Brezhnev's quest for arms control. Many economists, academicians, government officials outside the defense-related ministries, and local party secretaries had interests that conflicted with the accelerated weapons buildup advocated by the military in Moscow. They urged restraint in the face of provocation and held out hope for renewed progress on arms control.

Even after Reagan announced his defense modernization program, articles in *Pravda* and *Izvestia*, the party and government newspapers, continued to assert that the Soviets had "all we need to safeguard security." Commentators persisted in tying Soviet policy to the economic burden of the arms race, as Brezhnev had been doing for years, and repeated their warnings that nuclear war would leave no winners. One *Izvestia* author, using a line of reasoning later picked up by Mikhail Gorbachev, connected the loss of resources to the arms race with unsolved problems of ecology.[18]

Moderates claimed in 1982—and subsequently went on claiming—to see growing resistance to Reagan's program in Washington, obviating any need for a Soviet counterbuildup. While the military press in Moscow eagerly reported Reagan's political victories in Congress, the Communist party newspaper observed that "enlightenment" was setting in among members of Congress, who were depicted as increasingly hostile to the administration's defense budgets. Aleksandr Bovin, veteran commentator for *Izvestia*, noted "changes in the tone of speeches and statements delivered from Washington. There is . . . now less stupidity, less cheap bravado, less of that cowboy daredevilry."[19] The political controversy over an appropriate Soviet reaction to Reagan's buildup was still raging when, late in 1982, Leonid Brezhnev died.

THE POLITICS OF ARMS CONTROL SINCE BREZHNEV

In his last days Brezhnev had been called to a meeting with his generals, who apparently demanded action in response to the Reagan buildup. Now, as the leadership's energies turned to the choice of a new general secretary, the military had its victory. The selection quickly narrowed down to two old-timers on the Politburo: Yuri Andropov, recent head of the secret police, and Konstantin Chernenko, a Brezhnev crony resistant to change in either domestic or foreign policy. The Politburo chose Andropov, who enjoyed strong support within the defense establishment.

Because he lived only fifteen months after becoming general secretary, Andropov will always remain something of a mystery in foreign policy terms. But one of his statements in 1983 may give us a hint of his attitude to arms control: He began his term by ridiculing those who expected moderation in Washington.[20] A known advocate of sweeping reform in the Soviet economic structure, Andropov probably saw a rejuvenated economy as the key to defense policy. If growth rates could be pumped back up to 5 or 6 percent annually, the leadership in Moscow would escape Brezhnev's dilemma. Defense budgets could expand more rapidly again without damage to consumer well-being, investment in agriculture, or the crucial development of new energy sources in Siberia. Andropov seemed impatient with arms control, four fruitless years after the failure of SALT II. When Washington began delivering intermediate-range nuclear missiles to Western Europe late in 1983, Soviet delegations walked out of the recently resumed Geneva arms negotiations.

Then, early in 1984, the top Communist party post fell vacant again with Andropov's death. The Politburo, unable to agree on a more vigorous, longer-term leader, named the ailing Chernenko to succeed his old rival. Behind the scenes, though, a relative newcomer to the leadership, fifty-two-year-old Mikhail Gorbachev, was starting to run the show. Even before Gorbachev's formal appointment as general secretary following Chernenko's death in March 1985, Moscow and Washington announced they were resuming negotiations on three related aspects of the arms race: strategic offensive weapons, intermediate-range nuclear weapons, and the militarization of space. The USSR proposed a 50 percent cut in strategic systems, a ban on "space strike" weapons, and the removal of all U.S. and Soviet nuclear missiles from Europe.

What is Gorbachev's thinking about the military rivalry between East and West? So far he seems to be keeping open several very different options for Soviet policy. Some depend on arms control. If Washington agrees to continue the ban on space-based strategic defenses, and if negotiated reductions in strategic delivery systems take place, the new Soviet leader has an opportunity unknown to his predecessors. He can actually stop the growth in military spending, investing additional resources in the civilian economy. One specialist in Soviet defense policy, MIT's Stephen Meyer, estimates that Moscow would have to reduce military spending to 10 percent of Soviet gross national product (from nearly 16 percent at present) for Gorbachev to reach his economic goals.[21] Alternatively, and again only if nuclear arms control succeeds, he can divert funds from the strategic arms race to modernize Soviet conventional forces, as military leaders like Ogarkov have been urging.

So far the resumed Geneva negotiations and a series of top-level summit meetings have produced no breakthrough on strategic arms control, despite agreement in 1987 to eliminate the far less numerous U.S. and Soviet intermediate-range nuclear weapons in Europe. Gorbachev's policy initiatives have focused on restructuring the Soviet economy and improving its efficiency. To break down the conservative resistance facing his economic reforms, he has sometimes linked them to defense policy in a way that suggests a third option. A reformed economy with faster growth rates will be necessary, he has argued, if Moscow is forced to match the defense buildup of Reagan's America.[22] Failing arms control, the Soviet Union will need to modernize its own strategic forces, making its missiles "smarter" to overcome new American defenses and building exotic missile defense technologies of its own. Gorbachev has developed a foreign policy agenda calling for cooperation between East and West in settling regional conflicts, and he has made some bold innovations in arms control negotiations. If these fail to produce results, however, a revitalized Soviet economy could make the next round in the arms race more affordable for him than for his predecessors.

Controversy:
DO THE SOVIETS THINK THEY CAN WIN A NUCLEAR WAR?

Yes! Soviet strategic doctrine differs fundamentally from Western thinking about nuclear war. While U.S. strategies are retaliatory in nature and include concepts of "sufficiency" in nuclear arms, Soviet military thought is offensive in nature. As Richard Pipes, who became an adviser to President Reagan, pointed out in 1977, Soviet doctrine calls for "not deterrence but victory, not sufficiency in weapons but superiority, not retaliation but offensive action."[23]

The vast array of weapons in the Soviet strategic arsenal shows Moscow is serious about fighting a nuclear war with capitalism and winning. The Soviets have enough land-based warheads to launch a first strike against U.S. missiles with only a part of their own ICBM force. Their desire to preempt—destroying Western forces before they can be used—requires highly accurate counterforce-targeted ICBMs, and these they have in abundance.

Americans must understand that the Russians just don't think like the rest of us. For them there is no such thing as "enough" weapons. Only with a nuclear arsenal vastly superior to their opponents' can they hope to "win" a nuclear war in any meaningful sense, achieving the kind of damage limitation that warfighting scenarios require. To the Soviet Union arms control is just an elaborate hoax, designed to buy time for a further buildup by Moscow. Their occasional soothing words only mask an aggressive impulse: to prepare for a nuclear attack on the West.

NO! It is true that Soviet leaders have never been content with a simple assured destruction capability, nor have they been satisfied with a weapons arsenal inferior to their opponents'. But neither has Washington. Many of the same forces driving American thought in more ambitious directions are at play in Moscow. Defense industrial establishments in both political systems depend on ever-growing budgets and new generations of weapons for their institutional prosperity.

Strategic doctrines based on war-fighting scenarios are popular among military officials of both superpowers. The military is naturally interested in how to fight a war if one breaks out and impatient with arguments about how much is "enough" to deter an opponent. Thus "preemption" is to the Soviets what "damage limitation" is to Americans: an answer to the question "What if deterrence fails?" and a justification for more weapons, whatever their current number. With this mind-set, the military on both sides will always be suspicious of negotiations to limit weapons, and arms control treaties will always seem to favor the enemy.

It is the task of the political leadership in both countries to put these views of the defense community into broader perspective, a job that has been done better at some times than at others. In Soviet politics succession crises tend to favor the claims of the military. General secretaries secure in their power, though, take a different line from the generals. They often speak of "having all they need" to deter attack on the USSR, they demand "parity" with an opponent rather than superiority, they decry the economic costs of the arms race, and they remind the military that nuclear war "can have no winners." These phrases are more than propaganda gestures; they reflect the Communist party leadership's attempts to control growth in defense budgets. They can also form the basis for negotiated arms control agreements of equal benefit to both sides.

SUMMARY: CODE WORDS IN THE SOVIET ARMS DEBATE

"further strengthen defense capabilities"—demand for a Soviet response in kind to new weapons acquisitions in the West.

imperialism—Lenin's theory that advanced capitalist societies are innately aggressive; universally accepted by Soviet thinkers today.

"Nuclear war has no winners"—used by critics of Soviet defense buildups since 1954 to oppose demands of war-fighting strategists.

"Nuclear war will destroy capitalism"—the militarists' response; assumes nuclear war can be won by socialism and justifies demands for more counterforce capabilities.

peaceful coexistence—cornerstone of modern Soviet foreign policy, asserting that war between socialist and capitalist states is not "fatalistically inevitable"; leaves open the question of how many weapons the USSR needs to deter capitalist attack.

rough parity—equivalence of strategic weapon systems between East and West, seen as existing since about 1970; it strikes some Soviets as a reason for arms control, others as justification to match every new U.S. weapon.

"We have all we need"—argument used repeatedly since 1954 to resist demands for a Soviet "counterweight" to every new weapon system.

FOR MORE DETAIL

George W. Breslauer, *Khrushchev and Brezhnev as Leaders* (Boston: George Allen & Unwin, 1982). A detailed account of the succession crises which brought the two leaders to power and of their policy choices once in charge.

David Holloway, *The Soviet Union and the Arms Race* (New Haven: Yale University Press, 1983). A recent classic on Soviet defense policy.

Joseph L. Nogee and Robert H. Donaldson, *Soviet Foreign Policy Since World War II*, 2d ed. (New York: Pergamon Press, 1984). Chapter 5 details the foreign policy content of the Khrushchev-Malenkov debates.

Samuel B. Payne, Jr., *The Soviet Union and SALT* (Cambridge, Mass.: MIT Press, 1980). A history of Soviet attitudes to arms control.

Richard Pipes, "Why the Soviet Union Thinks It Could Fight and Win a Nuclear War," *Commentary* (July 1977): 21–34. A prominent American conservative argues that Soviet strategic thought is fundamentally different from its Western equivalent.

Marshall D. Shulman, "What the Russians Really Want," *Harper's* (April 1984): 63–71. A useful counterpart to the Pipes article, placing Soviet military thinking in a broader political context.

V. D. Sokolovskiy, *Soviet Military Strategy*, 3d ed., ed. Harriet Fast Scott, (New York: Crane, Russak & Co., 1975). The touchstone of modern Soviet strategic doctrine, published in several editions in the 1960s, here with an introduction highlighting changes from each edition to the next.

Dan L. and Rebecca Strode, "Diplomacy and Defense in Soviet National Security Policy," *International Security* 8, 2 (Fall 1983): 91–116. Documents conflicting strands of thought on security issues within the Soviet leadership.

NOTES TO CHAPTER 5

1. Karl von Clausewitz, *On War.*

2. Karl Marx, *Capital,* vol. I, available in *The Marx-Engels Reader,* ed. Robert C. Tucker (New York: W. W. Norton & Co., 1978).

3. The subtitle of Lenin's essay *Imperialism.*

4. David Holloway summarizes Stalin's thinking about war and the doctrinal changes which occurred after Stalin's death in *The Soviet Union and the Arms Race* (New Haven: Yale University Press, 1983), ch. 3.

5. Ibid., p. 31.

6. Khrushchev's remarks on peaceful coexistence may be found in *Current Soviet Policies II,* ed. Leo Gruliow (New York: Praeger, 1957), pp. 29–38.

7. Joseph L. Nogee and Robert H. Donaldson document the Malenkov-Khrushchev debate over defense policy in their *Soviet Foreign Policy Since World War II,* 2d ed. (New York: Pergamon Press, 1984), pp. 110–11.

8. Dan L. and Rebecca Strode characterize them in this way in "Diplomacy and Defense in Soviet National Security Policy," *International Security* 8, 2 (Fall 1983): 91–116. They add that Brezhnev's defense budgets were designed "to placate the military leadership, which had grown furious with Khrushchev's erratic foreign policy, his interference in military spending, and his inadequate commitment to defense spending."

9. *Khrushchev Remembers,* ed. Strobe Talbott (Boston: Little, Brown & Co., 1970), p. 518.

10. John G. Hibbits emphasizes the political implications of Soviet military thought in "Admiral Gorshkov's Writings: Twenty Years of Naval Thought," in *Naval Power in Soviet Policy,* ed. Paul J. Murphy (Washington, D.C.: Government Printing Office, 1978).

11. George W. Breslauer, *Khrushchev and Brezhnev as Leaders* (Boston: George Allen & Unwin, 1982), pp. 85 and 96.

12. Brezhnev's speech was carried in *Izvestia,* March 31, 1971, and was translated as "Brezhnev: Central Committee Report," in *Current Soviet Policies VI* (Columbus, Ohio: American Association for the Advancement of Slavic Studies, 1973).

13. Support for and resistance to SALT I in Soviet politics are documented by Peter Volten, *Brezhnev's Peace Program: A Study of Soviet Domestic Process and Power* (Boulder, Colo.: Westview Press, 1982).

14. Leslie Gelb and Richard Halloran detailed the CIA estimates in "C.I.A. Analysts Now Said to Find U.S. Overstated Soviet Arms Rise," *New York Times,* March 3, 1983, p. A1.

15. See, for example, Colonel M. Ponomarev's commentary, *Krasnaia zvezda,* December 17, 1981, p. 3.

16. *Krasnaia zvezda,* January 12, 1982, p. 3.

17. General V. E. Tolubko, commander in chief of the Strategic Rocket Forces, in

an interview published in East Berlin by *Neues Deutschland*, January 16 / 17, 1982.

18. As examples, see Yu. Pankov, "Disarmament—An Ideal of Socialism," *Pravda*, October 30, 1981, p. 4, and Ye. Fedorov, "The Peace Policy and Problems of Ecology," *Izvestia*, December 9, 1981, p. 3.

19. A. Bovin, "The Process of World Renewal Is Invincible," *Izvestia*, January 1, 1982, p. 5.

20. See Andropov's statement on relations with the United States, published in the *New York Times*, September 29, 1983, p. A14.

21. Stephen M. Meyer, "Post-Iceland: No Change in Soviet Build-Up," *Washington Post*, October 19, 1986, p. H1.

22. After the debacle of the Reykjavik summit, Gorbachev commented that "under new conditions the people's efforts are helping to accelerate the growth of the country's economic potential and are thus consolidating its defense capabilities." Televised speech on October 14, 1986.

23. Richard Pipes, "Why the Soviet Union Thinks It Could Fight and Win a Nuclear War," *Commentary* (July 1977), p. 31.

PART III

ARMS
CONTROL:
HISTORY AND
CURRENT
OPTIONS

—

6

THE LEGACY OF THE PAST: PROBLEMS AND PROGRESS IN ARMS CONTROL

—

The 1980s have not been the easiest of times for arms control. After a series of agreements with the Soviet Union extending over twenty years, leaders in Washington began to doubt the wisdom of arms control toward the end of the 1970s. For some skeptics the reason was a growing Soviet advantage in weapons they considered the most important, especially ICBMs and IRBMs, while the United States remained ahead only in areas they thought less critical, such as bomber and submarine forces. Arms control had failed to achieve symmetry in the arsenals of the superpowers. Others looked askance at Moscow's behavior in Asia and Africa, where the tide of the seventies seemed to be turning against the West. Arms control had not suppressed Soviet aggression outside the nuclear arena. Still others feared a decline in defense contracting under a stricter arms control regime. The combination of jobs and profits in defense-related industries creates a strong constituency for military spending.

Arms control nonetheless enjoyed substantial popularity throughout the decade. No leader in the West dared campaign against it directly. Even those who opposed it for the moment offered some hope of better agreements in the future: "real" limits; drastic reductions; even the complete abolition of nuclear weapons. Polls of the American public showed large majorities favoring a halt to the U.S.-Soviet arms race, until respondents were asked whether they supported a freeze that would leave the USSR ahead. For its part, the Kremlin never accepted the demise of arms control. In the 1980s it repeatedly held out inducements to pull Washington back into negotiations: an immediate freeze on "nuclear arsenals"; a unilateral moratorium on nuclear weapons testing; what Moscow called a genuine zero option in Europe.

What accounts for the continuing interest in arms control? Incentives for both East and West include:

• The fear of nuclear war. The spectacle of the world's two superpowers building ever more and better weapons of mass destruction, as each tries to deter an attack by the other, causes anxiety. John Kennedy, for one, took arms control more seriously after the Cuban missile crisis had convinced him Moscow and Washington really might blunder into a war that would destroy both their countries. Intuitively many feel the chances of nuclear holocaust are less if arsenals dwindle instead of mounting. We have no way of knowing what Soviet leaders really think on this count, although their rhetoric associates the ongoing arms race with a growing danger of nuclear war.

• Pressure on governments in the United States and other democracies, coming from organized movements and broader public opinion. The weight of this factor is hard to measure, especially since popular movements ebb and flow so dramatically from year to year. Soviet leaders, with their control over the mass media and their one-party elections, feel less pressure from an informed public than do their counterparts in the United States.

• The costs of modernizing nuclear delivery systems and developing such capabilities as space-based defenses. Here the stronger incentive probably lies on the Soviet side, where a chronically strained economy must always give up other things of value to produce more weapons. In the last chapter we looked at some of these trade-offs and the support they generate for arms control in Soviet politics. In the West the same economic logic applies only at times of full employment or when political leaders give high priority to reduced public expenditures. Furthermore, any government, Communist or capitalist, which builds up its conventional forces to compensate for limits on nuclear weapons will end up spending more, not less.

• The suspicion that the other side will get ahead in an unlimited arms race. This consideration cuts both ways. Better American technologies, especially in computer guidance systems, probably account for some grudging acceptance of arms control within the Soviet military. The 1972 agreement cutting off competition in ballistic missile defense may have been "sold" to the Politburo by Brezhnev because U.S. ABM technology was likely to be superior. On the other hand, once a technology is developed on both sides, American Presidents cannot count on enduring public support for the long, expensive process of deployment. The interest Presidents Nixon, Ford, and Carter showed in negotiated limits on ICBM MIRVing derived in part from their fear that the Soviets could deploy more of these weapons over the long haul.

On the other hand, there is opposition to arms control among conservatives and defense officials on both sides. Unsatisfied with the proposition that each superpower already has enough to deter an attack by the other, the military starts with the question "What if war does break out?" It then asks, "How are we going to keep from being defeated?" As we saw in Chapters 4 and 5, that approach leads to demands for more weapons, both offensive and defensive. It also generates skepticism about agreements to give up weapons a country could use in fighting a nuclear war.

Political leaders in the Kremlin, the White House, and Congress have a broader role to play. While they cannot ignore the interests of their defense establishments, Presidents, general secretaries, and members of Congress have to balance pressure for more weapons against other uses for the same resources. Farming, housing, road building, health, and the high technology civilian industries that affect a nation's competitive position in the world economy—all compete for funding with the defense needs which preoccupy the military. Arms control stands the best chance when leaders in Washington and Moscow are sensitive to the costs of defense and strong enough domestically to organize constituencies averse to an unbridled arms race. The conjunction of such leadership on both sides at the same time creates a "window of opportunity" for arms limitation.

PERCEPTIONS: PARITY AND COMPLIANCE

As the historical review in this chapter will indicate, no arms control agreement restricts all forms of weapons at the same time.

Any such across-the-board disarmament, if it ever comes, must wait for some future when a radically new level of trust between nuclear adversaries has evolved. Under present circumstances arms control moves only by short steps, with two vital preconditions for each small advance: a shared perception of parity in the weapons under negotiation and an ability to verify compliance with the restrictions hammered out. The widespread perception that an arms control treaty locks one side into inferiority will undermine support for it. And ambiguity about either partner's adherence to its terms will lead to charges that an agreement is being violated. Treaties lacking these two preconditions are worse than no arms control at all since they erode confidence in the entire process.

Parity is an especially tricky concept. Sometimes, of course, its absence is obvious. When the United States had atomic (later hydrogen) bombs and the Soviet Union had none, there was little hope for a ban on nuclear weapons tests. When the number of Moscow's strategic launchers was only a fraction of Washington's, agreed limits on nuclear delivery vehicles remained out of the question. Serious negotiations for a nuclear test ban had to wait until the late 1950s, and it was not until the end of the 1960s, as the numbers of ballistic missiles deployed by the superpowers drew even, that the SALT process got off the ground.

By the 1970s measuring parity had grown more complicated. The United States was ahead in strategic bombers, as it always has been, and if one counted warheads rather than launchers, it still held the lead in submarine-based missile forces. But it was falling farther and farther behind the Soviets in ICBMs. Does that constitute parity? The debates over strategic doctrine from the Kennedy years forward (considered in an earlier chapter) essentially revolve around this question. Some thinkers emphasize a survivable capacity for countervalue retaliation—assured destruction—and are happy to trade American superiority in SLBM warheads for Soviet superiority in warheads based on land. Others—the "damage limiters"—consider ICBMs more valuable than other systems and denounce as Western inferiority what their rivals call *rough parity*.

The SALT agreements of 1972 and 1979 failed to require reductions in Moscow's ICBMs that would bring them down to American levels. As we will see below, SALT I lumped SLBMs and ICBMs together, fixing launcher totals that left the USSR ahead of the United States in missiles by nearly 25 percent. In exchange, it allowed Washington to keep its advantage in bombers. The agreement was immediately attacked in the U.S. Senate, which insisted that the next treaty limiting strategic arms set equal aggregate totals for strategic delivery vehicles. SALT II did that, and it also regulated warheads; but its intricate formulas still permitted the Soviet Union more ICBMs with far more warheads than the United States had on its land-based missiles. Taking into account the continuing American advantage in SLBMs, the agreement added up to parity in some eyes. To Ronald Reagan and his supporters, it seemed to codify Moscow's war-fighting advantage.

Verification is a second prerequisite for success in arms control. Anyone giving a public presentation on the subject is bound to face the question "But can we trust the Russians to keep their word?" Relations between the superpowers are intensely competitive, and neither relies on the honesty of the other. But trust is not a precondition of arms control so long as each side can see whether the other is cheating. For the process to work, only observable activities can be banned.

A major breakthrough for verification came in the early 1960s, as satellite reconnaissance began letting Moscow and Washington spy on each other with impunity. Previously each had only the spottiest glimpse of the other's airfields and missile sites, gathered from secret agents and, in the case of the United States at least, overflights of the opponent's territory by aircraft. To make arms limitation possible, President Eisenhower had sought to legalize aircraft surveillance with his "Open Skies" proposal. The Soviets, whose passion for military secrecy is legendary, predictably refused. Their downing of an American U-2 spy plane over Soviet territory in 1960 dramatized the need for nonintrusive means of verification such as satellites.

The superpowers now maintain an array of satellites positioned to cover each other's entire territories twenty-four hours a day. Since optical observations can be impeded by darkness or bad weather, infrared sensors in orbit assist them. Ballistic missile deployments, the subject of the first strategic arms limitation agreement, are now easy to monitor. So are the scorching exhausts of missiles being fired. Most of the extensive tests done by Soviets and Americans before they put new weaponry into operation can be observed.

Besides satellite reconnaissance, the nuclear superpowers monitor each other's activities from ships and aircraft just offshore or near Pacific test ranges and from listening stations that intercept transmissions from weapons being tested. Together these capabilities constitute the *national technical means* of verification sanctioned by the arms control treaties of the 1970s, and they let Moscow and Washington learn a great deal about their opponents' forces. We can see how many warheads are on a delivery vehicle when it is tested, for example, and as long as messages coming from it during testing are not put into code (as long as the telemetry is not encrypted), we can estimate the accuracy of delivery fairly closely.

Even though we commonly hear that our reconnaissance satellites can "read the license plates on cars in Moscow," there are still some things we cannot find out by national technical means. Satellites can count aircraft and missile silos, but not the warheads mounted inside a missile's nose cone. That makes verification difficult for any treaty which limits MIRVing, as we will soon see in the case of SALT II. Cruise missiles pose a similar dilemma for arms control since they are small enough to fit inside the body of an aircraft or to be hidden inside a submarine. The recent squabble over a Soviet radar facility at Krasnoyarsk provides another example. The ABM Treaty of 1972 forbids its signatories to place missile-tracking radar anywhere except along the peripheries of their territories. Since Krasnoyarsk lies deep inside Soviet Asia, a radar there violates the treaty if it serves to track missiles. But does it? Washington says yes; Moscow, no. In an age of multipurpose radar there may be no way of knowing without on-site inspection. A recent rare visit by U.S. congressmen to the Krasnoyarsk site, as well as the verification measures in the 1988 INF Treaty, may foretell provisions for on-site inspection in future arms control agreements.[1]

The negotiating teams that put together arms control accords thus have several tasks to complete at the same time. In the first place, they must put meaningful limits on the most important, current weapons of the superpowers; otherwise the arms race goes on unimpeded. But the two sides rarely have these weapons in the same numbers and at the same stage of technical development. The second task, then, is to engineer some package of dissimilar weapons—missiles, aircraft, cruise missiles, missiles based on land, on submarines, etc.—that is of roughly similar importance in the American and Soviet arsenals. These will be restricted while other forms of arms will not. And then the treaty must specify limits on the weapons included in such a way that compliance with them is verifiable. A tough job, some say an impossible one. The following history of arms control shows how these tasks have been approached in the past. It may also help in choosing the best course for the future.

COMPLETE DISARMAMENT: THE FIRST RESPONSE TO NUCLEAR WEAPONS

The search for nuclear disarmament began inauspiciously in 1946, when Washington presented its *Baruch Plan* to the United Nations. Knowing it could not keep its monopoly on nuclear weapons forever, the United States asked other nations not to develop them. In exchange it would turn over control of its small arsenal of atomic bombs to an International Atomic Development Authority, which alone would have the power to mine fissionable materials and generate nuclear energy. It was to produce no nuclear weapons of its own and would be authorized to punish any nation attempting to acquire them. A reasonable plan? Only from the Western standpoint. Under its terms the United States would remain the sole nation privy to the secrets of nuclear destruction.

In the late 1940s Moscow was racing to build its own atomic bomb, while strenuously denying the significance of the nuclear revolution in weaponry. The Soviet counterproposal to the Baruch Plan asked Washington to destroy its nuclear stockpile before safeguards on the production of atomic bombs by other nations went into effect. An international monitoring body would be set up under the Soviet plan, too, but subject to control by the UN Security Council, where the USSR enjoyed a veto. Evidently the Kremlin hoped to test its own fission device before international provisions stopped it.[2]

With the first Soviet nuclear explosion in 1949, the Baruch

Plan was dead. In practice, the hope of abolishing nuclear weapons entirely was probably futile as soon as the first nation tested them successfully. Once we had learned how to make fission and fusion bombs, we had no way to forget the technology. As far as we can tell, there will never again be a time when humanity lacks the knowledge to build nuclear weapons. And given this knowledge, no nation is likely to accept total nuclear disarmament, trusting its adversaries not to sneak nuclear weapons back into production. Nonetheless, Moscow went on pleading for "general and complete disarmament" through most of the next decade, while both superpowers put together their hydrogen bombs. Only when they felt fully equal in the technology of nuclear explosions did agreement to limit them become feasible. By then it was no longer disarmament that was being discussed; it was arms control.

BANNING NUCLEAR WEAPONS TESTS

Michael Mandelbaum, author of a series of books on the nuclear arms race, points out that *arms control*—measures to restrict arsenals rather than abolish them—is a less ambitious enterprise than total *disarmament*.[3] No transfer of sovereignty to an international authority need be involved. The partners to an arms control agreement remain in control of their own weapons. If either sees the other violating the negotiated limits, it does not turn to the United Nations for enforcement. It can simply withdraw from the agreement on its own. The key to arms control, then, is not enforcement but mutual verifiability.

Verification became, indeed, the sticking point for the first nuclear arms control treaty worked out between the United States and the Soviet Union, the Limited Nuclear Test Ban Treaty of 1963. International pressure to stop nuclear explosions evolved in the 1950s, as radioactive rain from American and Soviet tests in the atmosphere spread around the world. In 1958 Moscow announced a unilateral moratorium on its testing program, and after initially rejecting the idea, the United States agreed to do the same. Negotiations for an international test ban agreement began, but they foundered on mutual suspicions of cheating. Even as satellites made it easier to verify a ban on testing in the atmosphere and outer space, underground tests remained hard to distinguish from earthquakes without on-site inspection.

In 1961 both sides abandoned their testing moratoriums in a climate of intense hostility between East and West. Ironically, the Cuban missile crisis of the following year, though it raised tensions to the breaking point for a short period, seems to have made President Kennedy and Soviet leader Khrushchev more amenable to dialogue over the longer run. Kennedy's June 1963 foreign policy speech at American University invoked the vision of greater cooperation between capitalist and Communist opponents to limit the nuclear arms race. At about the same time Moscow dropped its opposition to a Western plan for banning all nuclear tests except those underground. With remarkable speed Great Britain, the United States, and the USSR went on to sign a treaty to that effect in August 1963.[4]

The terms of the Limited Nuclear Test Ban Treaty as finally negotiated are simple and easy to verify. The signatories undertook not to carry out any nuclear explosion, including weapons testing, "in the atmosphere; beyond its limits, including outer space; or under water, including territorial waters or high seas."[5] Underground tests were not prohibited and continue to this day, though restricted by two lesser treaties of the 1970s. In the last stages of the bargaining, Moscow had offered to allow three on-site inspections per year if underground testing was included, but London and Washington had held out for at least seven. No one knew, though, whether a comprehensive nuclear test ban was likely to pass the U.S. Senate, where a two-thirds vote is required for treaty ratification. Critics insisted that a cessation of all tests would keep the United States from developing improved ICBMs and the ABM interceptors it was working on in the 1960s.

The Limited Nuclear Test Ban Treaty remains in force indefinitely and has been signed by more than 100 nations. Unfortunately these do not include France and the People's Republic of China, whose small but growing nuclear forces are independent of the superpowers. Even so, the agreement has all but eliminated testing in the atmosphere, as France and China voluntarily moved to underground tests in the 1980s. The United States and the Soviet Union go on testing nuclear weapons at an undiminished rate, as Figure 6-1 shows, but below rather than aboveground.

EARLIER NONNUCLEAR ARMS CONTROL AGREEMENTS

The 1963 treaty limiting atmospheric testing marked the beginning of an era in nuclear arms control, with new Soviet-American agreements issuing forth every few years until the end of the 1970s. It was not, however, the first time the two powers had agreed to limit armaments. As early as the 1920s, both subscribed to naval agreements seeking to curtail a multilateral arms race in warships. Those treaties were scuttled by Japan's burgeoning imperial designs before the Second World War.

The Soviet Union and the United States had also been signatories to the Geneva Protocol of 1925, prohibiting the use of poison gas and bacteriological weapons in war. In Washington, though, the Senate refused to ratify the protocol. Arguments about its effect on American policy flew back and forth sporadically for fifty years, until in 1975 the Ford administration succeeded in getting ratification. Interpretations of the treaty still vary. For example, would the chemical defoliants used by the United States in Vietnam have been a violation? For its part, the United States has charged the Soviet Union and its client states in Afghanistan and Southeast Asia with using prohibited agents (the infamous "yellow rain") against insurgencies there.

A treaty on Antarctica immediately preceded the limited nuclear test ban. Dating from 1959, the Antarctic Treaty sought to preserve the auspicious international exploration of that frozen continent, specifying that it "shall be used for peaceful purposes only." The treaty prohibits "any measures of a military nature, such as the establishment of military bases and fortifications, the carrying out of military maneuvers, as well as the testing of any type of weapons." Nuclear explosions and the disposal of radioactive waste materials in Antarctica are also banned. Because the parties to the treaty have the right to inspect installations in all areas of the continent, verification of the treaty's

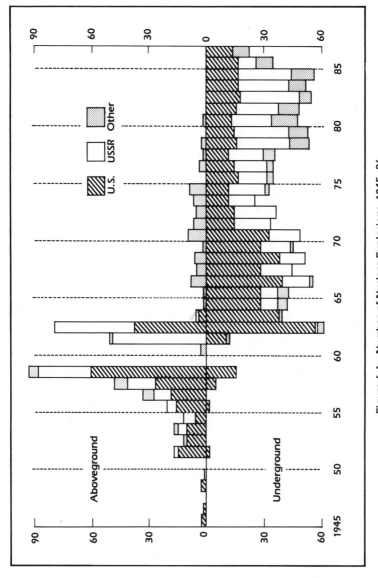

Figure 6-1—Number of Nuclear Explosions, 1945–86
(from *World Armaments and Disarmaments: SIPRI Yearbook*, 1987)

comprehensive provisions has been possible, and it remains a source of general satisfaction to the community of nations.

THE OUTER SPACE TREATY

After the Limited Nuclear Test Ban Treaty the next step in arms control came with the 1967 treaty governing the exploration and use of outer space. It reflected the experience gained by the super-powers in their negotiations over Antarctica and the testing of nuclear weapons. In line with the treaty preserving the polar continent as a weapons-free area, the Outer Space Treaty set out to protect another environment from the nuclear arms race. And like the limited ban on nuclear tests, it accepted the principle of arms control by small increments. President Eisenhower had proposed as early as 1960 that the terms of the Antarctic agreement be extended to outer space and celestial bodies. For several years, though, the Soviets refused to separate the issue from their proposals for "general and complete disarmament." Only when Moscow's attitude shifted did an agreement become possible.

The Outer Space Treaty, like its predecessors, was easy to understand and readily verifiable. Parties to the treaty agree "not to place in orbit around the Earth any objects carrying nuclear weapons or any other kinds of weapons of mass destruction, install such weapons on celestial bodies, or station such weapons in outer space in any other manner." The accord demilitarizes the moon and other celestial bodies entirely, prohibiting their use for establishing military bases, testing weapons of any kind, or conducting military maneuvers.

To date the hostile powers of the planet have managed to keep weapons out of space, with the exception of the partial orbits of ballistic missiles on the way to their targets. That achievement now seems highly precarious, though. The "weaponization" of space may be starting, and without even requiring a violation of U.S. or Soviet treaty commitments. Note that the Outer Space Treaty bans in space only certain types of weapons: nuclear or any other weapons of "mass destruction." Conventional explosives used to destroy satellites or antisatellite weapons that kill by impact fall into neither of these categories. The same is probably true of lasers placed in space since they accomplish pin-point, not mass, destruction.

Both the United States and the Soviet Union have tested anti-satellite weapons, and both are working on laser technologies that carry destruction from earth to space and vice versa. If we are interested only in keeping nuclear weapons earthbound, our existing agreements may be adequate. If it is space weaponization we want to prevent, broader measures will have to be adopted, and the agreement will have to come soon.

NUCLEAR NONPROLIFERATION

The nuclear age has brought us a few pleasant surprises along with its grim realities. Prominent among them, of course, is the absence of war among the nuclear powers. A close second is the slowness with which nuclear weapons have spread from the superpowers to other nations. By the mid-1960s only five countries had exploded nuclear weapons: the United States (1945), the USSR (1949), Great Britain (1952), France (1960), and China (1964). Since then two decades have passed with only India exploding what it called a "peaceful" nuclear device in 1974. How much arms control has to do with this good fortune is an open question. Probably the reluctance of the nuclear states to pass along their destructive technologies accounts for most of it, since smaller states find the resources and know-how to build the bomb hard to come by. But three important agreements codify the world's efforts to halt nuclear proliferation.

The Limited Nuclear Test Ban Treaty was the first of these. Proponents of a complete ban on testing—aboveground or below—believed it would stop nonnuclear signatories from becoming nuclear powers. The agreement's tolerance of underground testing represents a major flaw in this regard. When India became the sixth nuclear nation, it did so without violating the limited test ban, which it had signed a decade earlier. It simply conducted its nuclear test underground.

A second step toward nonproliferation was taken by the Latin American nations in 1967, when they agreed to prohibit nuclear weapons in their region. Parties to the Treaty of Tlatelolco, which

Cuba has not signed, abjure the testing, production, or acquisition of nuclear weapons. Outside nations with possessions in Latin America acceded to the agreement in a protocol, and a second protocol binds the United States, the Soviet Union, Great Britain, France, and China to respect the denuclearized status of the zone.

But the landmark agreement on this issue is the worldwide Treaty on the Nonproliferation of Nuclear Weapons signed in 1968. The outcome of a decade of haggling among the nuclear powers, it seeks to stop the spread of nuclear weapons entirely. To do so, it divides the world into two categories—nuclear weapons states and nonnuclear weapons states—and imposes obligations on the treaty's adherents according to this status:

1. Nuclear weapons states contract "not to transfer to any recipient whatsoever nuclear weapons or other nuclear explosive devices" or to assist any nonnuclear weapons state in acquiring them. Along with all other parties to the agreement, they are prohibited from providing "special fissionable material" to nonnuclear weapons states.

2. On their side, nonnuclear weapons states undertake not to receive or manufacture nuclear weapons or nuclear explosive devices. They accept safeguards arranged through the International Atomic Energy Agency "with a view to preventing diversion of nuclear energy from peaceful uses to nuclear weapons or other nuclear explosive devises."

3. In exchange for their compliance, nonnuclear states are guaranteed the benefits from peaceful applications of nuclear energy, which all parties to the treaty are required to share with them.

4. The spread of nuclear weapons from one state to another is generally described as *horizontal proliferation.* Most of the treaty aims at its prevention, but Article VI contains a provision demanded by the nonnuclear states to stop so-called *vertical proliferation,* the piling up of more nuclear weapons by the existing nuclear powers. By its terms all parties undertake "to pursue negotiations in good faith on effective measures relating to cessation of the nuclear arms race at an early date and to nuclear disarmament. . . ."

How well has the Nonproliferation Treaty worked? Since it took effect, only one new nation, India, is known to have set off a nuclear explosion. Israel is generally assumed to be ready for one on short notice, however,[6] and both South Africa and Pakistan seem close to a nuclear weapons capability. France, China, and India all refuse to sign, though France has announced its intention to behave as if it were a party to the treaty.

The reprocessing of spent fuel from nuclear reactors into weapons-grade plutonium poses the greatest current threat of nuclear weapons proliferation. The more advanced nations, such as Canada, France, and the United States, sell technology and fuel for nuclear power plants to the many nations interested in generating power this way, whether the recipients have agreed to the Nonproliferation Treaty or not. Turning spent fuel—for example, the plutonium produced by some nuclear reactors—into weapons may soon be within the grasp of countries like Argentina, Brazil, South Africa, Taiwan, South Korea, Pakistan, Iraq, and Iran. Pakistan is thought to be near a nuclear weapons capability, based on energy technology provided by the United States, and Israel in 1981 bombed an Iraqi nuclear reactor it suspected of producing weapons-grade materials. Given the recent history of deadly regional conflicts involving these countries, one has to wonder how long the nuclear peace of the past forty years can last.[7]

THE FIVE-YEAR QUEST FOR SALT I

When the United States and the Soviet Union signed the Nonproliferation Treaty in the summer of 1968, they had already begun preparing for the first negotiations on strategic delivery systems. The arms control agreements of the previous five years, promising though they had been, did nothing to limit the means both superpowers now had of attacking each other. The 1960s were, in fact, a time of ferocious competition in missile deployments, when Moscow and Washington raced to get their ICBMs and SLBMs on-line. By late in the decade the contest had come to include strategic defenses, too; if either side developed its ABM systems successfully, the other would have to plunge into a further vortex of missile proliferation.

So it was that Lyndon Johnson approached the Soviet leadership in 1967 with a proposal to negotiate restraints on the strategic arms race. His administration suggested limiting offensive and defensive weapons at the same time since more missiles stimulated interest in defenses, while success with strategic defenses would lead to the deployment of more missiles. The American initiative came at an awkward time for the Kremlin, though; a triumvirate of new leaders was still consolidating its power there in the wake of Khrushchev's removal in 1964. Divisions were greatest between the new general secretary of the Communist party, Leonid Brezhnev, and the Soviet premier, Aleksei Kosygin. In the crossfire between these two rivals, arms control probably served as a political weapon, leading Moscow to give contradictory answers to Johnson's first queries.

Asked about the U.S. proposal to include ballistic missile defense in a Strategic Arms Limitation Treaty (SALT), Kosygin at first pleaded, in effect, "How can you expect me to tell the Russian people they can't defend themselves against your rockets?"[8] Instead, he suggested an agreement to limit only ballistic missiles themselves, in which the USSR was approaching parity with the United States. The Soviets subsequently reversed course, urging that an ABM agreement be struck at once, while deferring limits on offensive weapons. Once negotiations finally got under way, however, the Soviets consented to simultaneous restraints on defensive and offensive systems.

The American policy of linkage, making strategic arms control contingent on Soviet behavior unrelated to the nuclear arms race, occasioned further delay in getting SALT off the ground. The first talks, scheduled for the fall of 1968, were canceled by Washington when Soviet troops invaded Czechoslovakia in August of that year. It was the end of 1969 before they at last got started.

As is often true of arms control, these postponements made agreement more complicated. Soviet ICBMs, which were fewer than American ones when Johnson originally proposed a treaty, came to equal and then exceed them in number as the haggling over SALT went on and on. Thus, while the Johnson administration had thought of SALT as a freeze that would leave the United States ahead in numbers of missiles, Nixon's negotiators could hope at best for parity.[9] By 1972, when limits on missiles were finally imposed, the asymmetries in force posture were much greater than even a year or two earlier. The resulting "unequal ceilings" brought the agreement under attack in the West before its ink was dry.

SALT I: THE ABM TREATY

In final form, SALT I consisted of two parts. One was an "interim agreement" on offensive missiles designed to expire in five years, by which time a permanent treaty governing offensive strategic arms was expected to replace it. The second was a treaty "on the Limitation of Anti-Ballistic Missile Systems," of indefinite duration, though subject to review every five years. The latter remains in force today, constituting one of the most airtight and effective impediments to the superpower arms race. Both were the result of lengthy negotiations in Helsinki and Vienna, aided by a "back channel" connecting President Nixon's national security adviser, Henry Kissinger, directly with the Soviet ambassador in Washington, Anatoly Dobrynin. It was in this back channel, and at a five-day Moscow summit between Brezhnev and Nixon, that the final deals were struck.

The glory of the ABM Treaty lies in its thoroughness and its precision. It begins by banning deployment of ABM systems for the defense of Soviet or American territory and then allows two carefully defined exceptions: one cluster of 100 land-based interceptors around the capital of each nation and a similar cluster around an ICBM site. Two years later a protocol to the treaty further reduced the allowed number to just one cluster of 100 interceptors, around either the capital or an ICBM site. The USSR has kept 64 interceptors around Moscow, while the U.S. Congress opted to close the ABM site at Grand Forks, North Dakota. With each superpower holding more than 10,000 strategically deliverable nuclear warheads, the treaty has essentially eliminated strategic defense, although Moscow's tiny cluster might be helpful in an attack of the size of China could mount. It indisputably lets the Soviet Union keep experimenting with interceptor technology; half of its 64 interceptors were recently upgraded.

The treaty's prohibitions go well beyond deployment. With a stringency almost unknown in the history of arms control, it binds each superpower "not to develop, test, or deploy ABM systems or components which are sea-based, air-based, space-based, or mobile land-based." The development, testing, or deployment of MIRVed ABM launchers is likewise ruled out. Until 1983 these provisions kept the military in both Washington and Moscow from one of the most lucrative and destabilizing opportunities offered by the arms race: experimenting with exotic technologies that could neutralize an opponent's assured destruction capability. With only a few dozen land-based, single-warhead interceptors allowed, Moscow cut back the budget of its Strategic Defense Forces, and Washington followed suit.

Three other provisions of the ABM Treaty are worth noting:

- Ballistic missile defense by interceptors normally involves two sets of radar: perimeter acquisition radar, to locate incoming missile warheads as they approach a nation's territory, and site radar, to track warheads after they have entered a country's airspace and to direct interceptor rockets toward them. To preserve this distinction, the treaty binds each party "not to deploy in the future radars for early warning of strategic ballistic missile attack except at locations along the periphery of its national territory and oriented outward."

- To ensure compliance with its terms, the treaty authorizes each signatory to use "national technical means of verification" (discussed above); it requires each party "not to interfere with the national technical means of verification of the other" and "not to use deliberate concealment measures which impede verification." It thus blesses the "spy satellites" of both Moscow and Washington.

- A Standing Consultative Commission is set up to hear questions of compliance raised by either side. Over the years a number of legitimate Soviet and American complaints have been cleared up in this private fashion.

As arms control agreements go, the ABM Treaty is a model of brevity, comprehensiveness, and specificity. Despite these qualities—or possibly because of them—it has its critics. The fundamental source of opposition is the strategic logic it imposes on the superpowers, a situation of mutual assured destruction (MAD), in which neither can ward off a nuclear strike by the other. Damage limiters in the military and at research institutions on both sides regret this enforced vulnerability, preferring a free hand to devise strategic defenses for their countries.

In the past few years some of the treaty's definitions have also begun to unravel. We have alluded to the Soviet radar at Krasnoyarsk, where current technologies make it hard to distinguish radars with different purposes. President Reagan's renewed interest in strategic defense from space raises some additional ambiguities. Where, for example, does research on space-based ABM systems (not prohibited) leave off and the forbidden "development" begin? What constitutes a "component" of an ABM system (which cannot be developed, tested, or deployed), and what is merely a "subcomponent" (which is not mentioned in the treaty)? When a laser beam destroys a dummy missile, is that a test of an ABM component?

If it is to retain its effectiveness, the ABM Treaty needs mutual clarification soon. One proposal, for example, would define "research" as what goes on in a laboratory, unobservable by satellite reconnaissance, while extending the treaty's prohibitions on development and testing only to observable activities. Without some kind of agreed clarification the superpowers are likely to charge each other with more and more violations, until the treaty as a whole ceases to be viable.

SALT I: THE INTERIM AGREEMENT

The accord on ballistic missile defense came more easily than the second part of SALT I, whose final terms were worked out in a last-minute rush at the May 1972 summit in Moscow. In the first case negotiators were dealing with weapons still largely undeployed; in the second, with missiles the superpowers had been deploying for more than a decade. Strategic offensive weapons posed a variety of problems for the Soviet and American teams charged with capping the arms spiral:

1. The two sides had different concepts of what was "strategic." The Soviets argued, logically, but in their own self-interest, that any weapon with which one nuclear power could strike the territory of another was strategic. Conveniently for them, U.S. forward-based systems (such as aircraft with nuclear weapons stationed in Europe)

would fall within the limits they proposed, while Soviet systems with the same range would not. American negotiators insisted that forward-based systems were substrategic because their ranges were less than intercontinental. SALT I circumvented the issue of bomber range entirely, limiting only SLBMs and land-based missiles of intercontinental range. But the meaning of "strategic" continued to vex arms control, as a 1985 Soviet proposal to include the Pershing II and American GLCMs in strategic arms negotiations showed.

2. By the early 1970s the Soviet Union had yet to reach parity with the United States in submarine-launched missiles, and for a while they demanded that these be excluded from the agreement. They gave in on the question, but the treaty limited SLBMs to those "operational and under construction" at the time of signing. In view of the hectic schedule of SLBM construction by the USSR and a series of delays in the negotiations, this way of setting the ceiling ultimately left Moscow with more nuclear-missile submarines carrying more SLBMs than Washington had.

3. The USSR had larger ICBMs than any in the U.S. force and a program of replacing older missiles with heavier versions. Since both sides were rushing to MIRV their land-based missiles (U.S. MIRVing actually began before the treaty was signed), larger ICBMs with more throw weight would soon extend the Soviet advantage. Washington demanded and got treaty terms limiting this conversion process, but no agreed definition of a "heavy missile" could be reached.

On one point both sides concurred: The Interim Agreement would limit only missile launchers, not the numbers of warheads U.S. and Soviet missiles could carry. Here a paradoxical logic, not uncommon to the arms race, came into play. The idea of MIRVs had sprung up in Washington during the 1960s as a response to the Soviet ABM program—if Moscow began building ballistic missile defense, the United States would need more warheads to overwhelm it—but with strategic defenses virtually eliminated under SALT I, the momentum of MIRVing continued unabated. American leaders refused to bargain away an innovation in which their side was ahead, while the Soviets did not want MIRVing banned until they had caught up in the technology.

What, then, did SALT I achieve? Its principal virtue (or vice, depending on one's view of strategic defense) was in ruling out ballistic missile defense on any significant scale. The Interim

Agreement was far less effective, but it did freeze deployments of ballistic missile launchers at a level where they have remained ever since. By its terms the superpowers agreed "not to start construction of additional fixed land-based intercontinental ballistic missile (ICBM) launchers after July 1, 1972." They undertook "not to convert land-based launchers for light ICBMs, or for ICBMs of older types deployed prior to 1964, into land-based launchers for heavy ICBMs of types deployed after that time." And they pledged "to limit submarine-launched ballistic missile (SLBM) launchers and modern ballistic missile submarines to the numbers operational and under construction" on the day the Interim Agreement was signed.

It seemed likely in 1972 that without negotiated constraints the Soviets would soon have twice the number of U.S. SLBMs. SALT I stopped that. In addition, Moscow consented to reduce the number of ICBMs it had already deployed if it was allowed to complete the subs it had under construction. Thus the current Soviet total of 1,400 land-based missiles falls well short of what the USSR had in the early 1970s and is probably a fraction of what could have been produced by now. Without SALT I the United States could likewise have built many times its current number of ICBMs.

The Interim Agreement infuriated critics on all sides. Its net effect was to codify Soviet numerical superiority in both ICBM and SLBM launchers. In ICBMs the ceilings were roughly 1,400 for Moscow and 1,050 for the United States. For SLBMs a protocol to the agreement spelled out the new arithmetic: 710 SLBMs on no more than forty-four subs for the United States; 950 SLBMs on no more than sixty-two boats for the USSR. Advocates of SALT I in Washington pointed out that it left the Western advantage in bombers untouched; that the United States had the lead in MIRVing its ICBMs; that with 40 percent more submarines, the Soviets still had fewer on station at any time than the United States; that the agreement provided only a temporary cap to the arms race until a more equitable treaty could be hammered out. Conservatives deplored the unequal missile totals of SALT I and insisted, "Never again!"[10]

Left-wing opponents of the nuclear arms race were equally incensed. Though satisfied with the ABM Treaty, they viewed the Interim Agreement as an invitation to a superpower contest in MIRVing. The agreement's launcher limits came just as militarists on both sides were shifting their sights to warhead proliferation. And its prohibitions were in terms of deployment only, leaving undisturbed the prospect of further testing by both sides in the quest for greater warhead accuracy. In Moscow for a short time after SALT I was signed, the public claim was that the ABM treaty eliminated the need for more offensive weapons. Within a month or so, however, this wistful view had disappeared from the Soviet press.[11] A new superpower race was on, this time to more highly MIRVed, more accurate missiles that would make nuclear deterrence even less stable than before.

In retrospect, two lessons may be drawn from SALT I. First, delay is almost always to the detriment of arms control. Had the missile ceilings of the Interim Agreement been set even one year earlier, they would have been much more nearly equal. And second, the best place to halt a new arms technology is before either side has tested it successfully. Once Washington or Moscow has a system ready to deploy, stopping it is next to impossible. Everyone knew when SALT I was signed that the next strategic arms treaty would have to limit MIRVing. Seven years and several thousand warheads later the next step was made.

ARMS CONTROL AND THE POLITICS OF THE 1970s

By 1972 Leonid Brezhnev had firm control over the Soviet Communist party. He had gone to the party congress the previous year to present a "peace program"—better relations with western Europe, more trade with the West, negotiated limits to the arms race—which became the centerpiece of his foreign policy. While many in the Soviet military remained suspicious of arms control, some of détente's most vocal critics in Moscow died or were removed from power. At just the same time, however, the U.S. presidency underwent a dramatic decline in authority.

The Nixon administration followed the signing of SALT I with a major shift in personnel at the State Department's Arms Control and Disarmament Agency, bringing in more skeptics to help formulate U.S. positions. Before another round of strategic arms negotiations could make any headway, the President's power began slipping away with the series of revelations about Watergate. His resignation in 1974 abruptly placed in the White House a leader of less stature, Gerald Ford, whose tenure was to be limited to two and a half years. In 1977 the presidency turned over again, and Jimmy Carter had the job of piecing together an agreement to succeed the expiring SALT I.

While the weakness in American leadership slowed progress in arms control considerably, it did not put a stop to it. We have mentioned the 1974 protocol to the ABM Treaty which cut the allowed number of interceptors in half. The same year a Threshold Test Ban Treaty tightened the screws on underground nuclear weapons testing, still going in under the provisions of the partial test ban of 1963. The new treaty limited underground testing to explosions of 150 kilotons or less and restated the ultimate goal of ending "all test explosions of nuclear weapons for all time." Since underground weapons tests are indistinguishable from nuclear explosions conducted for peaceful purposes, the United States and USSR signed a companion agreement on peaceful nuclear explosions (the PNE Treaty) in 1976, imposing the same 150-kiloton limits on them.

The Threshold Test Ban and PNE treaties may or may not have prohibited anything essential to the East-West arms race. Their fine print did include some precedent-setting agreements to exchange detailed information on testing sites and, in certain specified cases, to allow on-site inspection by observers from the other side. But the treaties were signed at a time of growing hostility to arms control in Washington, where the Committee on the Present Danger was warning officials and the public about the growing threat from Moscow's MIRVed ICBMs. Though presented to the Senate by President Ford, neither treaty was ratified.

SALT II: THE VLADIVOSTOK ACCORDS

What, then, about SALT? The Interim Agreement of 1972 had been signed with the understanding that it would lead quickly to a tighter set of restrictions on strategic delivery systems. Unfortunately technology proved swifter. Both superpowers MIRVed their strategic forces rapidly in the 1970s, the Soviets concentrating on ICBM warheads, the Americans on MIRVed SLBMs. Moscow developed the Backfire bomber, considered by some to have an intercontinental range. Washington turned to cruise missiles for its bomber fleet, which was to be upgraded with the new B-1. By the time SALT II came down to the wire at the end of the decade, each side faced a greatly enhanced threat from the nuclear forces of the other.

The first breakthrough toward SALT II came with the Vladivostok Accords between President Ford and General Secretary Brezhnev in 1974, erecting a structure for the eventual treaty. In brief, the two leaders committed their countries to:

- Limit the deployment of new types of strategic arms.
- Set equal aggregate limits of 2,400 strategic delivery vehicles (ICBMs, SLBMs, and heavy bombers) for each side.
- Allow only 1,320 of each superpower's strategic delivery vehicles to be MIRVed.

Arms control enthusiasts gaped in disbelief at the Vladivostok framework. Its launcher totals were those already reached by the Soviet Union, they exceeded what the United States currently had, and the degree of MIRVing permitted was well beyond what either country had done so far. It would take years' more racing just to reach the new ceilings. Critics of arms control noticed that most of the hottest issues had been swept under the rug. What number of warheads would be allowed on MIRVed delivery vehicles? Would cruise missiles be counted? Was the Backfire a heavy bomber? Did Soviet heavy ICBMs count equally with light ICBMs? Would anything ever have to be reduced?

Ironically, when the next American President came to office and tried introducing real cutbacks, his initiative gave the SALT process a severe jolt. Unimpressed by Vladivostok, Jimmy Carter suggested revising its framework in March 1977. He surprised the Soviets with a proposal to reduce the ceilings in SALT by about 20 percent, forcing Moscow into significant reductions in its delivery vehicles. Carter's proposal went further: It would restrict MIRVed ICBMs on both sides to the number of American

Minuteman IIIs and require a 50 percent cut in the number of Soviet heavy missiles.

From the Western standpoint the new administration's "comprehensive proposal" made fine sense. It meant reductions, not just higher and higher ceilings, and it mandated greater symmetry in the strategic forces of the United States and the USSR. In the eyes of Moscow, it was anathema. The burden of symmetry fell on the Soviets, who would have to make virtually all the cuts; the Americans offered to give up only what they had yet to produce, the mobile MX missile. More fundamentally, Carter was pulling out of the basic SALT structure Brezhnev had sold to his Soviet colleagues during several years of internal bargaining: a set of ceilings in SALT II to regulate the superpower competition until 1985, followed by actual reductions in SALT III. Soviet Foreign Minister Andrei Gromyko bitterly rejected the U.S. proposal. His deputy, Georgi Kornienko, privately reminded Carter's chief negotiator, Paul Warnke, that "Brezhnev had to spill blood to get the Vladivostok accords."[12]

Stunned by the Soviet rebuff, Carter and his staff fell back upon the 1974 framework. After two more years of negotiation, in which basic issues often took a back seat to comma placement and the phrasing of footnotes, the ceilings of Vladivostok finally became the elaborate SALT II treaty of 1979. Its principal features are summarized in Figure 6-2, on page 170. One of the treaty's great weaknesses is its complexity. Its prohibitions are stated in so much detail, with so many addenda and agreed statements, that its exact terms are hard to keep straight. To explain the underlying principles of SALT II to the public proved more than the Carter administration could handle.

SALT II: END OF THE ROAD FOR STRATEGIC ARMS CONTROL?

Like SALT I, the 1979 treaty begins with strategic launcher limits, but this time the totals are equal and include heavy bombers. Initially, the ceiling was to be 2,400 ICBMs, SLBMs, and intercontinental bombers for each party, as specified at Vladivostok, but by the end of 1981 it would be lowered to 2,250, forcing the

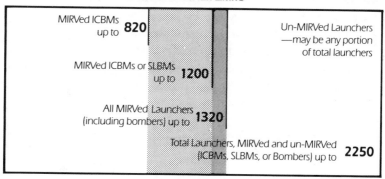

Figure 6-2—SALT II Limits

Soviets to dismantle some of their oldest ICBMs. Unlike SALT I, the second strategic arms limitation agreement then went on to limit MIRVing. Only 1,320 strategic delivery vehicles on each side could be MIRVed; of those, only 1,200 could be MIRVed missiles (ICBMs or SLBMS), and only 820 could be MIRVed ICBMs. No more fixed ICBM launchers could be built, and the number of heavy ICBM launchers could not be increased. SALT II thus put a cap on the rapidly expanding Soviet ICBM force without requiring any significant reduction in it. Only one "new type" of ICBM could be tested or deployed by either side. Moscow had proposed a complete ban on new types of ICBMs, but Washington now insisted on one exception to allow for its MX missile.

For each category of launcher, separate MIRVing limits were stipulated: For current types of ICBMs the maximum existing number of reentry vehicles on each, for SLBMs a limit of fourteen warheads each, and for ALCMs on heavy bombers an average limit of twenty-eight per bomber. The one new type of ICBM could have no more than ten warheads. Here the effect was to let the Soviet Union keep its existing edge in ICBM MIRVing, except for any new highly MIRVed MX missiles the United States might choose to deploy. In exchange, SLBMs (in which the West was superior) could be MIRVed more highly than they currently were. The Soviet Backfire bomber was excluded from the treaty's limits once Moscow had pledged not to give it an intercontinental range.

SALT II as a whole was to extend until the end of 1985. Two related issues, cruise missiles and mobile ICBMs, were treated in a protocol that was to last only through 1981. As in SALT I, the Soviets had agreed to exclude American forward-based systems in Europe from the aggregates of SALT II. But the protocol did ban deployment of intermediate-range ground-launched and sea-launched cruise missiles (like the GLCMs Washington was readying for Great Britain, Italy, Belgium, the Netherlands, and West Germany) until the end of 1981. It prohibited the testing and deployment of mobile ICBM launchers (such as the MX in its shell-game mode) for the same period.

The MIRVing limits in SALT II posed a new problem for verification. Since satellites are not able to observe the number of warheads on a missile, the best way to make sure an opponent is not deploying more than the allowed number is to observe its missile tests. Each missile would henceforth be counted as carrying the maximum number of warheads its type had been tested with. The telemetric information transmitted during testing thus became crucial to verification, as SALT II acknowledged in a roundabout way. In a "common understanding" the superpowers reserved their right to encrypt telemetry but promised not to engage in that practice when it "impedes verification of compliance" with the treaty.

In Washington SALT II raised howls of protest. Conservatives, who had hoped arms control would cut back Soviet counterforce capabilities, denounced it as a sellout. They saw a window of vulnerability opening up, as Moscow completed the MIRVing of ICBMs it was allowed under SALT II. For the United States to pull even with the USSR in land-based forces now would require hundreds of new MX missiles. On the left, SALT II was criticized for legitimizing another round in the arms race. Just as the Soviets could go on with their MIRVing, Washington could add thousands of warheads to its ICBMs, SLBMs, and cruise missiles before it bumped up against the SALT ceilings. The treaty's verification provisions were also controversial, especially since the revolution in Iran had just deprived the United States of some of the best listening posts it used to monitor Soviet missile tests.

Even before the Red Army invaded Afghanistan in the last days of 1979, the chances of a two-thirds vote to ratify SALT II in the Senate seemed slim. With Soviet troops in Kabul, Jimmy Carter withdrew the treaty from consideration. The 1970s—the era of SALT—were over. For the 1980s the American electorate chose a President keenly hostile to arms control in its existing form. Ronald Reagan would have "deep cuts" in strategic forces, or he would have no arms control at all. He mistrusted the ABM Treaty, which kept the United States from defending itself against Soviet missiles. He wanted new ICBMs, new SLBMs, new bombers, and new cruise missiles for the American strategic arsenal, and in Europe he began the deployment of U.S. intermediate-range missiles which his predecessor had endorsed.

The next eight years produced no more East-West agreements to limit strategic nuclear forces, although the unratified SALT II continued in an eerie limbo—discredited but still roughly observed by both sides. Whether arms control had a future seemed very much in doubt. In the final two chapters we look at the Reagan administration's arms control proposals, Soviet responses to them, the 1988 INF Treaty, and some of the major current options for reversing the nuclear arms spiral.

Controversy:
SHOULD SALT II HAVE BEEN RATIFIED?

YES! It was far from the ideal agreement but much better than no arms control at all. Taken together with SALT I, it would stop the arms race from getting even farther out of control than it already has. By 1985, for example, the United States had reached its SLBM launcher limits under SALT. Adding more to its Trident forces would mean taking older submarines out of commission if the SALT limits were followed. Similarly, the Soviets could easily achieve a higher degree of ICBM MIRVing than SALT II allows them. Their SS-17s, SS-18s, and SS-19s can each hold twice the number of warheads they have mounted on them so far. Only the MIRVing limits of SALT II prevent Moscow from doubling the damage it could do in a first strike.

The 1979 agreement has a number of advantages that often go unnoticed. While it imposes a subceiling for MIRVed ICBMs (820), for example, there is no parallel limit on MIRVed SLBMs, a less threatening and less vulnerable system. SALT II thus encourages the superpowers to "go out to sea" with their strategic missiles. It prohibits development, testing, and deployment of rapid-reload ICBM launchers, a potential technology which, if deployed by either side, would mandate far more retaliatory counterforce weapons for the other.

SALT II spoke of a successor agreement, to be concluded "well in advance of 1985," which would scale back its temporary ceilings and require mutual reductions in strategic forces. Despite the 1980s rhetoric about "deep cuts" in strategic weapons, we would be better off if SALT II had been ratified and a SALT III erected to replace it.

NO! SALT II was fatally flawed. It would have locked America into permanent inferiority in the weapons that count most, MIRVed ICBMs. The task of arms control must be to force reductions in the Soviets' destabilizing land-based missiles. The ceilings in SALT II permit Moscow to go on MIRVing its ICBMs until every one of them has the most warheads ever tested on its type. Then the Soviets are allowed one new type of ICBM with ten warheads per missile.

The SALT process only channels the arms race in new directions. It needs to be scrapped for a radically different approach. The focus will have to be on ICBMs, not all three legs of the triad lumped together. The USSR will have to give up at least half of its land-based forces and scale the remaining ones back to throw weights equivalent to those of U.S. ICBMs. Even if there had been a SALT III, it would not have accomplished that.

If Moscow continues holding out against real arms control, Washington had better be ready to resume the nuclear arms race and to win it.

SUMMARY: MAJOR U.S.-SOVIET ARMS CONTROL AGREEMENTS (WITH DATE SIGNED)

Geneva Protocol (1925)

Antarctic Treaty (1959)

Limited Nuclear Test Ban Treaty (1963)

Outer Space Treaty (1967)

Latin American Nuclear-Free Zone Treaty (1967)

Nuclear Nonproliferation Treaty (1968)

Biological Weapons Convention (1972)

SALT I—ABM Treaty (1972)

SALT I—Interim Agreement (1972)

ABM Protocol (1974)

Threshold Test Ban Treaty (1974), unratified by United States

PNE Treaty (1976), unratified by United States

SALT II (1979), unratified by United States

FOR MORE DETAIL

Raymond Garthoff, "SALT I: An Evaluation," *World Politics* (October 1978): 1–25. What the first strategic arms limitation treaty did and did not achieve.

John Newhouse, *Cold Dawn: The Story of SALT* (New York: Holt, Rinehart and Winston, 1973). How SALT I was negotiated.

Glenn T. Seaborg, *Kennedy, Khrushchev, and the Test Ban* (Berkeley: University of California Press, 1981). The first major treaty governing nuclear arms from the standpoint of a prominent scientist involved in achieving it.

Gerard Smith, *Doubletalk: The Story of the First Strategic Arms Limitation Talks* (New York: Doubleday & Co., 1980). A principal negotiator gives his account of the SALT process.

Leonard S. Spector, "Silent Spread," *Foreign Policy* 58 (Spring 1985): 53–78. On the weakening of nuclear nonproliferation and what could be done to stop it.

Stockholm International Peace Research Institute, *World Armaments and Disarmament: SIPRI Yearbook* (London and Philadelphia: Taylor & Francis, published annually). Facts and commentary on the current state of the arms race.

Strobe Talbott, *Endgame: The Inside Story of SALT II* (New York: Harper & Row, 1979). A journalist details the lengthy efforts which produced SALT II.

United States Arms Control and Disarmament Agency, *Arms Control and Disarmament Agreements: Texts and Histories of Negotiations* (Washington, D.C.: Government Printing Office, 1982). A short summary introduces each arms control treaty through SALT II.

Thomas W. Wolfe, *The SALT Experience* (Cambridge, Mass.: Ballinger Publishing Co. 1979). Classic narrative of the elaborate SALT process.

NOTES TO CHAPTER 6

1. William J. Broad, "Soviet Radar on Display," *New York Times*, September 9, 1987, p. A1.

2. The Baruch Plan and Soviet counterproposals are discussed in Michael Mandelbaum, *The Nuclear Question* (Cambridge, England: Cambridge University Press, 1979), ch. 2.

3. Ibid., p. 37.

4. The negotiating history of the limited test ban is given by a Kennedy administration insider, Glenn T. Seaborg, in *Kennedy, Khrushchev, and the Test Ban* (Berkeley: University of California Press, 1981).

5. The texts of this and subsequent U.S.-Soviet arms control agreements can be found in a U.S. Arms Control and Disarmament Agency publication, *Arms Control and Disarmament Agreements: Texts and Histories of Negotiations* (Washington, D.C., Government Printing Office, 1982).

6. An Israeli nuclear technician, Mordechai Vanunu, claimed in 1986 that his country had been building nuclear weapons for twenty years and had a stockpile of up to 200 nuclear warheads. See the account of Vanunu's trial for betraying Israel's nuclear weapons secrets in the *Boston Globe*, August 31, 1987, p. 4.

7. On the threat posed by "ambiguous proliferation" to countries such as Israel, India, South Africa, and Pakistan, see Leonard S. Spector, "Silent Spread," *Foreign Policy* 58 (Spring 1985): 53–78.

8. John Newhouse, *Cold Dawn: The Story of SALT* (New York: Holt, Rinehart & Winston, 1973), pp. 89–95.

9. Warner R. Schilling, "U.S. Strategic Nuclear Concepts in the 1970s," in *Strategy and Nuclear Deterrence*, ed. Steven E. Miller (Princeton: Princeton University Press, 1984), pp. 183–93.

10. The Senate's Jackson amendment, prohibiting future agreements which set U.S. "levels of intercontinental strategic forces inferior to the limits provided for the Soviet Union," was taken to require equal launcher totals in SALT II. See Strobe Talbott, *Deadly Gambits* (New York: Vintage Books, 1985), ch. 10.

11. Michael J. Deane, *Strategic Defense in Soviet Strategy* (Washington, D.C.: Advanced International Studies Institute, 1980), ch. 5.

12. Kornienko's remark to Warnke is quoted by Strobe Talbott in his account of the SALT II negotiations, *Endgame* (New York: Harper & Row, 1979), p. 73.

7

ARMS CONTROL IN THE EIGHTIES

—

For most of the 1980s arms control was running on a treadmill. Negotiations to reduce nuclear arsenals would start up, stumble along, and break down in mutual recriminations between Moscow and Washington. They would resume with dramatic proposals to eliminate whole categories of weapons, to cut other categories by half, to end the nuclear era by the close of this century. Optimistic predictions were issued by both sides, though rarely at the same time, only to be followed by denunciations in which each superpower accused the other of scuttling the entire process. What was wrong?

Breakthroughs in arms control generally require what is sometimes called a window of opportunity, one of those critical moments when leaderships in both the United States and the Soviet Union are seriously interested in progress, are firmly in control of their domestic political processes, and are willing to compromise, to give up things they value in return for concessions by the opposing side. Through the mid-1980s there was no such window. In Washington a conservative government was more interested in racing than in reducing. Moscow in the early eighties saw a trio of leaders come and go, committed to old ways of doing business and unreceptive to new approaches. One round of arms control talks foundered on Washington's determination to place new weapons in Europe. A second generated proposals too sweeping to form a realistic basis for a near-term accord. At times the superpowers seemed close to discarding all that had been achieved in arms control. Only in the talks on INF, a category in which the United States had no weapons until 1983, did agreement prove attainable.

A NEW BROOM IN WASHINGTON

The Reagan accession produced an icy climate for East-West relations. A President who knew what he wanted—and got it—in domestic policy took longer to develop a coherent policy on the arms race. His administration was torn between conflicting ambitions for the international power which comes with growing military strength and for the prestige that drastic cuts in nuclear weapons might bring. On the one hand, Ronald Reagan wanted all the elements of a nuclear war-fighting capability. He rightly identified ICBMs as the most destabilizing of current weapons, and he insisted on having more of them. The 100 MX missiles he demanded from Congress would have added 1,000 highly accurate warheads to U.S. arsenals, and the D-5 warhead would upgrade American SLBMs to serve a counterforce function. At the same time Reagan argued that proliferating U.S. strategic bombers and cruise missiles should not bother the Soviets because of their long flight times to target. The B-1 bomber began deployment under the new President, and the nation's older B-52s started taking on ALCMs by the thousand. The 1980 Republican platform had called on the United States "to achieve overall military and technological superiority over the Soviet Union,"[1] and Reagan acted as if he thought that goal could be reached.

On the other hand, the administration declared arms control to be a top priority. It would, however, be an arms control far different from SALT, with its high ceilings and negligible impact on existing arsenals. Arms control that only limited what the superpowers could build next struck Reagan as worse than useless. It simply codified the perceived Soviet supremacy in nuclear war-fighting capabilities. The U.S. administration of the 1980s dreamed of something more dazzling: stability at much lower levels of nuclear weapons, perhaps their eventual elimination from the face of the earth. Regrettably, in the short run, the arms race might have to proceed at an even hotter pace.

With these contending aims, the Reagan leadership presided over six years without arms control. By 1986 the administration was announcing its intent to breach the limits of the SALT treaties. If this result was due partly to contradictions inherent in the President's policies, the hiatus in arms control also owed much to institutional divisions within his government. He had brought into the State Department a set of officials who wanted negotiated agreements to halt the arms race, while at the head of the Defense Department he placed Caspar Weinberger and his lieutenants—staunch opponents of arms control. The proposals State came up with to move arms control forward were vetoed by Defense, seeking to stall arms control while it assembled the array of weapons it wanted.

On one side, Secretary of State George Shultz and his deputy Richard Burt joined with experienced negotiators like Paul Nitze in trying to edge the administration toward positions the Soviets might take seriously. At the opposite pole, Weinberger and Richard Perle at Defense struggled to shore up more hard-line positions.[2] The arbiter of similar interdepartmental disputes under previous administrations had been the President's national security adviser, most prominently Henry Kissinger, who served Richard Nixon in that capacity during the bargaining for SALT I. But under Reagan the national security adviser was largely stripped of his authority in the arms control process. Within seven years six successive incumbents had rotated through that post. The upshot was a series of hashed-together proposals for arms control that struck the Soviets as preposterous and even administration insiders as confused.

At the fulcrum of policy formulation in Washington stood the President himself. Contending factions brought their disputes to him for resolution, and more often than not Reagan sided with the secretary of defense. The President seems rarely to have focused on arms control during his first term. As a veteran Washington observer, Strobe Talbott, puts it, "In the Reagan Administration, only when arms control was a political exercise, either within the U.S. or within the alliance, did it capture the President's attention."[3]

Compared with previous Presidents, Reagan was slow to learn the specifics of the arms race. While his administration made *throw weight* (the mass of warheads, decoys, and other material heavy Soviet missiles can place on a trajectory toward the United States) a major negotiating issue, Reagan confessed to not fully understanding what "this throw-weight business is all about." His unscripted public comments on the arms race sometimes rambled far from the facts, as when he told a group of congressmen that ICBMs were the most destabilizing weapons because "land-based missiles have nuclear warheads, while bombers and submarines don't."[4]

Under a divided administration and with little leadership on the issue from the President, arms control languished in Washington. Not until the fall of 1985, when arms control loomed as the central issue in his first summit meeting with Mikhail Gorbachev, did Reagan try to get control of the process in which his subordinates were forging American positions. Some who went to Geneva with him that November reported that the President was for the first time "on board" the arms control wagon.

A PARADE THROUGH THE KREMLIN

If Washington lacked firm leadership on arms control in the 1980s, Moscow also bore its share of responsibility for the hiatus. By the time the new American President had his first proposals ready to make public, the Communist party general secretary who had carried the ball for détente in the Politburo was besieged and dying. Leonid Brezhnev had seen SALT from its timid beginnings to its bitter end; he spent his last months staving off Soviet military leaders, who criticized his continued advocacy of restraint in the face of Reagan's defense buildup. When Brezhnev died late in 1982, his aged comrades in the leadership held to his basic line on arms control but lacked the force of his personal commitment.

Much was heard in the early 1980s about Moscow's lack of interest in arms control. The Reagan administration often talked about what it would take to bring the Russians back to the bargaining table, about the incentives that could get them interested in serious negotiations. Even as seasoned a scholar as George Kennan wondered, in the light of the Soviet invasion of Afghanistan, whether "hard-line elements" had not broken through to positions of dominance in the Kremlin, preserving Brezhnev as "a figurehead."[5] This fear proved to be unfounded. Until Brezhnev's death the old guard in Moscow adhered doggedly to the arms control agenda it had agreed on in the mid-seventies: a series of SALT agreements limiting nuclear arms incrementally, with SALT III taking the ceilings of its precursor and lowering them to produce actual reductions. The problem was that SALT had become unpalatable to the Americans, that it would take too long to eliminate Soviet ICBM advantages under the old formulas.

There may have been one point when the Communist party leadership considered abandoning arms control in favor of an unconstrained arms race. Yuri Andropov, named to succeed Brezhnev in November 1982, was widely regarded as a political patron of the Soviet defense establishment. His years of service with the KGB, which he headed until becoming party secretary, made him popular with the intelligence services, the military interests, and the conservatives in the party apparatus who were most suspicious of détente. Alarmed when Brezhnev refused to respond in kind to the Reagan buildup, they probably saw in Andropov a figure who would give defense a higher priority.

In his foreign policy Andropov exhibited less patience with the United States than did his predecessor. He criticized as naive those in Moscow who still hoped the moderates would win out in Washington, frustrating Ronald Reagan's plans. And when a Soviet "peace campaign" failed to prevent the deployment of new U.S. missiles in Western Europe late in 1983, Andropov had his delegation walk out of the Geneva arms control negotiations without setting a date for their resumption.

Andropov passed from the scene at the start of 1984, and a second temporary replacement for Brezhnev moved up to general secretary. The Politburo's choice of Konstantin Chernenko, a former crony of Brezhnev's, dispelled the impression of a drift away from détente in the Soviet leadership. With Chernenko at the helm it was the status quo ante for policies in Moscow; everything simply reverted to the way it had been under Brezhnev. There were no radical reforms to shake up the economy, no new departures in foreign policy. By the end of the year the United States and the Soviet Union had agreed to start talking about arms control again, and when Chernenko died early in 1985, the new negotiations continued without so much as a day's pause.

ARMS CONTROL AND THE GORBACHEV AGENDA

Even before his accession to the Communist party leadership in March 1985, Mikhail Gorbachev was probably pulling the strings in the Chernenko Politburo. He had narrowly missed becoming Andropov's direct successor; by the time he made a widely televised visit to the West late in 1984, he had become the undisputed heir apparent. Very likely it was Gorbachev who took the initiative in getting Soviet delegates back to the bargaining table in Geneva and who selected as Moscow's new defense minister a career soldier with little history of policy independence. Once he became general secretary, Gorbachev moved swiftly to engineer a Politburo he could control, excluding Defense Minister Sergei Sokolov from full membership in the central party leadership and eventually replacing him with a handpicked successor, Dimitri Yazov. Brezhnev's longtime foreign minister, Andrei Gromyko, was kicked upstairs to a ceremonial position, while his replacement, Eduard Shevardnadze, lacked foreign policy experience. Gorbachev was going to be his own man in foreign policy, eliminating competitors inherited from the past and preserving as much independence as possible from the special interests that infect politics in the USSR, just as they do in the United States.

Under Gorbachev, Soviet policy began moving in some new directions. Experiments with decentralized decision making spread through more of the economy, and the pace of production quickened. Efforts to bridge the chasm between the Soviet Union and socialist China—a country undergoing radical economic changes of its own—gathered steam. And in arms control Soviet proposals shifted away from a fossilized adherence to SALT and toward a grander display of policy innovation.

The new general secretary placed improved relations with the United States at the top of his policy agenda. He brought back from Washington the longtime Soviet ambassador, Anatoly Dobrynin (veteran of SALT I and SALT II), putting him in charge of the powerful International Department in the Communist party apparatus and establishing a new arms control section within that department. A corresponding organization to deal with arms control was set up in the Soviet Foreign Ministry, adding to the civilian expertise available on the subject. Addressing the Communist Party Congress after he had been in power a year, Gorbachev emphasized the prospects for cooperation between the superpowers. He saw "signs of a change for the better" in U.S.-Soviet relations and linked superpower disarmament to the health of the Soviet economy, as well as to broader international progress on third world development and environmental preservation. Concluding his speech, Gorbachev proposed "the use for the well-being of world society, above all of the developing countries, of a part of the resources which will be freed as the result of a reduction in military budgets."[6]

When it came to the renewed arms control talks in Geneva, Gorbachev made some dramatic and sweeping proposals: the removal of all nuclear weapons from Europe, a "guarantee that the arms race is not carried into space," and "the complete liquidation before the end of the present century of weapons of mass destruction." This grandiose approach to disarmament, dealing with arms race issues "in their totality," as Gorbachev put it, was less promising than it sounded, however, and certainly nothing new for Moscow. Proposals for "general and complete disarmament" have often marked the Soviet response to ambitious Western initiatives at times when substantive progress in arms control seemed far away. In Gorbachev's case they probably represented a grandstanding reaction to the Reagan administration's own public relations exercises: its proposed 50-percent cuts in nuclear weapons and its hoped-for defenses to make nuclear weapons obsolete.

Before arms control could get anywhere in the 1980s, these bold visions on both sides had to make way for less glamorous, more incremental, more precisely formulated superpower proposals that could support serious negotiation. Neither Reagan nor Gorbachev was in a position to sell complete nuclear disarmament to his political constituents back home, especially to the military. A U.S. plan to cut strategic nuclear weapons on both sides in half, for example, was approved by the Joint Chiefs of Staff in 1985 only because it had little chance of succeeding.[7] More concrete proposals for arms reduction, with specific warhead and launcher totals, clear definitions of what systems are to be limited, and reliable means of verification, began coming out of Washington and Moscow in 1986. They were not the first such initiatives of the 1980s. A handful of realistic proposals had been sprinkled in among the superpower press releases of earlier years. By taking a closer look at them, we may get some idea of how the next arms control agreements could be put together.

ROUND ONE BEGINS

The 1980s opened with the spectacular failure to ratify SALT II, which set back strategic arms control by years. The eighties also found most other East-West negotiations on ice. Discussions on limiting antisatellite weapons (*ASAT*) had started up in 1979 and closed down later the same year. Great Britain, the United States, and the Soviet Union had opened talks on a comprehensive nuclear test ban—one to include underground tests—in 1977, but these, too, were suspended in 1980. In one area, though, Moscow's differences with Washington seemed narrow enough to merit immediate further effort: the intermediate-range nuclear forces outside the bounds of SALT.

Even as Jimmy Carter approached the 1980 election that cost him the presidency, he took one more stab at arms control, sending a delegation to meet with the Soviets in Geneva on INF. In a month of desultory exchanges that broke off after the Reagan landslide, the two sides staked out the positions dividing them. The United States wanted equality of forces between the two superpowers. In the wake of NATO's dual track decision (see Chapter 3), it claimed the right to add intermediate-range missiles to its nuclear arsenal in Europe until their number equaled the SS-20s, SS-4s, and SS-5s deployed by the USSR. Furthermore, the equal missile totals were to be global: Soviet SS-20s in Asia would count along with their INF in Europe since the new missiles were mobile. By contrast, Moscow proposed a freeze on INF, claiming that East and West were already equal in that category.

It would halt SS-20 deployments in Europe—but only in Europe—
if Washington agreed not to put its cruise missiles and Pershing
IIs there.

With Ronald Reagan in the White House, INF once more offered
the most promising opportunity for U.S.-Soviet negotiations. In
the fall of 1981, soon after announcing his plan to modernize U.S.
strategic forces, the President set forth his zero option for the INF
talks then resuming in Geneva. In a speech to the National Press
Club, Reagan explained his proposal: "The United States is prepared to cancel its deployment of Pershing II and ground-launch
cruise missiles if the Soviets will dismantle their SS-20, SS-4, and
SS-5 missiles."[8] The zero option was simplicity itself, easily
intelligible to the American public and eminently fair, as long as
you accepted the premise that Moscow needed no counterpart to
British, French, and Chinese nuclear forces.

To the Brezhnev Kremlin, however, it seemed anything but
fair. It required the USSR to do all the reducing; Washington gave
up missiles that did not yet exist, while Moscow had to eliminate hundreds of weapons already in place. When the negotiators
for the two superpowers met in Geneva, the Soviet Union adopted
a quite different stance. It was willing to get rid of two-thirds of
its intermediate-range nuclear forces in Europe if the United States
did the same. As we saw earlier, the Kremlin was concerned not
only with the projected American cruise and Pershing II missiles,
but with U.S. forward-based aircraft already in Europe and the
nuclear missiles of Britain and France, which together presented
an arsenal equal to the Soviet INF in Moscow's view. To call
attention to the Soviet position and cultivate Europeans hostile
to the new U.S. deployments, General Secretary Brezhnev went
on in March 1982 to announce a unilateral Soviet cessation of its
INF buildup in Europe. Playing to the gallery, he suggested a "real
zero option" as the long-term Soviet aim, the complete removal
by all parties on both sides of all tactical and medium-range nuclear
arms from Europe.

With such disparate negotiating positions—one seeking to bring
Soviet intermediate-range missiles down to zero, the other
equating American aircraft with the missiles of the USSR—there
was little hope of progress, and none occurred. But after several
months of stalemate the chief INF negotiators for the two superpowers, Paul Nitze and Yuli Kvitsinsky, did make one realistic

attempt at a breakthrough. Their so-called walk in the woods in the summer of 1982 brought arms control as close to a victory as it was to come for the next five years.

ROUND ONE NEARLY SUCCEEDS

Paul Nitze, Reagan's man on INF during his administration's first term, had been active in American foreign policy for all of the nuclear arms race to that point. Principal author of NSC-68, the document which urged U.S. rearmament against the Soviet threat in 1950, Nitze was again vocal in the 1970s, as the terms of SALT unfolded. In the face of treaties he thought were giving Russia more than the United States, he helped form the Committee on the Present Danger and spoke out against ratifying SALT II. When Reagan chose him to meet with the Soviets in Geneva on INF, the appointment made clear that Washington would not be satisfied with just any treaty.

At the same time Nitze was personally committed to getting an INF agreement during Reagan's first term. He was therefore willing to go beyond his formal negotiating instructions, which adhered stubbornly to the zero option in 1982, and to sound out his opposite number in private with a more imaginative proposal. Nitze had a hunch the Soviets were more concerned over the Pershing II, with its short warning time to the USSR, than with prospective American cruise missiles in Europe. He tried suggesting the complete cancellation of the Pershing II if the Soviets agreed to dismantle most of their SS-20s in Europe. The elements of Nitze's package appear to have been:

- Abandonment of U.S. plans to deploy the Pershing II in Europe; its short-range relative, the Pershing I, could be upgraded, but not to intermediate range.

- A limit on American GLCM deployments in Europe to seventy-five launchers, each with four missiles.

- Moscow's elimination of all but seventy-five of its SS-20s in Europe.

- A freeze on SS-20s in Soviet Asia at the current number of ninety.

The head of the Soviet INF delegation, Yuli Kvitsinsky, had, like Nitze, a long history of involvement in arms negotiations. How far he was authorized to go in these private discussions is unclear. The terms of Nitze's deal, after all, required a major Soviet concession in principle: Washington's INF deployments would not be entirely stopped. Furthermore, the Soviets were asked to agree to unequal warhead totals in Europe. The seventy-five American GLCM launchers would carry 300 warheads, while the seventy-five SS-20s had only 225. When he had heard Nitze out, Kvitsinsky concurred that each negotiator should submit the idea to his government, not as a proposal by either side, but as a "joint exploratory package."[9]

Returning with the news from Geneva, Paul Nitze found the Reagan administration suspicious of his adventurism and, in many cases, openly hostile to the terms of his "walk in the woods." The package not only abandoned the high road of the zero option, allowing both superpowers to keep intermediate-range nuclear forces, but also left the United States with only cruise missiles in the face of Soviet ballistic missiles. Furthermore, it gave the USSR an advantage in global launcher totals: For the ninety SS-20s allowed in Asia, the United States would have no counterpart. The Nitze-Kvitsinsky deal in effect allowed Moscow the offset it had wanted for the nuclear forces of third powers. The Defense Department would have none of it, and the Soviet government, learning that the United States was about to reject the package, issued its own public denunciation. It was back to stalemate in Geneva.

Round One Collapses

As 1982 ended and the year for the scheduled deployment of U.S. missiles in Europe began, negotiations for an INF agreement continued. Now the Soviet Union, headed by Yuri Andropov, launched a series of initiatives designed to turn European opinion in favor of Soviet positions and, if possible, to ward off the American deployments. Andropov began offering to cut back the European portion of his country's intermediate-range missiles if the United States abandoned its plans. He first proposed to reduce Soviet missiles in Europe to 162 (of roughly 240 SS-20s already in place), exactly equaling the missile totals of Great Britain and France. In response to Western criticism that this would still leave Soviet warhead numbers ahead of NATO's, Andropov went further. He was "prepared to reach agreement on the equality of nuclear potentials in Europe both as regards delivery vehicles and warheads with due account, of course, for the corresponding armaments of Britain and France."[10]

Would the mobile SS-20s Andropov was promising to remove from Europe be dismantled, or would the USSR simply redeploy them east of the Ural Mountains, where they could still strike Europe? For months Washington objected to Andropov's proposals on the basis of this ambiguity. Not until the summer of 1983, with the new GLCMs and Pershing IIs almost ready to go in, did the Soviet leader make clear that the excess SS-20s would be "liquidated." As it turned out, this was to be Andropov's last offer.

In 1983 the United States did finally budge from Reagan's zero option position on INF, but its altered stance came only as the first cruise missiles were arriving at Greenham Common in England. The plan Paul Nitze presented in Geneva that November still insisted on equal global totals for U.S. and Soviet intermediate-range missiles. The proposed total was no longer zero, however, but 420 warheads on each side. The United States would restrict its GLCM and Pershing II warheads to that number if the USSR agreed to cut its SS-20s in Europe and Asia to 140. That was about the number of Soviet missiles implied in Andropov's scheme to let his country's warhead totals equal those of a modernized British and French force. But two major differences set the latest American proposal apart from Andropov's:

1. The Soviets were talking about reducing only their missiles *in Europe*. Nothing was said about SS-20s in Asia.

2. In exchange for its INF reductions in Europe, Moscow expected Washington to abstain from any new INF deployments. Washington's plan allowed most of the 572 American GLCMs and Pershing IIs to go in.

In fact, Soviet and American leaders had been pursuing irreconcilable objectives from the time the talks resumed in 1981.

Many in the first-term Reagan administration were determined to have U.S. intermediate-range missiles in Europe. Brezhnev and Andropov were determined to keep them out. Theirs was a true zero-sum game, with no mutually profitable outcome possible. At the end of 1983 Washington got its way, the first deployments in Great Britain and West Germany getting started right on schedule. The price, though, was a year-long hiatus in arms control negotiations, not only those dealing with INF but also the parallel set of discussions to reduce strategic nuclear arms, which Moscow had insisted all along could proceed only if the United States kept its missiles out of Europe. When the first Pershing II reached its station in Germany, Andropov recalled his negotiators from Geneva, setting no date for their return.

Strategic Arms in Round One

When the Reagan administration had been in office nearly a year and a half, it made public its first plan for strategic arms limitation. The key elements of the President's thinking on the superpower strategic arsenals were that they should be drastically reduced, not simply capped, and that the counterforce-capable ICBMs of the Soviet Union, posing the worst threat to the United States, should bear the brunt of the cuts. His subordinates in the State Department, the Arms Control and Disarmament Agency, and the Defense Department disagreed so fundamentally on how to approach these goals that it took months longer to produce a policy that had been the case with INF. By May 1982, however, the administration was ready with a proposal for resuming negotiations on strategic arms, negotiations Reagan now dubbed Strategic Arms Reduction Talks (START).

The American position envisioned a two-stage agreement, restricting intercontinental ballistic missiles from the outset while leaving bombers and cruise missiles, in which the United States had an advantage, untouched until the second stage. Washington proposed a launcher limit of 850 per side for ICBMs and SLBMs, with missile warheads for each superpower restricted to 5,000, only 2,500 of which could be ICBM warheads. These would have been deep cuts indeed, since existing launcher totals were two or three times the proposed number, and existing missile warheads for each side already numbered more than 7,000.

The kicker in the plan was its special treatment of ICBM warheads. In this aspect of their strategic arsenals, Moscow and Washington possess very asymmetrical forces. The Soviets keep roughly three times as many of their warheads on ICBMs as does the United States, while U.S. SLBM warheads outnumber those on Soviet SLBMs by nearly the same ratio. An ICBM warhead limit of 2,500 would actually exceed present American totals, while forcing the USSR to give up more than half its land-based force. Another aspect of the START proposal, also aimed at eliminating most of Moscow's land-based missiles, would impose "equal limits on ballistic missile throw-weight at less than current U.S. levels" in the second stage of the agreement.[11]

For these reasons Soviet leaders—first Brezhnev and then Andropov—turned the Reagan proposal down flat. As with the zero option for Europe, they saw in the American START position a demand for unilateral disarmament by the USSR. In response, they put forward a plan of their own for cutting strategic nuclear weapons, one that encompassed areas of U.S. superiority and left the heaviest Soviet ICBMs intact. Moscow's proposal was essentially derived from SALT II, taking its ceilings and lowering them. It called for:

• An overall limit on strategic delivery vehicles, including bombers along with missiles, at 1,800 for each side—a 25 percent cut in the overall ceiling imposed by SALT II

• A SALT-like subceiling of 1,200 MIRVed missiles and bombers armed with cruise missiles and down from the earlier 1,320

• An inner sublimit of 1,080 MIRVed ICBMs and SLBMs

• A sublimit of 680 MIRVed ICBMs, high enough for Moscow to keep all of its SS-18s and SS-19s, with no ceiling on throw weight

• A complete ban on all forms of long-range cruise missiles

President Reagan regarded the Soviet plan as an attempt to keep U.S. land-based forces vulnerable by retaining the several thousand highly accurate ICBM warheads the USSR had aimed at them. As some of his own advisers pointed out, though, the administration's START proposal itself did nothing to close the window of vulnerability. Under its 850 launcher limit for missiles, the American land-based arsenal might consist, for example, of 500 existing Minuteman ICBMs, each with 3 warheads, and 100 new MX missiles with 10 warheads each. That would make up the allowed 2,500 ICBM warheads for the United States. But those 600 aimpoints—U.S. ICBMs in their silos—would still be targeted by 2,500 Soviet land-based warheads. This *warhead-to-aimpoint ratio* of more than four-to-one would preserve Moscow's ability to destroy Washington's ICBM force in a first strike using only a part of its arsenal.

In the light of this logic the Reagan proposal underwent some slight revisions before the START talks closed down, along with negotiations on INF, at the end of 1983. The United States indicated its willingness to accept a higher launcher total—perhaps 1,250—and a marginally higher missile throw weight ceiling, somewhat above current U.S. totals. Moscow made only one significant change in its position: It would reconsider its proposed ban on cruise missiles. And there things rested until the Soviets walked out. The fundamental issues of which strategic weapons to include in START and what framework of ceilings to impose were still unresolved.

ROUND TWO: INF, STRATEGIC ARMS, AND SPACE WEAPONS

For arms control, 1984 was the year that got away. While the two sides engaged in recriminations, each blaming the other for the deadlock, each declaring its willingness to move forward if the other would quit blocking progress, the nuclear arms race rumbled along. The Kremlin leadership apparently hoped for two dividends from its adjournment of the Geneva talks sine die: a European reaction to American INF deployments that would bring them to a halt and the election in 1984 of a new U.S. President more favorable to arms control. It got neither. The Reagan administration, for its part, was in no hurry. A sparkling economic recovery at home augured victory for the incumbent in November, even with no new arms control agreement to show for his four years in office.

As had happened before with such interruptions, however, events during the delay made subsequent negotiations even more difficult. The new American missiles in Europe, especially the Pershing II, were going in quickly. In response, the USSR announced it was moving some of its shorter-range nuclear missiles (primarily its SS-22) forward to East Germany, where they could reach most of the targets covered by INF stationed on Soviet territory. In the next negotiating round the United States would point out the need to limit these, too, if INF ceilings were to have any meaning. Strategic arms also continued piling up. Washington began deploying the B-1 bomber, put the MX missile into production, and added warheads to its ALCMs and SLBMs. The Soviets started production of two new ICBMs (one new and one updated, according to Moscow): The first, the SS-24, was a mobile replica of the ten-warhead MX; the second, the SS-25, was a single-warhead mobile ICBM foreshadowing the American Midgetman. Soviet SLBM warheads also proliferated.

But the most dramatic change in the superpower equilibrium came from Ronald Reagan's Strategic Defense Initiative. The President's surprise 1983 plan to make nuclear weapons "impotent and obsolete," though dogged by skepticism in the scientific community, was beginning to find support in Congress. As preparations for reconvening the Geneva negotiations gained momentum late in 1984, Moscow insisted that any reductions in strategic offensive weapons be tied to an American reaffirmation of the 1972 ban on space-based ballistic missile defense. When a new round of negotiations finally got under way in January 1985, it thus had three arenas: "space weapons" (in which the Soviets wanted to include antisatellite as well as strategic defense systems), strategic offensive arms, and INF. As outgoing Soviet Foreign Minister Andrei Gromyko put it, "the view has prevailed that the question of either strategic weapons or intermediate-range nuclear weapons cannot be examined without the question of space. . . ."[12]

Again INF seemed to offer the earliest chance for an accord. In place of Paul Nitze, who had come close to a breakthrough in the first round, President Reagan sent a career diplomat and Nitze deputy, Maynard Glitman, to head the new INF discussions. By contrast, the President's chief delegates on space and strategic weapons, Washington lawyer Max Kampelman and former Texas

Senator John Tower, respectively, were known enthusiasts of the U.S. defense buildup and opponents of SALT II.

On the Soviet side, with Mikhail Gorbachev taking over at the top, Soviet negotiating positions again began to move. For a time Moscow had reverted to counting U.S. INF in Europe as part of the West's strategic arsenal, suggesting that these could be treated only as a package together with space weapons. As negotiations proceeded, however, Soviet representatives spoke of a possible "interim" agreement on INF alone, not linked to progress in the other two types of systems. Secretary of State Shultz saw the revised Soviet stance as "a grudging acceptance of the presence of some U.S. INF missiles in Europe defending our allies."[13] Early in 1986 Moscow went farther, offering to settle for a bilateral INF agreement between the United States and the USSR if Washington pledged not to transfer nuclear missiles to other countries, such as Great Britain.

Responding to these new offers from the other side, the Reagan administration also adopted a revised INF position. The President made public a proposal to eliminate all U.S. and Soviet intermediate-range weapons worldwide within three years, an idea which differed little from the American zero option of five years earlier. Other reports, though, quoted a comment by negotiator Glitman that the United States was prepared to "limit each side to 140 medium-range missiles launchers that are within striking range of Europe."[14] In a March 1986 speech Paul Nitze, who remained a close adviser to Reagan on arms control, used the same INF figure but tied it to "concurrent proportionate reductions in Asia" by the Soviet Union.[15] If Washington were modifying its insistence on global INF totals for both superpowers, that flexibility might bode well for an agreement on intermediate-range forces.

On issues of strategic defense, there was also a small but significant narrowing of East-West differences, possibly as a result of the Reagan-Gorbachev summit in November 1985, when American and Soviet leaders met for the first time in this decade. Moscow began speaking favorably of an arrangement that would let research on ballistic missile defense go ahead, while pinpointing the forms of testing and deployment that would remain off limits to both sides. Washington, although sticking to its vision of a "defense-dominated" future, offered a five-year prohibition on deploying space-based BMD, during which time reductions in offensive weapons would proceed.

On the third aspect of the Geneva negotiations—strategic offensive arms—the superpowers still seemed far apart. For one thing, every Soviet proposal remained contingent on an indefinite ban on strategic defenses. For another, the strategic weapons in question differed according to whose plan one looked at. The Reagan administration was still concentrating on 50 percent reductions in ballistic missile warheads (the figure 40 percent was sometimes reluctantly mentioned) with special restrictions on ICBMs. The President added a proposal to limit long-range bombers and ALCMs, though in a way that would let the United States keep what it already had. The Soviets late in 1985 came up with a new START framework of their own, also promising to cut strategic arms in half. But the Soviet plan counted bombers with their payloads along with ballistic missiles in the totals to be cut, thereby asking Washington to do at least as much reducing as Moscow. One aspect of the Soviet proposal—a 3,600-warhead ceiling for warheads deployed "in any one basing mode,"[16] might provide a formulation helpful to the negotiations since it would mandate roughly symmetrical cuts in Soviet ICBMs and U.S. SLBMs.

In two other ways the superpower START proposals were at odds. Washington would prohibit all mobile ICBMs (a technology in which the USSR is currently ahead), while allowing other forms of modernization within the numerical totals set by any agreement. Moscow, by contrast, would conveniently prohibit all new strategic weapons not yet tested by either side, ruling out a whole series of U.S. missiles and bombers being developed in the 1980s, while keeping the mobile missiles it had already tested.

The arms control process suffered yet another jolt in June 1986, when the White House announced that the United States would abandon the limits of SALT I and II before the end of the year. A subsequent set of meetings to discuss American intentions and charges of Soviet treaty violations produced only more acrimony. And then a second face-to-face meeting between Reagan and Gorbachev produced a fundamental shift in the terms of the arms control dialogue.

FROM ICELAND TO AN INF ACCORD

One of the most bizarre episodes in the history of arms control took place in October 1986, when the two superpower leaders got together at a reputedly haunted house in Reykjavik, Iceland. The Soviets arrived, as Gorbachev was to say several days later, "with constructive and most radical arms reduction proposals in the entire history of Soviet-U.S. negotiations."[17] In a series of personal consultations with the American President, Gorbachev offered to eliminate all U.S. and Soviet intermediate-range missiles in Europe, with subsequent talks to deal with INF in Asia and shorter-range INF. In addition, he proposed cutting all strategic nuclear weapons on both sides in half. The President, after meeting with his advisers, responded by suggesting the elimination of all nuclear missiles of all sorts worldwide over a ten-year period.

For a few euphoric hours reports from Iceland foresaw a nuclear-free world by the end of the century. On the final day of the summit, however, Gorbachev indicated that all the agreements reached in principle so far were contingent on Washington's giving up its efforts toward strategic defense, a concession President Reagan was unwilling to make. Instead of a dramatic breakthrough in arms control, the summit had produced the most profound disappointment. On INF, it even represented a setback since the leaders left Reykjavik with any agreement in that "basket" of the negotiations once again linked to the problematic future of SDI.

In another sense, however, the Soviet position at the Iceland summit augured well for an INF agreement. Moscow was now talking about intermediate-range weapons in terms of U.S. and Soviet missiles, leaving aside the nuclear-capable aircraft in the European theater whose complicating effects were examined in Chapter 3, and accepting the Western view that the United States could not negotiate away French and British weapons. Although the next year was to bring no measurable progress on strategic offensive or space-based systems, it did produce a very gratifying breakthrough to an INF accord.

The chances for success on INF improved suddenly in the spring of 1987, when Gorbachev for the last time unlinked that issue from the stalled negotiations on strategic defense. The plan he put forward, drafted at the Reykjavik summit, would have forced withdrawal of all U.S. and Soviet intermediate-range missiles from Europe over five years, leaving each side 100 warheads outside Europe.[18] In the months that followed, the Soviets agreed to the elimination of these weapons, too, clearing the way for a global ban on superpower missiles in the INF category.

As mentioned in Chapter 3, however, a further obstacle arose when Washington demanded the right to convert its Pershing II missiles into "short-range INF"—missiles with ranges between 300 and 600 miles—arguing that Warsaw Pact superiority in these systems would result from a treaty abolishing longer-range INF. Gorbachev, whose freedom to innovate on arms control matters seems greatly to exceed his predecessors', responded by offering to abolish all short-range INF also, as long as West Germany's Pershing I was included. The United States, though astonished by the development, took Gorbachev up on his offer, and the way to an INF accord was cleared when, in August 1987, West German Chancellor Helmut Kohl pledged to dismantle the Pershing I if a superpower agreement on INF was reached and carried out.

And so in December 1987 Mikhail Gorbachev traveled to Washington to sign an INF Treaty. President Reagan's dream of eliminating an entire category of missiles had been realized in terms of intermediate-range forces. The new treaty required the dismantling of all sites at which missiles such as the SS-20, Pershing II, and Tomahawk GLCM had been deployed, it forced the United States and the USSR to destroy all their land-based missiles with ranges between 300 and 3,400 miles over a period of three years, and it banned further production of such weapons. And for the first time it allowed each superpower to station teams of inspectors on the other's territory to ensure that production of the banned missiles had stopped.[19]

The INF agreement did raise several major questions, which became the focus of the Senate's ratification debate in early 1988. What would become of extended deterrence as a strategy once NATO was again without U.S. ground-based missiles in Europe? Would some compensating changes in NATO's conventional weapons be needed as a result of the accord? Could the ban on production of intermediate-range missiles be verified with the inspection rights each party had secured under the treaty?

The greatest question of all, however, was whether the INF Treaty could serve as a stepping-stone to future reductions in the immense strategic nuclear arsenals held by Washington and Moscow. These had grown steadily during the 1980s; by the time of the third Reagan-Gorbachev summit in 1987 they numbered several thousand more than they had at the beginning of the decade. Unless strategic weapons could be cut, the achievements on INF would be overshadowed by towering mountains of new ICBMs, SLBMs, and airborne nuclear weapons. As Gorbachev departed from the United States, the interrelated issues of strategic defense and strategic offensive arms still posed formidable obstacles to the reinvigorated East-West dialogue.

CONCLUSION:
CURRENT ISSUES IN STRATEGIC ARMS CONTROL

In the late 1980s a series of outstanding issues still frustrated hopes for reducing strategic offensive weapons. They included questions such as:

- Which strategic weapons are to be reduced? Should an agreement focus solely on ballistic missiles or count long-range aircraft along with them?

- Should there be special limits on ICBM warheads, not applicable to SLBM and bomber payloads?

- How can megatonnage be equalized, if at all?

- Should mobile ICBMs be prohibited, restricted, or encouraged?

- And—a question crucial to the future of the arms race—will modernization be allowed within the numerical ceilings imposed by an agreement, or will new weapons be prohibited?

Negotiations on strategic offensive arms are further complicated because of their linkage by Moscow to an agreement limiting weapons in space. On these weapons, a further series of questions arises:

• Is strategic defense a good idea or a destabilizing development?

• Should the existing ABM Treaty be discarded, or will the superpowers commit themselves to observe its provisions for a stated time period?

• If space-based defenses are to be restricted, where should the line be drawn? Will research be allowed? Will testing?

• Is it too late to rule out antisatellite weapons in space?

• Should nuclear weapons be placed in space, either for ASAT purposes or for ballistic missile defense, or should they continue to be prohibited?

The final chapter of this book outlines some of the principal current ideas for moving arms control ahead, with their conflicting answers to these essential questions.

FOR MORE DETAIL

Newspaper accounts in the *New York Times* make up the best source for current developments in the Geneva arms control negotiations. For recent works that chronicle some aspects of these negotiations in the 1980s, see:

Robbin F. Laird and Dale R. Herspring, *The Soviet Union and Strategic Arms* (Boulder, Colo.: Westview Press, 1984).

John T. Murphy and Phil Braudaway-Bauman, "Current U.S. and Soviet Nuclear Arms Negotiating Positions, and a Possible Compromise" (Brookline, Mass.: Institute for Defense & Disarmament Studies, October 1985).

Paul H. Nitze, "Negotiations on Nuclear and Space Arms" (U.S. Department of State, Current Policy No. 807, March 1986).

Strobe Talbott, *Deadly Gambits: The Reagan Administration and the Stalemate in Nuclear Arms Control* (New York: Vintage Books, 1985).

NOTES TO CHAPTER 7

1. "1980 Republican Platform Text," *Congressional Quarterly Weekly Report* 38, 29 (July 19, 1980): 2030–56.
2. The best account so far of Reagan administration policies on arms control is contained in Strobe Talbott, *Deadly Gambits: The Reagan Administration and the Stalemate in Nuclear Arms Control* (New York: Vintage Books, 1985).
3. Ibid., p. 171.
4. Ibid., pp. 237 and 273n.
5. George F. Kennan, *The Nuclear Delusion: Soviet-American Relations in the*

Atomic Age (New York: Pantheon Books, 1983), pp. 161–62.

6. *Pravda,* February 26, 1986, pp. 2–10.

7. Michael R. Gordon, "Experts Criticize Reagan Proposal for Weapons Cuts," *New York Times,* July 13, 1986, p. A1.

8. *Public Papers of the Presidents of the United States: Ronald Reagan 1981* (Washington, D.C.: U.S. Government Printing Office, 1982), p. 1065.

9. For details of the "package" and its ultimate fate, see Talbott, op. cit., pp. 116–51.

10. Excerpts from Andropov's speech appeared in the *New York Times,* May 4, 1983, p. A16.

11. U.S. Department of State, "The Strategic Arms Reduction Talks" (Current Policy No. 389), May 11, 1982.

12. Excerpted in the *New York Times,* January 14, 1985, p. A5.

13. Excerpted in the *New York Times,* October 15, 1985, p. A6.

14. Michael R. Gordon, "Arms Talks Adjourn with No Gains," *New York Times,* March 5, 1986, p. A3.

15. Nitze's speech was published by the U.S. Department of State's Bureau of Public Affairs as No. 807 in its Current Policy series, "Negotiations on Nuclear and Space Arms."

16. For a detailed comparison of U.S. and Soviet START positions at the end of 1985, see John T. Murphy and Phil Braudaway-Bauman, "Current U.S. and Soviet Nuclear Arms Negotiating Positions, and a Possible Compromise" (Brookline, Mass.: Institute for Defense & Disarmament Studies, October 1985).

17. As translated by the official Soviet press agency Tass and published in the *New York Times,* October 23, 1986, p. A12.

18. *New York Times,* March 1, 1987, p. 1.

19. The *New York Times* published the full text of the INF Treaty on December 9, 1987, pp. A24–25.

8

OPTIONS IN ARMS
CONTROL

—

On many critical issues of arms control, the positions of the superpowers remain far apart. The points of contention are numerous, and future progress is likely to occur fitfully with countless invitations to discouragement. As the 1987 breakthrough on INF demonstrates, however, arms control has been stalled not because it has nothing to offer but because the political will to achieve it has sometimes been lacking. There continue to be a number of possible next moves, each of which might add to the experience of successful cooperation and facilitate further negotiations. Our next steps must be chosen carefully, so that stability for both sides increases as the process goes along and so that public confidence can be maintained, even in periods of deadlock.

What, then, should the next step be? Does it make more sense to focus on nuclear weapons, whose testing we were nearly able to ban more than twenty years ago, or on their delivery vehicles, the subject of more recent arms control treaties? Should we simply call a halt to deployments, or is anything short of drastic reductions useless? Is it enough to limit the numbers of our weapons, or does the qualitative improvement of our arsenals need to be halted? Does the militarization of space—with antisatellite technologies and exotic ballistic missile defenses—pose so acute a threat that we must deal with it first?

While it is important to weigh the relative merits of various arms control proposals, we must avoid letting the best become the enemy of the good. Very likely there are numerous paths to productive outcomes, any one of them preferable to paralysis. This chapter sets out some of the most viable current alternatives in arms control, arranged in no particular order of precedence. Each has visible merits and enthusiastic supporters in the United States and elsewhere. Each has disadvantages, limitations, and possible dangers associated with it. Our job is to inform ourselves on the options and then to make our choices.

A COMPREHENSIVE NUCLEAR TEST BAN (CNTB)

On August 6, 1985—the fortieth anniversary of the Hiroshima bombing—the Soviet Union announced a unilateral moratorium on all nuclear tests, calling on the other nuclear powers to join it. Had they done so, they would have plugged the last hole in a series of agreements limiting nuclear explosions, from the limited test ban of the early 1960s through the unratified treaties of the mid-1970s which restricted underground nuclear tests to 150 kilotons or less. Interest in a comprehensive ban dates from the Khrushchev-Eisenhower years, when a similar Soviet moratorium ushered in three years without nuclear explosions by Britain, the United States, and the USSR. In the decades since then, however, the nuclear powers have been unable to agree on the verification, desirability, or even the importance of a complete test ban.

Those who favor a *CNTB* consider it the next logical step in arms control. The Center for Defense Information, a private Washington-based organization, calls a ban on all nuclear explosions the "most significant and achievable arms control measure at this time."[1] It would, according to its advocates, prevent the superpowers from developing a "third generation" of more sophisticated weapons to enhance their nuclear war-fighting capabilities. By reducing each side's confidence in its ability to carry off a first strike, a test ban could minimize the incentive to start a nuclear war.

Other arguments for a comprehensive test ban emphasize its longer-term benefits for arms control. Nuclear proliferation, for example, may be impossible to avoid if existing nuclear powers go on developing their arsenals. The 1968 Nonproliferation Treaty, test ban proponents point out, commits the nuclear states to a disarmament they have yet to begin. The fact that China, which has shunned the existing partial test ban, now professes its willingness to sign a comprehensive prohibition on nuclear tests, suggests the appeal a CNTB could have to states on the verge of the nuclear threshold. Supporters of a CNTB believe its enactment, a step that could be taken immediately and without elaborate negotiation, might serve to loosen the 1980s logjam in other forms of arms control.

As the history of the issue suggests, though, a comprehensive nuclear test ban has determined opponents, especially among government officials East and West with responsibilities for national defense. Many of them oppose a complete halt to nuclear testing on two grounds: (1) the chance that a nuclear state might cheat, gaining advantage over those who comply, and (2) the expected benefits to their own nations from continued nuclear testing.

The issue of verification has dogged the nuclear test ban since it was first conceived. President Eisenhower initially refused to join the 1958 Soviet moratorium, fearing that without on-site verification the USSR would be able to test nuclear weapons in secret. In 1963 negotiations seeking a comprehensive ban were defeated by the same problem: The Kennedy administration demanded several on-site inspections in each country annually, while Khrushchev would allow no more than three.[2]

Does current technology enable us to verify a comprehensive nuclear test ban by national technical means alone without intrusive inspections? Here the experts simply disagree. The seismographic technology of the 1980s can detect underground nuclear explosions down to very small ones, but below some level of explosive force it may be possible to conceal a test or disguise it as an earthquake. The Reagan administration now concedes that compliance with the unratified treaties of the 1970s, limiting underground nuclear explosions to 150 kilotons, could be verified by a system abbreviated as CORRTEX. By inserting cables parallel to the shafts where the superpowers conduct their tests, we could reliably determine how powerful the explosions were.[3]

U.S. ratification of the Threshold Test Ban and Peaceful Nuclear Explosions treaties might be auspicious for arms control generally, but it is still a long way from the ban on all nuclear tests which Moscow is demanding. For that, many specialists insist, each side would have to implant seismic monitors on the other's territory (as was recently done in the USSR by a private American group),[4] and both would need to inspect locations where they suspected an underground explosion had taken place.[5] Soviet statements have recently become more favorable to on-site inspection, raising the possibility that this obstacle to a CNTB may be overcome.

Even if a comprehensive test ban could be verified, many would still think it undesirable. The nuclear powers currently conduct a certain number of underground explosions each year to check the reliability of existing nuclear stockpiles. Most of the potential problems with aging warheads derive from their mechanics—the triggering devices that cause implosion, for example—and the performance of these parts can be certified without setting off a nuclear explosion. Nonetheless, there are those who doubt we could ever be confident of our existing weapons without at least a few nuclear tests annually.[6]

More fundamentally, opposition to a CNTB comes from advocates of force modernization. Many of the technical advances the United States and the USSR are planning for the next decade might be halted if neither could carry out further underground explosions. The warheads for mobile ICBMs and for counterforce-capable SLBMs—technologies both sides are going to want before the end of the century—cannot be developed, some scientists claim, without nuclear tests. This is, in fact, the precise argument made for a test ban by others who oppose further modernization. If improved counterforce capabilities on both sides are desirable, then continued nuclear testing may be necessary. (Soviet military officials appeared just as adamant on this point as American test ban opponents; the chief of the general staff, Sergei Akhromeyev, spoke publicly of the "military advantages" a unilateral Soviet moratorium gave the United States.[7]) If, on the other hand, we prefer to reduce counterforce capabilities on both sides, or at least to keep them at present levels, a comprehensive nuclear test ban might help. The only option not open is to allow further weapons development by one superpower while prohibiting it to the other.

Some aspects of space-based ballistic missile defense might also fall victim to a ban on nuclear tests. X-ray lasers, currently being developed by Washington for possible use against ballistic missiles, depend upon small nuclear explosions as their energy source. Under a comprehensive test ban treaty we might lose our chance to discover how this technology works. That, of course, is just what CNTB advocates suggest. They see the next round of the arms race, with its enhanced counterforce weapons and ballistic missile defense, as the most destabilizing yet, and they look to a ban on nuclear explosions to stop it in its tracks.

A NUCLEAR FREEZE

Were a complete ban on nuclear weapons tests to take effect, the nuclear arms race in most of its aspects could still go on. Strategic delivery vehicles, which have been the focus of modernization efforts since the late 1950s, would remain outside a nuclear test ban. So would most aspects of strategic defense, since they do not rely on nuclear explosions. With this in mind, critics of the arms race at the beginning of the 1980s formulated a more far-reaching proposal for arms control: the *nuclear freeze*. It includes a prohibition on nuclear weapons tests and thus subsumes the CNTB, but it goes much farther.

The aims of a nuclear freeze were set out in a joint resolution presented to the U.S. Senate and House of Representatives in 1982 by Senators Edward Kennedy of Massachusetts and Mark Hatfield of Oregon. The resolution called on the United States and the Soviet Union to "decide when and how to achieve a mutual and verifiable freeze on the testing, production, and future deployment of nuclear warheads, missiles, and other delivery systems. . . ."[8] The wording of the freeze resolution rules out not only weapons tests, which may or may not be indispensable to the arms race, but also tests of new ballistic missiles, such as the Midgetman or SS-25, cruise missiles of all sorts, and new strategic aircraft like the American Stealth or Soviet Blackjack bomber. The freeze would even prevent further production of existing weapons types and the deployment of delivery vehicles already produced but not yet deployed.

The freeze is a bid to halt the nuclear arms race more definitively than any arms control agreement the superpowers have reached so far. Its proponents point especially to one aspect of the arms race—qualitative modernization of strategic delivery vehicles—left outside the limits of SALT and START but subject to a freeze. With few exceptions, the arms control treaties of the 1970s and the Reagan administration's proposals in the 1980s impose only quantitative limits on strategic weapons, setting ceilings at one level or another on the numbers that can be deployed. They do little or nothing to stop the superpowers from replacing existing delivery vehicles with newer, more accurate, and therefore more threatening versions. Freeze advocates point out, for example, that the highly MIRVed, counterforce-capable SS-18—the reason American ICBMs are now vulnerable to attack—could not have supplanted earlier, less menacing Soviet missiles if a freeze had been in effect in the 1970s.

The crux of the nuclear freeze is its ban on the testing of new delivery vehicles. Freeze advocates maintain that this unique aspect of the proposal makes it politically more astute than competing plans to end the arms race. A new weapon that exists only in the mind's eye—without benefit of testing to demonstrate what it can actually do—will have a harder time finding support among leaders in Washington or Moscow. Politicians are more likely to commit resources to programs whose benefits they can observe.

In the early 1980s the nuclear freeze developed a broad following within the American electorate. Opinion polls showed the public favoring it by large margins, and dozens of local referenda calling for a freeze were passed by voters. The Soviet leadership did what it could to encourage the freeze movement in the West, publicly endorsing the idea, but in terms so vague (usually a freeze on "nuclear arsenals") as to leave the actual Soviet attitude toward the proposal in question.[9] The movement reached its crest in August 1982, when a freeze resolution failed by two votes of passage in the U.S. House of Representatives.

Opposition to a freeze takes three forms: (1) concern about verification, (2) commitment to weapons the freeze would prohibit acquiring, and (3) fear that it would get in the way of actual reductions in nuclear stockpiles, inducing the superpowers to keep what they already have. Verification issues center on the proposal's inclusion of weapons production in the list of banned activities. While satellite reconnaissance can show Moscow or Washington when its opponent deploys additional strategic delivery vehicles, converts missiles to more highly MIRVed forms, or tests new delivery systems, neither side can tell exactly what goes on in the factories where the other produces nuclear weapons. Some freeze advocates point out that the location of these factories is known and that their complete shutdown by mutual agreement should be verifiable. Others would settle for a "quick-freeze," banning only the testing and deployment of strategic delivery vehicles, while the more complex problems of a broader freeze—possibly to include on-site inspection—are negotiated.[10]

Even if verification posed no difficulties, the nuclear freeze would still arouse opposition. Precisely because it halts modernization of nuclear forces, anyone with a favorite new weapon which seems critical to either superpower's defense posture will oppose a freeze until that weapon is in place. In the early 1980s it was most commonly the MX missile whose advocates held out against the freeze. The Soviets had already begun deployment of their equivalent to the MX; a freeze would stop the United States from catching up. Similarly, defense planners critical of the MX because of its vulnerability wanted a new generation of survivable counterforce weapons: the Trident II SLBM and the mobile Midgetman ICBM. By the mid-1980s the USSR had already tested two mobile versions of its ICBMs. Would it be sensible to deprive the West of this technology once the Soviets already had it?

If a nuclear freeze generates opposition because it prohibits too much, it can also be criticized for accomplishing too little. The Reagan administration, for example, came to office committed to deep reductions in existing weapons systems, while wanting to modernize what was left. It therefore condemned the freeze on both counts. If the nuclear arms race were halted as of, say, 1984, what incentive would the Soviets have to negotiate away anything in their existing weapons inventory? How could Washington persuade Moscow to eliminate the thousands of ICBM warheads which had opened a window of vulnerability for American land-based forces?

Freeze advocates see a ban on further modernization as improving the climate for negotiated reductions. A "negotiators' pause" in the arms race might actually make reductions easier to agree on since the technology would not be continually outrunning the negotiators. The United States would have to trade reductions in areas of its strength—its new air-launched cruise missiles, for example, or its new Ohio-class submarines—for cutbacks in Moscow's most powerful ICBMs. But proponents of a freeze consider this kind of negotiated outcome more likely in the context of a freeze than in conditions of an ongoing arms race.

STRATEGIC BUILD-DOWN

One proposal to permit continued modernization of nuclear forces while cutting back their numbers is a *strategic build-down*, sometimes referred to as the Cohen-Nunn build-down after the two senators who introduced the idea. As originally put forward by Senators William Cohen (a Maine Republican) and Sam Nunn (the Georgia Democrat who now chairs the Armed Services Committee) early in 1983, the build-down simply meant a U.S.-Soviet agreement to destroy two nuclear warheads for each new one deployed. According to Senator Cohen, "It has as its theoretical underpinning the notion that weapons modernization could be stabilizing and that modernization could and should be combined with nuclear arms reductions."[11]

Proponents of a strategic build-down prefer it to a nuclear freeze for several reasons:

- The very desire of defense planners to improve strategic weapons would compel them to reduce the numbers of those weapons. This is what Senator Cohen means when he refers to the build-down as "a plan for reductions paced by modernization." Technological progress, previously a motor of the arms race, becomes instead a brake.

- A build-down agreement would not dictate the composition of either superpower's forces. Unlike SALT II, it would not require more effort by the United States than by the Soviet Union to reach a common set of ceilings. Unlike the START proposals, it would not impose greater restructuring on Moscow than on Washington.

• A guaranteed build-down would logically draw both superpowers toward more survivable, less highly MIRVed missiles and thus a more stable strategic relationship. If each knew that it was going to have progressively fewer warheads, not more and more of them, the incentive to deploy them in less vulnerable modes, with fewer warheads on the average delivery vehicle, would be great. Thus SLBMs would become preferable to ICBMs, and single-warhead mobile ICBMs—like the proposed Midgetman or SS-25—more desirable than the MX or additional warheads on the SS-18.

By late 1983 the Reagan administration had endorsed the build-down, appending it to its START proposals in Geneva as an appealing way to achieve deep reductions in strategic inventories. Along the way, however, the proposal had become more complex. The simple two-for-one warhead trade-in of the initial version had been supplanted by the following set of guidelines:

• Each warhead installed on a new MIRVed ICBM would require eliminating two existing warheads. In the Reagan administration's version, only ballistic missile warheads, not bombs or cruise missiles on aircraft, are covered by this and the next two provisions.

• New warheads on SLBMs or small single-warhead ICBMs would force reductions at a lower ratio, perhaps three for two.

• Even if a side were not adding more warheads through modernization, it would still have to make annual reductions of, say, 5 percent in its ballistic missile warheads.

• Bombers would be treated in less carefully specified ways, with some limits on air-launched cruise missiles and a trade-off of U.S. bomber carrying capacity for missile throw weight on the Soviet side.[12]

From the standpoint of a skeptic, the build-down in this revised form loses some of its original appeal. Apart from its greater complexity—the seemingly inevitable fate of any evolving arms control option—the proposal has taken on many of START's objectionable features. It treats warheads on ballistic missiles in detail, while providing only vague terms for building down bomber forces, currently the principal U.S. advantage and the leg of the triad to which Washington is now adding warheads the fastest. In the same vein it puts the highest price tag on MIRVed ICBMs, the best-developed weapon in the Soviet arsenal. Moscow is less likely to consider the strategic build-down a viable approach to arms control if it is seen only as a new bottle for the old wine of START.

More fundamentally, the build-down idea in any form gives ground for doubt about its implications for stability. The claim of its proponents that the build-down provides an incentive to move toward mobile forces is correct. Simultaneously, however, it encourages an increasingly accurate force since new warheads are almost certain to have the most advanced characteristics their designers can give them. Improved accuracy has an effect exactly opposite that of mobility: It renders an opponent's forces more vulnerable. It was, after all, the combined effect of MIRVing and accuracy improvements that built crisis instability into the superpower relationship in the first place. Opposition to continued force modernization on either side is based on the desire to stop increases in accuracy before they raise the first-strike incentive too high.

The net effects of a strategic build-down are thus hard to calculate. To the extent that it brings a reduction in warhead-to-aimpoint ratios, as it seems likely to do, it gives greater stability to the nuclear stalemate. To the extent that it raises the accuracy of the average warhead, it tends in the direction of instability. Its peculiar mixture of quantitative reductions with a qualitative arms race leaves the overall result of a strategic build-down a legitimate matter for debate.

AN ASAT TREATY

Since the early 1960s the superpowers have observed each other's military activities from space, counting missile launchers and aircraft, watching troop concentrations and movements, monitoring tests of nuclear delivery vehicles. While other forms of intelligence gathering continue to function—seismic monitoring, for example, and the illegal procurement of secret documents by agents in each country's capital—satellite reconnaissance now tells us most of what we know about the weapons capabilities of our opponents.

The same satellites engage in more sinister activities as well. Just as Soviet satellites can verify U.S. compliance with arms control agreements, so they can track American vessels on the high seas, putting Moscow in a better position to conduct naval warfare if a conflict breaks out. The United States, from its side, plans to use satellite communications to make its next-generation SLBMs as capable as current ICBMs in a possible counterforce assault on the Soviet Union.[13] Because an enemy's satellites can tell it so much about our defenses, efforts to build antisatellite (ASAT) weapons began almost as soon as the first satellite went into orbit.

Starting in the 1960s, the USSR constructed a land-based ASAT system which it had tested twenty times by 1982. The Soviet weapon, launched by an ICBM, chases enemy satellites through space, overtaking them after one or two orbits and destroying them with a conventional explosion. Relative to current American ASAT technologies, the Soviet system is extremely primitive. Since it can be fired only from fixed launch sites, it must wait until the target satellite is in the correct position to be attacked, and even then it takes several hours to catch its victim. It will probably be fairly easy to deflect with protective countermeasures. Out of twenty test trials, it has failed eleven times.[14]

By contrast, the United States is putting together an ASAT system capable of being launched from high-flying aircraft around the globe. Its much smaller rockets attack satellites in space with skillfully guided warheads, homing in on infrared radiation from their targets and adjusting course to collide with them. If deployed, the U.S. system should be able to destroy objects in orbit much more quickly than its Soviet counterpart. It will also be a great deal harder to detect, complicating any future attempt to regulate the ASAT competition.

In 1982 the Communist party leadership in Moscow announced a unilateral moratorium on ASAT testing, inviting the United States to resume negotiations on a treaty banning antisatellite weapons. The Reagan administration showed little interest in doing so. It wanted a chance to equal or exceed Soviet accomplishments before it discussed any agreement that might halt ASAT testing. In 1985 the President's national security adviser,

Robert McFarlane, commented, "We have to test, and we have to test now," adding, "This will lead to stability by having some equivalent capability."[15] The U.S. ASAT program has been working under a congressionally imposed handicap, however, since legislation passed in the mid-1980s prohibited tests of the American weapon against objects in space, as long as Moscow's moratorium continued.

Critics of the East-West competition in ASAT systems, including many in Congress, give a number of reasons for nipping the technology in the bud. The United States cannot deploy antisatellite capabilities without allowing the USSR to resume its ASAT program, which could eventually threaten Washington's ability to observe Soviet military activities and to control its nuclear forces in wartime. As usual with arms control matters, we have to decide whether it is better for both sides to have ASAT capabilities or whether we are better off if neither does. Some opponents of ASAT argue that nuclear war could even be started accidentally by actions taken initially in space. A nuclear power fearing attack, for example, might decide to destroy its opponent's satellites as a defensive measure. This ASAT attack could easily be misinterpreted by the other side as the first move in a nuclear war started by the original power, leading it to launch a war neither intended in the first place.[16]

Because of the dangers they see in the race to "Star Wars," many critics of the ASAT competition prefer a treaty prohibiting its further development. Nothing in existing law stands in the way of the technologies involved. The Limited Nuclear Test Ban Treaty, while it bans nuclear explosions in space, has no provision against nonnuclear explosions there. Similarly, the Outer Space Treaty, while it stops the placement of nuclear and "other weapons of mass destruction" in orbit, says nothing about the more modest devices needed to destroy satellites. And the ABM Treaty, though prohibiting ballistic missile defenses based in space, does not stand in the way of systems explicitly dedicated to antisatellite warfare.

The ultimate argument against an ASAT treaty, however, is the near impossibility of keeping ASAT and BMD technologies distinct. Many aspects of the Strategic Defense Initiative—from ground-based lasers to "smart rocks" to particle beams launched from space—would also make ideal antisatellite weapons. Indeed, most technologies for disabling ballistic missiles in flight would have an easier time if used against satellites, which are a good deal more delicate.[17] If SDI is to go ahead, then, the United States must be allowed to test weapons with an ASAT capability. Proponents of an ASAT treaty view this as another reason for abandoning the drive toward strategic defense.

REVISING THE ABM TREATY?

The decisive issue of arms control in our time is likely to be strategic defense. Seen by its advocates as the answer to nuclear vulnerability and by its adversaries as the ultimate arms control prevention program, ballistic missile defense has become crucial to the course of negotiations on offensive nuclear weapons. At the Reykjavik summit in October 1986, Gorbachev made all the Soviet proposals to reduce offensive systems, whether intercontinental or intermediate in range, contingent on agreement between Washington and Moscow on strategic defense. Reagan, by contrast, insisted on the right to deploy ballistic missile defense, even as the missiles BMD seeks to neutralize are eliminated.

An East-West agreement on strategic defense could take one of two basic directions: The terms of the existing ABM Treaty could be tightened to make sure new technologies do not outrun its prohibitions, or the treaty could be revised or abrogated to allow testing and deployment of BMD in space-based modes. The first was essentially what Gorbachev proposed in Iceland. Because the "development" of space-based defensive systems, ruled out by the ABM Treaty, is too vague a term to be useful, and because the treaty's signatories disagree on what are "components" of an ABM system and what are not, the Soviet leader suggested a strict interpretation of the treaty which would limit research and testing of space-based defenses to the laboratory for ten years.[18] The Kremlin was proposing to reinforce the treaty by making it both more specific and more verifiable. Henceforth those BMD activities each superpower could see from its satellites would be prohibited.

This was not what the White House wanted. The United States could never hope to determine how effective a defensive shield it could build against ballistic missiles if its tests were limited to the laboratory. It needed to try lasers and particle beams based in space against missiles and warheads in flight. At Reykjavik, Washington therefore suggested a lenient interpretation of the ABM Treaty for ten years; during that period the USSR and the United States would undertake "strictly to observe all its provisions while continuing research, development, and testing, which are permitted by the ABM Treaty."[19] At the end of ten years, with all "offensive ballistic missiles" of the two superpowers eliminated, "either side could deploy defenses if it so chose unless the parties agree otherwise."

When the Reagan-Gorbachev meeting in Iceland produced no agreement, the participants launched intense public relations campaigns suggesting that it had been a near miss. Except for the obstinacy of the other side on strategic defense, each maintained, a stunning breakthrough could have been achieved in the battle against offensive weapons. All ballistic missiles, possibly all nuclear weapons could have been dismantled by the end of the century. Anyone familiar with the history of arms control, however, has grounds to question these official accounts. The "quibble" over strategic defense is, in fact, the crux of the matter, and the attitudes of East and West on the issue remain diametrically opposed. The limitation of strategic offensive weapons has been, from its beginning in SALT I, contingent on an agreement to forswear an arms race in strategic defenses.

Without agreement on the meaning or future of the ABM Treaty, it is hard to imagine where arms control can go next. What number of offensive weapons each side thinks it needs depends not only on how many weapons the other side has but also on its expectations of how its own weapons will perform. Whether they face strategic defenses or not is thus no small matter. As long as the issue of space-based defenses remains unresolved, Washington and Moscow are free to propose whatever limits on offensive systems they think will please the public, knowing that no actual agreement is likely to result. To reach the next arms control accord, a more incremental, if somewhat less popular, approach will probably be necessary.

ARMS CONTROL IN THE FUTURE: BY INCHES OR BY MILES?

As the alternatives presented in this and the previous chapter suggest, a number of possible agreements to limit the nuclear arms race are available to us. Some are more eye-catching than others. The nuclear freeze, for example, enjoyed great popularity for a few years, but it had an inherent political flaw: Anyone in Washington or Moscow who favored any new weapon carrying nuclear arms had a reason to oppose the freeze. Similarly, if the Reagan administration's proposals to cut nuclear delivery systems by half or to abolish ballistic missiles entirely were put into effect in one fell swoop, they would offend the interests of so many powerful constituencies in both political systems as to be practically unattainable.

Over the past forty years the nuclear arms race has generated entrenched bases of support for new weapons systems in both East and West. In the Soviet Union these include the armed services, major industries supplying those services, the intelligence agencies, and party bureaucracies at national and regional levels with functions relating to defense industry. In the United States more than just public institutions are involved in a defense-industrial complex. Besides the civilians and uniformed personnel employed by the Pentagon and other security agencies, many of the nation's largest corporations are defense contractors, and much of the labor force has learned the skills of defense-related trades. Our most prominent research institutions, universities included, rely on weapons-related contracts for their prosperity, and most members of Congress come from districts where military bases or defense industries are located.[20]

This does not make arms control impossible since there are countervailing interests in any political system which would benefit from a restructuring of public expenditures away from defense. But the powerful influence of defense-related interests does have important implications for the future of arms control:

- It makes more attractive those proposals, like the Cohen-Nunn build-down, which allow new weapons to be developed, tested, and deployed as older ones are dismantled. The same political logic—a drive to ensure contracts and jobs related to defense and to avoid damage to the institutional interests of the military—explains the nature of most past arms control agreements, which restricted some aspects of the nuclear arms race while allowing it to go forward in other directions.

• If arms control is to become something different—if it is to bring significant reductions in arsenals, prohibit new technologies sought by defense-related interests, and reduce what Washington and Moscow spend on weapons—it will have to be done incrementally and with attention to the interests which benefit from it. Diverting federal dollars from defense to education, road building, or housing construction actually creates more jobs in these civilian industries than it destroys in defense industry. But these employment gains by people who have yet to receive them are far less politically salient than the current jobs of defense workers who will be thrown out of work. Defense budgets have been reduced in the past, but the task can best be accomplished gradually and by a political leadership able to dramatize the positive achievements of peaceful conversion.

In light of these political realities, future progress in arms control is likely to take place by small increments. Throughout the 1980s arms control experts pointed to an INF agreement as the most easily achievable next step, one which could break the ice and encourage additional measures requiring East-West cooperation. That view has proved correct precisely because intermediate-range weapons make up such a small and expendable part of nuclear arsenals on both sides. An INF accord does not bring the nuclear era to an end or even result in a nuclear-free Europe. But it creates an improved climate for discussing more significant and elusive goals, such as reduced conventional forces in Europe and negotiated reductions in the far more massive strategic nuclear forces of the superpowers.

Similarly, the most feasible next move in strategic arms control is probably a small one. Appealing as it may be to talk about eliminating all nuclear weapons or dismantling all ballistic missiles, these are longer-range goals not attainable with just one more arms control treaty. In fact, their ultimate achievement becomes more doubtful the longer the present hiatus in strategic arms control continues. Current negotiations between Washington and Moscow focus on the less ambitious goal of cutting strategic nuclear warheads in half over a period of several years, an approach still drastic enough to raise powerful opposition among defense specialists in both Washington and Moscow. If that, too, proves too large a bite to swallow, a more acceptable basis for agreement might be something like the following:

- Take the ceilings of SALT II, intricate as they are, and reduce them by 25 or 30 percent, as the Soviets suggested early in the 1980s. The number of allowed delivery vehicles, and the number of those in various categories which could be MIRVed, would fall below present levels.

- As a concession to American concerns, make the required reductions in MIRVed ICBMs somewhat more stringent. If overall ceilings were cut by 30 percent, for example, the treaty could require a 35 percent reduction in the allowed number of MIRVed ICBMs, forcing Moscow to begin dismantling some of its most threatening weapons. Soviet superiority in land-based warheads would not be eliminated, but it would be significantly reduced.

- In exchange, put more stringent limits on the new U.S. offensive technologies of most concern to the Soviet Union: air-launched and sea-launched cruise missiles. Because current Soviet air defenses are largely useless against cruise missiles, their deployment by the United States in large numbers will force a major new defense expenditure by Moscow. A treaty limit of perhaps 1,000 ALCMs on each side would scale back the new American system to levels the Soviet leadership might accept. Sea-launched cruise missiles with more than the shortest ranges may have to be banned entirely, since their nuclear and conventional versions are practically indistinguishable.

None of this would end the nuclear arms race once and for all. Even the modest reductions outlined, however, would need selling to defense establishments in both countries. In this regard the hypothetical agreement has a chance of success because it satisfies a long-standing demand of the military on each side—reductions in its opponent's most threatening system—in exchange for dismantling weapons of its own. The proposed framework also has the merit—dubious from a logical standpoint but attractive politically—of permitting modernization of the reduced strategic forces to continue. A shift from highly MIRVed to single-warhead mobile ICBMs would be one likely result. But to avoid instability in the new strategic balance, accuracy improvements in SLBMs would have to be ruled out.

In some such manner are the arms control agreements of the future likely to be produced. Only as one negotiated reduction is followed by another will we reach the point of eliminating major categories of nuclear weapons altogether. If the process seems tedious and strewn with obstacles, consider the alternative: an arms race without limit, costing enough to render both superpowers second-rate societies by the twenty-first century.

FOR MORE DETAIL

The Defense Monitor, serial publication of the Center for Defense Information, Washington, D.C.

Alton Frye, "Strategic Build-Down: A Context for Restraint," in *The Nuclear Reader: Strategy, Weapons, War*, ed. Charles W. Kegley, Jr., and Eugene R. Wittkopf (New York: St. Martin's Press, 1985). Outlines the intricacies of various build-down proposals.

George F. Kennan, *The Nuclear Delusion: Soviet-American Relations in the Atomic Age* (New York: Pantheon Books, 1983). Evaluates the arms control process and makes suggestions for improving it.

Edward M. Kennedy and Mark O. Hatfield, *Freeze: How You Can Help Prevent Nuclear War* (New York: Bantam Books, 1982). An explanation of the nuclear freeze proposal by two of its prominent advocates.

Herbert M. Levine and David Carlton, eds., *The Nuclear Arms Race Debated* (New York: McGraw-Hill, 1986). Presents current arms control issues, directly juxtaposing arguments for and against them. Chapter 3 evaluates SALT II, a comprehensive test ban, and the nuclear freeze.

Franklin A. Long, Donald Hafner, and Jeffrey Boutwell, eds., *Weapons in Space* (New York: W. W. Norton & Co., 1986). The technologies of ASAT and SDI, along with discussion of their merits.

Steven E. Miller, ed., *The Nuclear Weapons Freeze and Arms Control* (Cambridge, Mass.: Ballinger Publishing Co., 1984). Judging freeze proposals from the standpoints of Washington and Moscow.

Lynn R. Sykes and Jack F. Evernden, "The Verification of a Comprehensive Nuclear Test Ban," *Scientific American* (October 1982): 47–55. Makes the case that a CNTB can be verified.

NOTES TO CHAPTER 8

1. The Center for Defense Information's *Defense Monitor* has covered the issue of a comprehensive nuclear test ban several times. See, for instance, its Vol. XIV, No. 5 (1985), "Simultaneous Test Ban: A Primer on Nuclear Explosions."

2. Questions of verification in the 1963 negotiations are treated by one of the participants, Glenn T. Seaborg, in his *Kennedy, Khrushchev and the Test Ban* (Berkeley: University of California Press, 1981), ch. 14–18.

3. "Nuclear Testing Limitations" (statement by the President, March 14, 1986), *Weekly Compilation of Presidential Documents* 22:11 (March 17, 1986) pp. 364–65.

4. Michael R. Gordon, "U.S. Aides Are Looking to Gains at A-Test Talks Resuming Today," *New York Times* (September 4, 1986), p. A10.

5. For a more confident view on verification, see Lynn R. Sykes and Jack F. Evernden, "The Verification of a Comprehensive Nuclear Test Ban," *Scientific American* (October 1982): 47–55. Sykes and Evernden conclude that a network of fifteen seismic stations inside and fifteen outside the USSR could identify even small explosions "even if extreme measures were taken to evade detection."

6. A concise summary of the main arguments for and against a CNTB by Hugh DeWitt and Robert Barker is contained in *The Nuclear Arms Race Debated*, ed. Herbert M. Levine and David Carlton (New York: McGraw-Hill, 1986), pp. 123–37.

7. Gary Lee, "Soviets Successfully Use Nuclear Test Ban for International Campaign," *Washington Post*, August 31, 1986, p. A25.

8. The text of the resolution can be found in Kennedy and Hatfield's *Freeze: How You Can Help Prevent Nuclear War* (New York: Bantam Books, 1982), pp. 169–70. The same volume contains most of the arguments for a nuclear freeze.

9. One prominent émigré observer of Soviet politics argued in 1983 that Moscow would turn down a freeze if Washington offered to accept it. See Dimitri Simes, "Why Andropov Would Reject a Bilateral Freeze," in *The Nuclear Weapons Freeze and Arms Control*, ed. Steven E. Miller (Cambridge, Mass.: Ballinger Publishing Co., 1984).

10. Jane M. O. Sharp, "Exploring the Feasibility of a Ban on Warhead Production," and Franklin A. Long, "A Rapidly Negotiable, First-Stage Nuclear Freeze," ibid.

11. William S. Cohen, "The Arms Build-Down Proposal," *Washington Post*, October 9, 1983, p. C8.

12. Adapted from Alton Frye, "Strategic Build-down: A Context for Restraint," in *The Nuclear Reader: Strategy, Weapons, War*, ed. Charles W. Kegley, Jr., and Eugene R. Wittkopf (New York: St. Martin's Press, 1985), pp. 174–75.

13. Joel Wit, "American SLBM: Counterforce Options and Strategic Implications," *Survival* (July / August 1982): 163–74.

14. Soviet and U.S. ASAT technologies are described by William J. Broad in his *New York Times* article "Anti-Satellite Arms Issue: Proposal to Test American Weapon Spurs Debate over Its Impact on Hopes for Peace," August 21, 1985, p. A1.

15. Quoted by Gerald M. Boyd, "U.S. Will Proceed with an Arms Test on Space Target," *New York Times*, August 21, 1985, p. A1.

16. These and similar arguments are reviewed by Kurt Gottfried and Richard Ned Lebow, "Anti-Satellite Weapons: Weighing the Risks," in *Weapons in Space*, ed. Franklin A. Long, Donald Hafner, and Jeffrey Boutwell (New York: W. W. Norton & Co., 1986).

17. Ashton B. Carter, "The Relationship of ASAT and BMD Systems," in *Weapons in Space*, loc. cit.

18. Excerpts from Gorbachev's speech on the Iceland meeting were published in the *New York Times*, October 15, 1986, p. A12.

19. This remarkable rendering of the treaty's restrictions was contained in a State

Department text of the U.S. proposal, published in the *New York Times* on October 18, 1986, p. 5.

20. See, for example, the list of corporations and research laboratories acting as contractors for space-based weapons development, as reported by Steven J. Marcus, "Corporate Push for Space Lasers," *New York Times*, April 24, 1983, p. F4. A detailed account of institutions involved in Soviet weapons development may be found in Arthur J. Alexander, "Decision-making in Soviet Weapon Procurement," in *The Soviet Union: Security Policies and Constraints*, ed. Jonathan Alford (London: Gower for the International Institute for Strategic Studies, 1985).

GLOSSARY

—

ALCM

air-launched cruise missile. A small pilotless aircraft launched from a larger bomber, it flies at a low altitude to strike targets with high accuracy.

arms control

negotiated measures to restrict arsenals of weapons, rather than abolish them.

ASAT

antisatellite weapons.

assured destruction

deterring nuclear attack on a country by threatening the attacker with retaliatory destruction of its own society.

ASW

antisubmarine warfare.

ballistic missile

a missile whose fuel is burned early in its flight. When the booster burns out, the payload continues to its target on a ballistic trajectory, as a ball does when thrown.

Baruch Plan

Washington's original disarmament proposal to the United Nations, involving an international agency to control nuclear energy and prevent the development of nuclear weapons.

BMD	ballistic missile defense; a defensive system designed to destroy incoming ballistic missiles or their warheads. The term "antiballistic missile system" (ABM) was once used for BMD; President Reagan's version is called the Strategic Defense Initiative (SDI).
CEP	circular error probable. A measure of a weapon's accuracy, it is the radius of a circle drawn such that the weapon has a 50 percent probability of falling within the circle. The smaller the CEP, the more accurate the weapon.
CNTB	comprehensive nuclear test ban, including a prohibition against all underground nuclear explosions; proposed by the Soviet Union but not yet accepted by other nuclear powers.
counterforce capabilities	weapons that can be used against the military forces of an opponent, such as missile silos and command centers.
countervalue capabilities	weapons that can destroy an opponent's population and industry.
crisis stability	a condition in which no nuclear power feels it can gain by attacking first, even during an international crisis.
damage limitation	strategies designed to reduce the effects of an attack by a country's enemies.
deterrence	dissuading an opponent from undesirable actions it would otherwise take by threatening to do unacceptable damage in return.
disarmament	reductions in weapons, either unilaterally or by international agreement, with the aim of eliminating them altogether.
equal security	Soviet nuclear doctrine allowing the USSR nuclear weapons for which the United States has no equivalent, as an offset to the nuclear forces of other countries. SS-20s facing Western Europe and China are the best example.

extended deterrence	U.S. strategy of holding a nuclear umbrella over allies such as West Germany and Japan. According to this doctrine, the United States threatens to respond with a nuclear strike on the Soviet Union if its allies are attacked by Moscow's conventional forces.
FBS	forward-based systems, such as aircraft and missiles of intermediate range, under U.S. control but located in Europe, where they can strike the Soviet Union.
flexible response	multiple-options doctrine of the Kennedy era, allowing the United States to respond to Soviet military actions in kind.
horizontal proliferation	the spread of nuclear weapons from one nation to another or others.
ICBM	intercontinental ballistic missile, land-based and with a range in excess of about 3,400 miles.
imperialism	Lenin's theory that advanced capitalist societies are innately aggressive; universally accepted by Soviet thinkers today.
INF	intermediate-range nuclear forces, either ballistic missiles, cruise missiles, or aircraft, normally excluded from strategic arms negotiations because of their range—about 300 to 3,400 miles.
IRBM	intermediate-range ballistic missile, such as the Soviet SS-20 or the American Pershing II.
massive retaliation	Eisenhower's threat to respond to any Communist aggression with "massive retaliatory damage by offensive striking power."
MIRV	multiple independently targetable reentry vehicles; several warheads mounted on a single ballistic missile and capable of being aimed at separate targets.
mutual assured destruction	a situation in which each of two nuclear powers remains vulnerable to a second

strike by the other if it starts a nuclear war; often abbreviated as MAD.

MX   a new American MIRVed ICBM which carries ten highly accurate warheads, each with a 350-kiloton yield. Once intended to be mobile, it is now being deployed in fixed silos.

national technical means   satellite reconnaissance, radar tracking, telemetry interception, and other ways the superpowers use to verify each other's compliance with arms control treaties without on-site inspection.

NSC-68   position paper of the Truman administration, aimed at making the United States less dependent on nuclear weapons in a war with the Soviet Union.

nuclear freeze   according to its proponents, "a mutual and verifiable freeze on the testing, production, and future deployment of nuclear warheads, missiles, and other delivery systems."

peaceful coexistence   cornerstone of modern Soviet foreign policy, asserting that war between socialist and capitalist states is not "fatalistically inevitable"; leaves open the question of how many weapons the USSR needs to deter capitalist attack.

Pershing II   U.S. mobile ballistic missile of intermediate range and high accuracy, carrying only one warhead; 108 of them have been stationed in West Germany since the end of 1983.

preemptive strike   attack on an opponent's military forces, prompted by the belief that an attack by the enemy is imminent.

preventive war   unprovoked attack on an opponent's military forces.

rough parity   equivalence of strategic weapons systems between East and West, seen by Soviets as existing since about 1970; it strikes some as a reason for arms con-

	trol, others as justification to match every new U.S. weapon.
SDI	Strategic Defense Initiative. See BMD.
SLBM	submarine-launched ballistic missile.
SS-20	Soviet mobile intermediate-range ballistic missile with short firing time, high accuracy, and three warheads, able to strike targets in Europe or Asia but not in the United States.
strategic build-down	proposal requiring each nuclear power to destroy more than one nuclear warhead for each new one it adds to its arsenal.
strategic delivery systems	ICBMs, SLBMs, and long-range bombers.
strategic doctrine	any theory which matches the military capabilities of a country to its military objectives. For our purposes, a theory about the uses of nuclear weapons.
throw weight	the mass of usable objects a ballistic missile can place into orbit, including warheads, decoys, and the bus which guides multiple warheads.
Tomahawk GLCM	ground-launched cruise missile, deployed four to a launcher, stationed by the United States in Great Britain, West Germany, Italy, Belgium, and the Netherlands beginning in 1983. Combines high accuracy with the ability to evade radar detection by hugging the terrain of an opponent's country.
vertical proliferation	additions to the nuclear weapons already possessed by nuclear weapons states.
warhead-to-aimpoint ratio	the number of one country's accurate counterforce-capable missile warheads divided by the targets (primarily missile silos) on an opponent's territory that would have to to be hit in a first strike. Given current two-for-one crosstargeting, a warhead-to-aimpoint ratio of more than about two-to-one is thought to be destabilizing since it offers a nuclear power an incentive to launch a first strike.

INDEX

—

arms control (*continued*)
CNTB in, 200–201
conservative view of, 6
cooperative action established by,
11–12
crisis stability and, 8
Cuban missile crisis and, 146
defined, 219
delivery systems and, 7–8
détente and, 4–6
disarmament vs., 152
economic rationale for, 8–11
essential equivalence and, 107
first negotiations in, 5
under Gorbachev, 137–38
gradual steps for, 215–16
incentives for, 146–47
INF and, 67, 68, 69, 78–80
interdepartmental disputes on,
178
left view of, 6
military logic of, 7–8
negotiating teams for, 150
new international system and,
11–12
in 1960s and 1970s, 5–6
opposition to, 147
parity precondition in, 148–49
political will and, 199
popularity of, 145–46
SLCMs and, 46–47
Soviet aggression and, 145
strategic defense in, 211
verification requirement in, 149–
50
"window of opportunity" in,
176–77
see also specific treaties
Arms Control and Disarmament
Agency, U.S., 166
INF talks and, 188
Arms Control Association, 54
arms race:
counterforce capabilities and,
112–14
defensive, 58–59
driving forces in, 111–12, 213–14

early stages of, 4
MX missile in, 61–63
"negotiators' pause" in, 206
nuclear freeze and, 204
preferred weapons in, 56–57
tacit cooperation and, 4
unlimited, 146–47
Army, U.S., 59
under Eisenhower, 95–96
Army, Soviet, 130
ASAT treaty proposals, 210–11
see also Antisatellite weapons
assured destruction:
defined, 219
as single-purpose strategic doctrine, 88, 104
strategy of, 103–5
survivability requirement in,
104–5
see also mutual assured destruction
atomic bomb, 20–25
development of, 21–24
Stalin and, 4, 25, 122–23

B-1 bomber, 45
under Reagan, 45, 109, 177
B-52 bomber, 40, 177
upgraded, 45
Backfire bomber, 168
bacteriological weapons, 154
ballistic missile, 219
ballistic missile defense (BMD):
ABM Treaty and, 162
ASAT treaty and, 210–11
in damage limitation strategies,
98
debates on, 58–59
defined, 220
in INF talks, 192–93, 211–12
under Nixon, 106
origins of, 58
under Reagan, 110
SALT I limitations on, 59
Soviet response to, 151–52
see also Strategic Defense Initiative

Communist party (*continued*)
Andropov and, 180
ASAT testing and, 209
in defense decisions, 118–19,
126–29
International Department of, 182
Khrushchev and, 124
leadership selection in, 118–19,
126–29
Lenin and, 120
1961 Central Committee Plenum
of, 131
peace program in, 132
Politburo of, 119
Twentieth Congress of, 124
comprehensive nuclear test ban
(CNTB), 200–203
arguments for, 200–201
defined, 220
force modernization and, 202–3
opposition to, 201, 202–3
verification in, 201–2
computer guidance systems, 147
Congress, U.S.:
ASAT issue in, 210
defense costs and, 147
defense industry and, 213
freeze resolution in, 203–4
Geneva Protocol and, 154
INF debates in, 195–96
safeguard system and, 103
SALT I and, 149
SALT II ratification and, 172
SDI and, 191
test ban agreements in, 153
conscription, 106
containment policy, 90
conventional forces:
under Eisenhower, 94, 95, 101
extended deterrence and, 74–76
in flexible response strategy,
100–101
under Kennedy, 100–101
as massive retaliation alternative,
97–98
NSC-68 on, 91
nuclear development and, 90

volunteer army in, 106
of Warsaw Pact, 74–76
CORRTEX, 202
counterforce capabilities:
debates on, 112–14
defined, 220
in preemptive strike, 99
Soviet view of, 104
strategic doctrine and, 105
testing necessary for, 202–3
counterinsurgency, 101
countervailing strategy, 88, 107–8
under Carter, 106, 107–8
modernization in, 107
under Nixon, 106–7
countervalue capabilities, 99, 220
crisis stability, 43
ALCMs and, 46
arms control and, 8
defined, 220
MIRVing and, 50–51
crosstargeting, 49, 51
Cuba, 158
Cuban missile crisis, 4, 131, 146,
153
Czechoslovakia, 3, 76, 123, 160

D-5 warhead, 52, 109, 134
damage limitation strategies, 108–
11
ABM Treaty and, 162–63
assured destruction vs., 105
city avoidance and, 102–3
defined, 220
different approaches in, 98–99
as massive retaliation alternative,
98
under Reagan, 108–11
Davis, Lynn, 7–8
defense contractors, 213
Defense Department, U.S., 178
INF talks and, 186, 188
defense spending, U.S.:
under Carter, 133–34
civilian program resources and,
103, 109
constituency for, 145

Nitze, Paul, 178, 184
  background of, 185
  INF package formed by, 185–86
  as Reagan adviser, 192
Nixon, Richard, 41
  arms control personnel under,
    166
  BMD under, 106
  in Eisenhower's defense policy,
    96
  essential equivalence strategy
    under, 106, 107
  in SALT I, 160–61
  strategic doctrine under, 106–7
  Watergate and, 167
Nonproliferation of Nuclear Weapons Treaty (1968), 6, 20, 157–
  59
  compliance with, 158–59
  disarmament and, 201
  terms of, 158
North Atlantic Treaty Organization
  (NATO):
  countervailing strategy and, 108
  dual track decision in, 76
  equal security and, 70
  extended deterrence and, 74–76
  INF Treaty and, 195
  Soviet INF and, 72
North Vietnam, 3
NSC-68 position paper, 222
  economic considerations in, 93
  flexible response and, 100
  Nitze in, 185
  overreliance warning in, 96
  premises of, 91
  on targets, 91–92
nuclear balance of forces, 52–57
  in delivery vehicles and war-
    heads, 53–54
  differing estimations of, 53
nuclear fission, 20–23
  Einstein's formula and, 21
  "trigger" for, 21, 22
nuclear freeze, 203–6
  defined, 222
  force modernization and, 205–6

"negotiators' pause" in, 206
opposition to, 204–5
public support for, 204
"quick," 205
resolution on, 203–4
Soviet support for, 204
strategic build-down vs., 206–7
tests banned in, 203–4
verification of, 205
nuclear fusion, 25–27
nuclear power plants, 19–20
nuclear reactors, 159
nuclear umbrella, see extended
  deterrence
nuclear war, 29–35
  blast wave in, 30
  electromagnetic pulse in, 29–30
  fire storm in, 30
  genetic mutation and, 32
  initial radiation in, 29
  nuclear winter and, 31–32
  ozone depletion and, 32
  policy implications of, 32–35
  primary effects of, 29–30
  protracted, 109
  public fear of, 146
nuclear weapons:
  "cost-effective," 58
  deliverable vs. battlefield, 67
  delivery vehicles vs., 20
  development timetable for, 28
  divergent views on, 33–36
  elimination of, 35–36
  European protests against, 109–
    10
  kiloton ratings for, 22–23
  megaton ratings for, 23
  in regional theaters, 39
  third generation of, 200
  see also specific weapons
Nunn, Sam, 206
Nye, Joseph, 33

Ogarkov, Nikolai, 133, 137
Ohio-class submarines, 206
on-site inspections, 150
  for test bans, 153